More praise for
Recovering from the Loss of a Loved One to AIDS

"Plenty of practical advice, and it's not offered by the 'professional,' but by the person experiencing bereavement and by the person dying from AIDS. This is an inspiring book because it provides models for surviving. Just when the world seems too cruel, the survivor is offered hope."
—Roberta Temes, Ph.D.
Clinical Assistant Professor, Psychiatry
SUNY Health Science Center

"Authentic . . . Compassion and truth presented throughout—enabling professionals and laypersons to gain a greater understanding of the reality of loss due to AIDS. A most needed resource at a time when no one is exempt."
—Diana J. McKendree, M.Ed.
Psychotherapist/Consultant
Toronto, Canada

"Powerful . . . The strength of the book lies in the range of losses, reactions, and coping strategies."
—*Kirkus Reviews*

"It is impossible for a reader not to be touched by the wrenching details of [these] stories."
—*The Dallas Morning News*

"Sensitive, sound advice."
—*Feminist Bookstore News*

Also by Katherine Fair Donnelly

Recovering from the Loss of a Parent
Recovering from the Loss of a Child
Recovering from the Loss of a Sibling

RECOVERING

from the Loss of

a Loved One

to **AIDS**

●

KATHERINE FAIR DONNELLY

Fawcett Columbine • *New York*

A Fawcett Columbine Book
Published by Ballantine Books

This edition published by arrangement with St. Martin's Press, Inc.

Grateful acknowledgment is made to the following for permission to reprint previously published material:

Poem (Anonymous), published by *PWA Coalition Newsline*, 50 West 17 Street, New York, N.Y. 10011, Issue #77, June 1992. Toll-free hot line: (800)828-3280.

An Open Letter to the Parents of My Son's Lover, by Florence Rush, reprinted from *PWA Coalition Newsline*, 50 West 17 Street, New York, N.Y. 10011, Issue #70, October 1991. Toll-free hot line (800)828-3280.

AIDS and Bereavement Care, by J. William Worden, Ph.D., reprinted from *Caregivers Quarterly*, 1078 Rice Street, St. Paul, Minn. 55117, Vol. 7, No. 2, Spring 1992.

Open Letter of Apology to Surviving Siblings, by Judith Haimes, excerpts reprinted from *Recovering from the Loss of a Sibling*, by Katherine Fair Donnelly, Dodd Mead, New York, NY © Katherine Fair Donnelly 1987.

Excerpts from *Losing a Loved One to AIDS: A Support Group Leader Talks About the Issues*, by Katherine Fair Donnelly, reprinted from *Thanatos*, Talahassee, FL, Vol. 18, No. 2, Summer 1993.

Library of Congress Catalog Card Number: 94-90793

ISBN: 0-449-90990-5

Cover design by Ruth Ross

Manufactured in the United States of America
First Ballantine Books Edition: June 1995
10 9 8 7 6 5 4 3 2 1

IN MEMORIAM

Tom Alexander (a.k.a. Tom
    Grella)
Larry Anger
Ross Byron Armstrong
Scott Charles Barr
Carol Bess Belove
Ronald J. Berne
Dr. Barry Binkowitz
Mark N. Bivens
Dolores Blackwell
Kenneth Britton
Angela Brown
Armida Brown
Faith Vanessa Brown
James F. Bruno
Jon Paul Calcaterra

Jack Campbell
Marcel Chabernaud
Renee Chabernaud
William Scott Cline
William R. Coady
Donald Commiskey
Michael Connolly
Christopher Covert
John J. Cristallo
Iris De La Cruz
Philip DeLisi
Darcella Devlin
Julio Cesar Dominguez
Robert Bruce Dorman
Randy Dunn
Terry Dunn

Daniel Eltinge
David A. S. Erb
Richard E. Eye
Rena Fenigshteen
David Ferguson
Mel Finan
Frank Freone
Hector Gonzales
James Gray
Richard W. Greene
Bob Del Grosso
Mikel Konig Harder
Alan Hauser
Harold Hawkes
David Hefner
John H. Herbst
Christian Hesler
Paul Edward Honeycutt
Richard Huot
Edward Jirak
Rosaire Jirak
Michael Knapp
Bill Knight
Anthony Kudes
Ernst Lauritzen
James M. Leventhal
Miles Looker
Bruce Macauley
Bohdan Maczulsky
John Mangano
Renee Martin
Samuel T. McDaniel, Jr.
John Natelli
William Navarro
Keith Nevel
Thomas Nichols

Kenneth D. O'Brien
Victor Ockey
Tim O'Hare
Robert Phillips
Rick Post
Burnett Poindexter
Charles S. Poindexter
Lisa Angela Poindexter
Magdelena Ribakoff
Samir Rizk
Dick (Richard G.)
   Robinson
James Rodriguez, Sr.
Kimberly Ann Rodriguez
Ramon Luis Rosa
Matthew N. Rush
Jim Saar
Bill Sabato
Mark Saunders
Bobby Scott
Marie Scribner
Richard J. Sebar
Steven Mark Showalter
Thelma Solomon
William Lee Steger
Jeff Storch
Abraham (Paul) Torres, Jr.
Xavier Valencia
Emily Vendemio
Joseph Vendemio
Bryon Walsh
Bob Ward
Wayne West
Joseph L. Whitfield
John Woodward
Ron Yost

[p o e m]

Do not stand by my grave and weep.
I am not there. I do not sleep.
I am a thousand winds that blow.
I am a diamond glint of snow.
I am the sunlight on ripened grain.
I am the gentle autumn rain.
When you awake in the morning hush,
I am the swift, uplifting rush
of quiet birds in circling flight.
I am the soft starshine at night.
Do not stand by my grave and cry.
I am not there . . . I did not die.

—author unknown

—PWA COALITION NEWSLINE

CONTENTS

ACKNOWLEDGMENTS

THIS book would not be possible without thanking

John H. Donnelly, Jr., whose guiding hand and heart were given many times into the wee hours in his untiring efforts to make this book one of hope and help to those who have lost a loved one to AIDS.

Franc Lacinski for his keen introspection and helpful information provided throughout the writing of the manuscript.

Judith Haimes, whose encouragement and faith bolstered me from the start to write a separate book for AIDS survivors.

George Witte, senior editor, who responded with compassion and enthusiasm for this undertaking and whose fine editorial touch added immeasurably to the final manuscript.

Jane Jordan Browne for her faith in the work and for placing it with a sympathetic publisher.

Matthew Rettenmund, who early on recognized the need for such a book and who passionately supported this work.

Ann McKay Farrell, assistant editor, for her special efforts, and Sona Vogel, copy editor, who saw that no detail was left unchecked and did a splendid job of it.

The many individuals kind enough to hear or read this manuscript in its various stages, permitting me their thoughts and comments, and who helped in many other ways: Angela Purpura, Dr. Roberta Temes, Ruth Hannon, Abe Malawski, Ann Magid, Kathleen Perry, Marjorie Martin, Ellen Martin, and Betty J. Kelly.

A Most Grateful Note of Thanks

To the bereaved survivors who participated in this book in a warm outpouring of compassion and sharing and who have permitted the use of their real names:

Midge Anderson, Joel Armstrong, Merri E. Armstrong, Arlene Binkowitz, Jerry Binkowitz, Ann M. Blake, Joe Calcaterra, Leonce Chabernaud, Michael Danilowski, William T. Davidson, Karen Dillard, Lisa Eltinge, Yoshua Eyal, Kathy Eye, Dan Frambach, Pat Fuller, Kelly Gonzalez, Maria Hefner, Nancy Hesler, Michael Jalbert, Rita Jirak, Deborah Klesenski, Barbara Koski, Ed Koski, Lisa Lahner, Terri Litz, George Marentis, Edward Marlatt, Nancy Miranda, Neil Nelson, Peter Newman, Melinda Broman Ockey, Rabbi Patricia Philo, Stephanie Poindexter, Paul Rapsey, Theresa Rodriguez, Cary Ross, Florence Rush, Sharie Schon, Herbert Schwartz, Ada Setal, Dennis Turner, and Michael Zients.

For others who requested confidentiality and privacy, this wish has been respected, and those names and locales or other identifying factors have been changed.

Thanks are also given to the many professionals who have helped to enlighten survivors about ways to help themselves: Greg Anderson, Patricia Corrigall, Sheila Crandles, Diane Grodney, Michael Miller, Diana McKendree, Paul Rapsey, Kathleen Perry, John Kennedy Saynor, Rori Shaffer, Roberta Temes, Jerilyn Woodhouse, and William J. Worden.

I would also like to thank Cindy Berman, Ruth Ross, and Sherri Rifkin at Ballantine Books.

INTRODUCTION

R E C E N T L Y I received a desperate telephone call from a mother seeking someone to talk to, someone who could understand her pain. Her son had died of AIDS.

I told her I thought there was a group near her for bereaved parents and that I would check to make certain.

When I called to make the inquiry, I was told that this mother could certainly come to their meeting but that she might not be especially welcome there.

The dialogue after that statement went something like this:

"Excuse me, would you please explain *why* this mother would not be made welcome?"

"Well, you see, parents who have lost a child, through a drowning or a car accident, for example, believe that this mother's child had a choice, while their children did not. That is the general mood she may encounter."

"Do you mean to say that this mother's pain is any less

than the pain of other bereaved parents because her child died of AIDS?"

"I'm simply trying to say that this is the mood she may find in this group and she may be better off trying to locate one that deals specifically with AIDS losses."

The exclusivity of grief! The prejudice I encountered in this least likely of places astonished me.

MOURNERS MAY also be denied the comfort of church, friends, and family. Whereas those whose loved ones have died from cancer, a heart attack, or an accident receive open support, such solace and consolation are not always forthcoming in an AIDS loss. Instead, a different message is often delivered:

THIS DEATH IS NOT AS WORTHY OF SUPPORT OR SYMPATHY!

No matter that a bereaved mother or father may know the worst anguish a parent can ever experience. No matter that a child's life is shattered by the death of a parent or grandparent. And what of those who shared a life, a bed, a dream, with a mate or companion? What of the terrible pain of brothers and sisters who mourn a sibling? Or a grandparent who is devastated by the loss of a dear grandchild—and in some cases is mourning both a child and grandchild simultaneously!

More to the point: Every person who dies deserves to be mourned, and every survivor needs to mourn. Do we not all belong to the human race? Is the pain of a survivor of an AIDS death any less than a survivor of any other death?

Where is the humanity? Where is the compassion?

THIS BOOK has been written for you—you who are mourning the loss of a loved one to AIDS. It offers the rare opportunity to share in the lives of survivors who have suffered an AIDS loss—their pain, sorrow, struggles, and love. Others have experienced such hurt and still live on. To know you are not alone is in itself a great source of encouragement, a source of hope.

Because AIDS is a particularly alienating disease, talking

things through with others in the same situation offers a pathway to recovering. Support groups provide survivors a place to connect with people who share the commonality of the experience, a safe haven where they are allowed and encouraged to tell their stories as often as they wish.

But what of survivors who live in rural areas where support groups or help may not be available? And what of survivors too afraid to seek out resources?

This book is really a support group! As you read along, you will hear real-life experiences and learn what happened to those who have been there. Their firsthand accounts of how they survived are far more intimate than any set of guidelines.

AIDS breaks all the rules when it comes to bereavement. Books on surviving the death of a loved one delineate stages of grief for mourners. But AIDS does not always permit such luxury. Often there is not time to reflect or to grieve one person's death before being hit with yet another—in some cases even back-to-back funerals.

Other complex issues surrounding AIDS deaths are addressed in this book. Some of them include:

• Aging mothers who, in their worst nightmares, never imagined they would be diapering their dying adult child.
• Parents who must come to terms with learning a child is both gay and HIV positive.
• Survivors who are traumatized by the clergy.
• Gay men who have provided extraordinary care and love to their partners but who may be subjected to insensitive or hostile treatment by families and hospital staff who fail to recognize their relationship to the one who has died.
• Surviving partners who worry, "Who will take care of me if I get sick?"
• Those who are HIV negative and feel guilty for not having contracted the virus that has affected a loved one.
• HIV positive men who are still fearful of outing themselves to their families.
• Survivors who are concerned about forming new and meaningful relationships. Many face the issue of

identifying themselves as HIV positive to new people.
• Wives infected by husbands who were unfaithful or had a hidden drug habit. (The bombshell usually falls after the death of the spouse.)
• Friends, who may also be business partners, faced with the loss of a personal relationship and the task of keeping their business afloat.
• Those who have lost many friends and are afraid to answer the phone, fearful of hearing about yet another death.
• Grown children who are shocked to learn that their parent (who is often a grandparent) is HIV positive. Some adult children suffer the loss of both parents when one is infected by the other.
• Children who may be subjected to rejection by friends and schoolmates because their parents or siblings have died of AIDS.
• Adolescents who are forced to assume a parental role, taking HIV parents to hospitals, bathing them, feeding them, giving medication, and perhaps caring for younger children.

So many issues. So much pain. So many pieces of flotsam swirling around in the heartache, the morass, of AIDS.

All of the participants in this book share a common goal of wanting to help others know they are not alone, that they are not crazy, and that all of these things happen to other people— real people who have given testimonials to what helped them survive the loss of a loved one to AIDS.

They tell it like it is—and it's tough.

But they found ways of recovering—and so can you!

—K.F.D.

PART ONE

●

chapter 1

LOVERS/LIFE PARTNERS

• *I feel so guilty. I keep wondering if I gave the disease to him. I have this awful thought that in some way I was responsible.*

• *His mother asked me for his ashes. It was the hardest thing I ever had to do, but I gave them to her. I wonder if she would have dared ask if we were recognized as spouses?*

• *Even though I was his primary caretaker and the one who saw to his every need, at the hospital I was treated as "just a friend."*

• *His family made the decision to bury him in their plot in a Jewish cemetery. That meant I could never be buried next to him because I'm Catholic.*

• *At work, I was forced to lie because I was afraid of losing my job. When my lover died, I told them it was my uncle, but the pretense was killing me.*

• *I was not only grieving the death of my lover, but wondering who was going to take care of me if I got sick.*

• *It was left to me to say when to remove the respirator. How horrible it was to say, "Yes, unplug it." I wanted him to live, but I knew I had to let him die in dignity, without more agony.*

We begin this book with the story of a survivor who had to deal with an AIDS death and with his own physical problems—a situation that many survivors find themselves facing.

When Cary Ross went to Washington, D.C., to visit the AIDS Memorial Quilt Project, he was accompanied by his guide dog, Kid, and five new friends. All of his old friends were dead.

Cary hadn't always been blind. He had been in and out of hospitals since he was ten, battling a congenital condition. At sixteen he lost the sight in his right eye, and he lost the use of his left eye four years ago. Later, Cary was to lose another battle when his lover Randy died of AIDS.

In Washington, Cary was desperate to find Randy's quilt. He describes the poignant and astonishing events of that day. "My friends were trying to help me find the panel, which had Randy's picture on it. They didn't know Randy from Adam, but they kept searching. No one could find it, and I was very dejected. As we started to leave, my dog, Kid, broke away and was rolling around on the ground. When my friends went to retrieve her, they yelled out, 'Cary, here it is! Here it is! Your dog found it!' Can you imagine! I knelt down beside the quilt, and I touched it. Suddenly I felt Randy's presence, and I started to cry. Then my friends started crying, too—for someone they didn't even know. It was incredible. Everyone was crying, and that release of tears supported us all."

Cary's dry sense of humor stands him in good stead when handling his own HIV positive status. "Right now," he jokes, "I have only three T cells. I call them Moe, Larry, and Curly." In a more serious vein, Cary comments on the trio. "With only three T cells, does that mean three days left? Three hours? Three minutes? According to all of the literature on AIDS, I should be dead, but I've never been sick. I don't have fevers or night sweats. I don't even catch a cold, knock on wood—and I've known others like that." Cary explains there is no accounting for why one person gets sick and the other doesn't, if the T cells are really an indicator. "Randy had three T cells for two years, but he was sick all the time, and he was a big, strapping guy, two hundred and five pounds, six feet two."

Cary looks back to memories of Randy's strength to help him through his own HIV infection. "When I first met Randy, I knew he was a special person, but he proved just how special when I lost the sight in my good eye. It was almost like a dramatic scene in a movie. I didn't want to saddle Randy at this young age with a blind person. I wanted to give him a way out of our relationship and told him my blindness wasn't part of the deal. I was busy with 'Woe is me,' but Randy quietly said, 'I love you, Cary. You are part of me, and you know I would never leave you.' "

Randy sought to bolster Cary and urged him to learn to do everything as a blind person so that his independence would be assured. His insistence that Cary not think of himself as being handicapped was of invaluable help to Cary during the holidays after Randy's death.

"At first, I wasn't going to do anything about Thanksgiving. I didn't feel thankful for a hell of a lot that day, but a couple of my friends were saying they didn't have any place to go. They had no family or no one who would accept them. So I said, 'Well, can you cook anything?' Each of us prepared a different dish. In a way, it was a kind of therapy. To top it off, I made the turkey. People asked me how I could cook a turkey if I'm blind. When Randy was alive we always made Thanksgiving, and I would always cook the turkey. When you cook a lot, you don't even look. We all sat around the table, sharing, eating, and it made the holiday a plus instead of a minus." Randy had prepared Cary for this sightless Thanksgiving, spent without Randy but not alone.

Although holidays and special dates can be difficult, one in particular was especially hard for Cary. "On Randy's birthday, I was an absolute mess. I kept thinking back to the last day he was in the hospital. It was so painful. He died in my arms. I was holding him, stroking him, and talking to him. I couldn't believe he died. So, on his birthday I was really at a low ebb and was thinking about calling his mother when the phone rang. It was his mom! She was calling because she was worried about *me!* Her name is Wilma Dunn, and let me tell you, she's a very special lady. In fact, Randy's whole family is terrific. When I went to Tennessee for the first time, we established a great relationship. They took me in and embraced me. They liked me from the start, and I have lots of nice memories to lean on. I've heard lots of horror stories about families who couldn't care less about the surviving lover, but Randy's family is the exact opposite."

Randy's mother came to New York during her son's hospitalization. Her presence made it easier for Cary to face his anguish. "What helped me get through it was I had to take care of his mom. I had to help her deal with it. I hugged her, and she held me. We supported each other, talking about it and trying to make sense of what was happening. It's hard to make sense of something you don't understand—and I'm living it. How do you make a mom understand that her son has just died?"

Cary felt a keen sense of compassion for Randy's parents. "I've never been a parent, but I tried to put myself in the place of Wilma and Ed, Randy's dad. I tried to picture what it must be like for them to lose this son they loved so much. His father is full of guilt for not having been able to come to New York. He was having ear problems, and his doctor told him he couldn't fly. He is such a great guy, and it really bothered him so much that he couldn't be here with his son. But then, nobody thought Randy was going to die."

Cary recalls the poignant last moments he spent with Randy and reflects on the value of tears. "The night before he died, Randy told me that he loved me. I was in such euphoria hearing him say that that it didn't hit me he was saying good-bye. He kept asking me to give him kisses, so I gave him kisses. He couldn't talk much because he was paralyzed on the right side of his body from a lesion in the left side of his brain—a lymphoma. He could only say a few phrases, so I didn't have anything to go on except key words. Like he would say 'Feet' when he wanted his feet rubbed. Then I would do that for him, rub his feet. What helped me get through those moments was that I cried a lot. I held nothing inside. I was not ashamed of that."

When Cary has a bad day, he calls somebody. He explains that all of his new friends have lost someone they loved to AIDS. "We call each other when we are down. There are times when I feel like a ninety-year-old man. These are the things you're supposed to talk about when you're in your eighties or older, not something you do in your twenties and thirties. We say things like 'I miss him so much.' Or 'I keep thinking he's going to walk in the door any minute.'

"I have dreams of Randy. Right after he died, I was lying in bed, sound asleep. Suddenly, I felt his body next to me. That's the God's honest truth, and I thought to myself, Oh, Randy, you're so cold. I'll just put my arms around you. Then I heard this moan, and it was my dog sleeping in a personlike position. That was not like her because she has her own bed. It was really strange. There was another dream in which Randy came to me, and we had a brief conversation about Susie, the little dog he left behind. She's a tiny little dog, with a flat face that only an owner could love. Soon after Randy died, Susie had gotten her hair cut and had a bath. It was just after that when Randy came to me in the dream. It was so real. He said in his little Southern accent, 'I've been out, but I wanted to see Susie. She looks real good.' When I asked, 'What are you doing here?' he said, 'I have to go now.' And that was it."

Cary was able to talk about his dreams and many other issues when he joined a bereavement support group for AIDS survivors. One of the problems Cary was grappling with was guilt. "There are decisions you make in the hospital, and later you feel guilt. Did you make the right decision? I allowed them to do some procedures on Randy that I was told would help him. I feel I did the best I could. I permitted them to do a brain biopsy on Friday. We got the diagnosis on Tuesday, and Randy was dead on Wednesday. So I had a lot of if-onlys. I know better now. I learned that 'if only' can be a killer if you allow it to be. I was able to share my emotions openly with the group at St. Vincent's Hospital [in New York].

"There were ten of us, all talking about our loved ones and our concerns about our own health, our loneliness, and the ability to go on. They would ask, 'How do you go on when your whole world has been blown apart?' I haven't found any answers for that. You just go on. You have to. You sort of just exist until you are ready. Not everybody is ready at the same pace. Some people want to wallow in their grief, and others are ready to move on. I feel that I'm ready to go on. I really grieved Randy's death before he died because of all the suffering. One of the things you can relate to in a support group is when you hear somebody else talk about the same things you've been going through. Realistically you know that others are also having a tough time, but you generally feel that you are the only one. Then, when you hear the others say these things out loud, you understand that you are not. Another thing that is so important in a support group has to do with who the facilitators are, who is running the group. At St. Vincent's, there are no words to describe Sister Pat and Brother Mike. They were fantastic. Everyone in the group commented on how outstanding and wonderful they were. When you know that someone is there for you, it means the world. And they were there for us whenever we needed them."

Cary has high praise for other groups that extended helping hands. "I made a very close friend at a Care Partners' group through the People with AIDS Coalition. The focus of the group was for those who were taking care of a loved one. What helped later was being able to go to the Gay Men's Health Crisis, where there are supportive groups for people who are HIV positive and also bereavement groups for survivors. I have met many new friends there. We form our own families because all of us are drawn together by our experiences. For some, we are the only family they have."

Cary admits to having one great fear—not a fear of death, but of the process of dying. He also tells of the steps he has taken to insure that his wishes are carried out if he should become incapacitated.

"I hope I don't have to go through what Randy had to endure or what other people I know have gone through. I hope when my time comes, it will be very fast. I hope I just go to sleep. Now with my T cell count, it seems very much like I'm looking it right in the eye. I had medical power of attorney for Randy, and I want to emphasize how important it is to have someone who knows about AIDS and who understands what to do with the power of attorney. I have a very close girlfriend, Terri. I met her fourteen years ago and she's a wonderful person—you couldn't have a better friend. I gave Terri the power of attorney because I knew my family couldn't handle it. I love my family, but they really don't know me. They know I'm gay, but that's about it. I don't want them to cause me stress. That could hurt me physically, and it's the kind of stress I want to avoid because I'm trying my best to live. Stress is a killer, so if you can relieve yourself of that wherever you can and however you can, then do it."

Cary is determined to live life as fully as he can. He has made new friends, goes to various support groups, some of which have social activities, and keeps in close contact with Randy's family. Cary still thinks about Randy, but time has given him a handle on his grief, and now he can talk about it without weeping. Like many other bereaved gay men, Cary is getting on with his life, reconnecting with the world rather than stepping back from it. In a sense, AIDS has created a stronger solidarity in the gay community—a community whose members heal within its ranks rather than as isolated individuals.

G A Y M E N bristle at the unfairness of families who interfere in their lives in areas that are personal and private; they maintain that such families would never ask a husband or a wife to leave one another in order to come home to die. "Families don't comprehend that they are intruding on a spousal relationship," is the complaint often heard. Lovers and life partners are viewed as a friend or a roommate, and because of that classification, families may cast aside the lover's wishes when it comes to making final decisions. Many life partners, in addition to the anguish of seeing their loved one dying, are outraged by the insensitive actions of the families after the death of the loved one.

One such survivor, Joel Armstrong, encountered problems with his lover's family. "Along with the mourning, there is always the complicated perception that gays have no rights. In my case, Jim was buried by his family in a Jewish cemetery, in their family plot. I had no say. What it means is that I can never be buried next to him. I have heard detestable and revolting stories about gays whose lovers died and they were not even allowed to go to the funeral!

"There is this feeling of 'All I've had to go through is enough, and all this other stuff seems incredibly unfair.' Watching someone you love die should be enough. Helping them through months and months of sickness should be enough. But people who are gay will suffer more, not only because of the stigma of the disease, but because of the lack of legal protection that would be afforded to a widow or widower."

Joel also comments on the inference that losing one's lover is an easier loss. "I've read in the bereavement books about how people say stupid things after a death because they don't know what to say. But, certainly, things were said to me and other friends I know who lost lovers that would never have been said to a widow. For example, 'It must be hard losing a roommate, but it's nothing like when I lost your father.' There's no acknowledgment of the emotional thing. We have a label for men and women who have lost their spouses, and we expect a certain kind of behavior from them—and they, in turn, expect their status to be recognized by others. If the bereaved spouse decides not to show up somewhere, it's 'Well, you know, she just lost her husband.' And, of course, all present say, 'Oh,' and shake their heads. And that's fine. But if it's 'Why didn't Joel show up?' the comment most likely would be, 'Well, you know, his *friend* died this year.' Somehow, that does not imply the same thing that someone's mother or grandmother or father has been through. The devastation caused by the death of one partner in a gay couple is not equated to that caused by the death of one in a recognized marriage. Widowhood is not accorded to gay couples."

Joel expounds on the strain such lack of recognition places on him. "It's hard to articulate, but the problem, even with my best friends, has been that there is not an acknowledged structure of a marriage. That makes it hard for people to have rules of reaction—how long should it be before someone gets over it? Gay men have faced 'Well, you have to get over it' sooner because it's not viewed as a marriage. You see it all the time— even the best of good-hearted and well-intentioned people are guilty. No matter how hard they try, they've grown up with role models. I have many liberal friends who still have trouble understanding what a gay relationship is."

Joel examines what "getting over it" means and offers his interpretation of the solicitous platitude. "Finding another human being in the gay world who wants to make the kind of commitment we had and to live with you as your great love, with all the obstacles against that, makes the possibility of such a relationship seem all the more singular. It's not like 'Well, I'm going to get over this. I'll just go out and meet another person.' I don't think gay survivors feel that way. It took me thirty-one years to find Jim, someone who wanted to make that kind of commitment, someone I could live with and who could live with me, someone who loved me to death, and I loved him as dearly. That's not waiting on every corner. It never occurred to me that I would be without him, and of course, being a person with AIDS, there inevitably comes the question of 'Who is going to take care of me if I get that sick?' But I began to look at what had happened around Jim's death, and I had to find all the different places in which there had been blessings and where there had been wonderful friends. I have great faith that those same angel people are going to show up when I get sick and need them."

Joel also has some excellent advice for friends and survivors who want but don't know how to help the bereaved. There are some definite ways, he indicates, and he provides some specific guidelines. "Don't call up and say, 'I'm happy to do anything for you. Just tell me what.' Instead, say, 'I'll be over in about a half hour. I've made a casserole. If you don't feel like eating it tonight, we can put it in the freezer.' Don't say, 'If you ever need me to run to the grocery store, let me know.' Rather, call up and say, 'Listen, I've gone to the grocery store and picked up an extra bag of Kitty Litter and some cat food. While I was there, I picked up some milk and cereal. I thought you may have run out of them.' The fact is at that point I was incapable—even though I had always been the big organizer—of organizing my own health or needs. And that is really what is being asked of you when people call and say, 'I'll do anything to help, just let me know.' That request says that, along with the job of mourning and being devastated, you must also engineer, plan, and command your own rescue. That's not what it's all about."

The people to whom Joel will always be grateful are the ones who just showed up. Joel adds, "Many came from my church. They didn't stay long unless they felt it was appropriate. Before they left, they did the dishes. They didn't say, 'I'll be happy to do those dishes if you want me to.' They went into the kitchen, saw there were dishes in the sink, and said, 'Oh, I was just washing my hands, so I thought I would wash these up, too. I didn't think you'd mind.' Those people were saints. There were times when I went to the grocery store myself, even though others had called and said, 'Let me know, and I'll go to the store for you.' To do otherwise meant I had to think—think who was available to call upon, think what grocery store would they go to, think what I would tell them to buy for me. All those details to *think* about. So my advice is, 'Don't ask, just do.' That is the greatest blessing someone can offer you when you are grieving— to get things done without your having to think about them. You just can't beat not having to think."

Joel cautions that this inability to think may go on for weeks or months. "Then it will become apparent that the bereaved person is functioning again. Some of the indicators will be if you come to the house and see things have been straightened up a bit, or the person is more animated in his conversation, or perhaps he or she may offer you a soda. Or you look in the refrigerator and instead of just pickles and crackers, you may see it neatly filled with foods. You will be able to observe positive changes, perhaps, in their personal appearance. Their clothing may be neater, or they may have gotten a haircut."

Joel devised a testing method that acted as a gauge for his progress. He felt as if he were coming back to the same planet everyone else was on, but he still felt very fragile. "I started having little tests for myself. Jim died in August. His birthday was in October. My birthday is in November. Then there was Thanksgiving, which was always a big day for us together. It had also been the previous year when we found out he had lymphoma. I started thinking, If you can just get through his birthday . . . Then, it was, If you can just get through your birthday . . . And then, If you can just get through Thanksgiving . . . After that, it was, If you can just get through Christmas . . . When I actually made it through Christmas, I felt that was my first graduation! I felt, I'm back in the world. I made it through Christmas without being a wreck all the time!"

There are certain things Joel still has not dealt with, and he realizes there will be good days and rough days. "I haven't been able to deal with removing his record collection, for example. I haven't been able to mobilize my forces. One of the things you read about in all of the bereavement books and hear about in the groups is that it takes what time it takes. I was doing very well after Christmas when suddenly, in February, I had about three weeks where I was laid low again. It had been six months since Jim's death, and I was depressed. Whereas before I had been so glad I was able to make it through Christmas, now it was like, My God, it's been six months without him. I didn't want to get out of bed. Everywhere I looked I saw Jim. I saw things about our life together. All I wanted to do was talk about him."

Joel found it irritating when friends and acquaintances walked on eggs if Jim's name came up in the conversation. "The thing that drove me crazy was when people tried to do the right thing by talking like Jim never existed. One day the subject of bad music came up, and Jim hated bad music. We were all laughing, and someone said, 'Remember how Jim hated bad . . .' and he suddenly stopped midsentence because he realized he had uttered Jim's name. He interrupted the conversation because he thought it would upset me to hear Jim's name. What is upsetting is that he no longer exists. People should go ahead and tell the funny stories, the bad stories, and the good stories, but not suddenly erase your loved one from all conversation. It makes the loss that much harder. You have lost the physical person, and initially, it appears that you are going to lose the ability even to acknowledge his existence because no one wants to talk about him. I found that very disturbing and had to have that discussion with my friends. For example, I couldn't stop saying 'we' because I had said 'we' for too many years and thought that way for so long. That was something many good friends had to think about and work hard on. They were honest and felt like they were doing it to protect me. However, by not talking about it, they were probably protecting themselves because then they didn't have to deal with their true feelings."

Joel joined a bereavement support group and tells of the knowledge he gained there. "One of the things I learned from the group is that grief was not going to be short and not going to be explainable. I couldn't control it. I couldn't say I'm going to be this way for this long and then in February I'm going to be fine, because in February I might have two weeks where I cried every day for who knows why. What I also learned was that I had not lost my mind. I discovered that physical ailments can be caused by grief. At one of the meetings I heard some of the other group members saying you might have leg pains. Well, my legs had been aching and aching. I asked what that had to do with grief, and they said some people carry the tension in that part of their body. Or you might have a sleeping problem and say, 'All I can do during the day is sleep and then at night I can't sleep for five minutes.' Then you go to the group and hear somebody saying, 'God, I don't know what to do. I think I'm going crazy. I can sleep all day long, but I can't sleep at night.' Just to know you are not crazy offers a tremendous relief."

Often Joel is asked by others, "What do you get from those groups?" He spells it out. "The one thing I can guarantee you is that someone has always had it worse on some level. If nothing else, that helps. There is always someone who has been locked out of their apartment with the police at the premises. There is someone who had to turn off their lover's respirator. There is someone who was told by their mother that they were going to burn in hell. Whatever scenario you want to dream up, someone has had it worse. But it was different things for different people, and it kind of balanced out. For example, the guy who had to turn off his lover's respirator was incredibly accepted in the lover's family. And the one who had been relatively easy with the physical thing had some awful stuff go on with the family. They say you are only given what you can bear. Everybody in my group seemed to be given pretty tough loads, but they were all bearing it."

Although Joel has only rave reviews for his bereavement

support group, he states that he would never have survived without his own therapist. He stresses the need for this before your loved one dies, where possible, and strongly urges survivors living in remote areas to seek out a source for a therapist early on. "I learned of my therapist by going to a friend's therapist and asking for a referral. If you are in a small town, either talk to a social worker in a hospital or ask a clergyperson about a referral to a professional. You want someone who is not prejudiced, a psychologist who has had exposure to grief. And even in the smallest town, if you can, I would talk to more than one psychologist. You will know when you have found the right person. The fact is you should never feel locked in to a single person. If somewhere inside of you it feels wrong, but that's the psychologist you started with, then you need to understand that can happen, and you must make a change. If you go into it saying 'I am going to talk to at least three people,' you will always come off better, particularly in a situation that is so complicated as AIDS and grief and dying. A survivor will be capable of looking for three people if he or she knows that can make such a difference.

"Actually, I believe you should start seeing a therapist before the death. Death is a transition of many things over much time. With AIDS, there is usually time to seek help beforehand. No matter how much you think death could happen, on some level we all think we are going to be the one person who escapes. Our lover is going to be the one person who is saved. Our parents are going to be the ones who live forever. It's just the human experience. In our society, I don't think we are at all prepared for death, period. I think it is a tremendous help if you begin the routine of 'I'll show up for this hour, and I can talk from my heart.' That takes a while to develop. But then it's very important in the grief process because it may be the only place and the only time that you have that response. And that kind of automatic response will help you enormously if it's built in. You will have developed that sense of 'It's Tuesday at three P.M. I'm going to talk about myself and how I'm feeling.' Then, when someone dies, the next Tuesday still feels like 'Well, that's what I do on Tuesday.' That routine really helps to keep you going."

* * *

I N T H E preceding account, we heard of the hurtful types of experiences gay men have with their lovers' families. But in some instances these painful encounters don't happen until after the death or shortly before. Neil Nelson tells of a heartbreaking decision he and his lover had to make.

"It had never been an issue for Rick to choose between me or his family. We were together for eight years, and during that time we spent almost every holiday with his family. Originally, they lived in New York only an hour or so away from us. Later, they made their home in Florida. We were a very close-knit family, and that's what made what happened later so difficult for me and Rick. His family felt he should come to Florida to die, and they made this pretty well known to Rick. No thought was given to my feelings. If I had been acknowledged as Rick's spouse, they would not have dared to ask that he leave our home and travel 1,500 miles to die. If I had been recognized as Rick's spouse, that demand would never have been made.

"As much love as Rick and I shared, so much caring, a lot of trust, a lot of dependency on each other, I think he was able to make the choice between his family's urgings and me because he saw [in me] an independence and an ability to take care of myself that was reassuring to him. By that time I was in a Twelve Step recovery program. I think he felt he could leave me and that I would be all right."

Neil believes that many families have no real concept of what a gay relationship is. Because of this lack of comprehension, the attitudes that prevail can cause bad feelings between surviving lovers and the families. "Most parents of gay people don't realize what the gay relationship is like—that there is a deep caring and a loving commitment. They may rationalize, 'My son is gay and he has a partner,' but people don't really want to visualize beyond that as to what this gayness really involves, especially any type of sexuality. This would probably not be acceptable to them and explains why they don't comprehend that it is a spousal relationship. In our case, the circumstances evolving around Rick's family were such that a lot of unresolved guilt, shame, and issues about his homosexuality were never resolved within his family unit. So, with the continued urgings of his family, in order for Rick to die in peace, I think he had to give himself over to them. When Rick realized that he was dying and that there was not much time left, he made the decision to go to Florida. He had this need to be with his family, particularly his mother."

Some painful and poignant moments followed that decision. On the morning he and Rick were scheduled to leave for Florida, Neil was literally disabled by his feelings. "I was escorting Rick down to Florida by plane. As I began to help him get ready to go, I felt so weak I could hardly walk. I couldn't speak. When I knelt to tie his shoes because he couldn't, we started to cry. It was very difficult. While I was packing the bags for him, I came across a little picture of us on a boat that was taken on a Hawaiian vacation. I showed it to Rick. I saw him try to smile, but I also saw the sadness in his eyes. I said softly, 'I'll just put this in your bag.' And, of course, we both started to cry again. It was so traumatic for me that I felt I began grieving his death at that point."

Having delivered Rick safely to his family, Neil was forced to return to New York to attend to business matters. Shortly thereafter, he was notified that Rick was in the hospital. Quickly he flew back to Florida. "One of the most difficult things was that there was never a moment when I could be alone with Rick. His family saw to that. I could not hold him in my arms when he died, and that made his death much worse for me."

In Neil's opinion, there is a topic yet to be adequately addressed in helping surviving partners. "There is a whole part of the AIDS healing process for partners that really hasn't been addressed—the double sense of loss of your lover and loss of his family. There have been times when I said, 'I wish Oprah would do a show on this—on AIDS surviving partners and their lovers' parents.' I have heard the whole gamut of stories, some of them horrors, but I have also heard very positive things about parents who have been extremely supportive. For example, when I went to my bereavement group, one of the guys told about how his lover's parents bought dual cemetery plots to include the surviving lover. I thought, 'What a comfort that would be, to have that kind of support.' But the whole topic needs to be addressed."

Neil shares what happened in his relationship with Rick's family. They had been very close and had always accepted Neil into the family. Suddenly, Rick's illness and death brought about a whole set of confrontations, and Neil was reeling from the changes in the attitudes of family members. "They were angry and became very nasty, to the point of being outright hostile. It made my grieving much more difficult because what I was experiencing was so contradictory to how I had experienced the family when Rick was alive. I had considered them almost as surrogate parents, particularly his mother. We became very close, since my mother has been dead for many years. After Rick's death, I almost felt a dual sense of grieving—that I had lost him and my surrogate family as well."

Neil describes the loneliness and despair he felt after Rick died and what helped him get through that painful time. "There was a long period after he died when there was a real sense of longing—a longing to physically touch him, to have some sort of attachment with him. It was breaking that physical attachment that became so difficult. I would wear his clothes, touch the things in the apartment that I knew he had held or had been in contact with. It was just that sense of longing to physically have him in my arms or to be able to reach out and touch him."

Before Rick died, he and Neil talked a lot about death. "It was very important for the two of us to talk about it," Neil stresses. "We had to deal with Rick's feelings about his dying. I felt if we could confront the inevitability of his death, we would both be able to accept it better. So we saw a social worker twice a week for the last two months of Rick's life. Rick was too sick to go out, so the therapy session was held in our home. We sat together on the sofa, with Rick in his pajamas and bathrobe. Holding each other, we shared our feelings—things like how I felt about surviving him and my anger at him for abandoning me. I would have to carry on alone. We had to deal with the writing of his will and things like that."

Neil claims the experiences he and Rick shared with the social worker in their home for eight weeks were invaluable beyond words. "It could never be measured in terms of money. But even though Rick and I had talked about his dying, and we were trying to prepare ourselves for that time, I was still totally unprepared for his death when it came. I guess the reason it was so shocking for me was that, despite all the preparation work we had done, I still thought it wasn't going to happen and Rick was not going to die. What *did* I think was going to happen? It was so obvious. And yet I reacted with such a sense of disbelief."

After Rick's death, Neil tells of various stages he experienced. "I went through so many stages, the denial, the anger, the five stages that Kübler-Ross talks about in the grieving process. My feelings have changed a lot since Rick's death over a year ago. There is an acceptance now, and I use the experience of Rick's death as a strength in my life. I try to look at the positive things in our life and the love we had for each other. I recognize our love as part of Rick's spirituality that lives on in me today. Right after Rick's death, I was so stunned that it overshadowed all other feelings. The immediate physical absence of that person is overwhelming. It has taken a year to accept his absence. Now I realize that the love we shared transcends his death.

"Today, it is evident to me that with the grieving process and all the events around the life we shared together, there is no clear-cut beginning or ending to our life. I feel that my grieving will go on, and a lot of the pain that came with Rick's death will be with me forever. Every day there may be an experience or event that will remind me of Rick and cause me pain. But today I am willing to accept that pain. By experiencing and working through these painful feelings, I will achieve the spiritual growth necessary to go on and generate new dreams. I think the fact that I am making new plans, living my life, and expanding in many new directions is evidence of that."

Neil expands on spiritual beliefs that helped in his healing. "In therapy one of the things I had to come to grips with was the sense of powerlessness over Rick's illness—that I was powerless over his AIDS, that I could not cure him, and that I was not responsible for it. I had to bring a spiritual element into my life. Sometimes I liken that strength to an inner light. It's almost as if I can beam the strength into me and feel a connection with Rick." The positive feeling that Neil receives from his spiritual beliefs gives him fortitude to go on. "I know that I will be all right and that I am not incapacitated from Rick's death. I do have my own identity and my own life. That gives me a sense of self-worth necessary to go on living a life that is rich in relationships with other people."

W E   H A V E learned of some of the difficulties a surviving lover had with his partner's parents. In the following account, we hear from a survivor who reached out to make sure his lover's parents felt included.

Tom Alexander was a good-looking young man. He had enjoyed a degree of success as a model and actor when he and Dennis Turner first met at a Twelve Step program. They called each other often and found they had lots of things in common. Dennis, a talented screenplay writer, tells of the growth in their bonding.

"Tommy and I went out to dinner. About a month later we moved in together—against the advice of many people, probably because of the age disparity. I was twenty years older. We stayed together until the moment he died. It was an incredible, growing relationship, often tough and sometimes argumentative. At other times we were in a power struggle, but both of us grew and nurtured each other."

Dennis reflects on the first time Tommy became ill. "We live in California, but Tommy first started getting sick when we were vacationing on the East Coast, where he ended up in the hospital. Up until then, he had indications but no symptoms. Tommy had told me the first night we were together that he was HIV positive. My reaction was that I was very sorry for him, and it saddened me. It didn't affect me in terms of my commitment to him, although I had no idea what it would turn out to be. But in knowing, I don't think I would have changed my mind. I think because I knew Tommy and his fear of abandonment so well, it made me overprotective in many ways. I would spend more hours at the hospital than were probably needed. I couldn't bear to think of him alone in the hospital room. I just had to be there. When he got out of the hospital and we came home, Tommy started to develop more medical problems."

Tommy had heard about a treatment in Switzerland. Dennis was decidedly in favor of trying it out. "I invited Tom's mother, who lived in New York, to join us because they had not spent that much time together in the last few years. We became quite close during that period and also when she was visiting us in California. It was a difficult and stressful time, but I admired her a great deal, and I knew how much she loved Tom. She was always supportive of our relationship, and there was never any negativity coming from her. Tom had been estranged from his father for about five years. His parents had been divorced when Tom was six, and I think he had an abandonment issue with his father that he carried with him for quite some time. When I met Tom, he and his father had not talked to each other for many years. However, when Tommy went into the hospital here in California, his father came, and they had an incredible closing in their relationship. His father was very supportive, and he stayed at Tom's bedside. Tommy ended up with the person he always had wanted—his dad. I also became very close to his father. This was a man who really did not understand the gay relationship. It was totally alien to him, but he put all that aside, and I think he grew in the time he spent at the house with us. Regarding Tom's other family members, there were five brothers and sisters, and they varied greatly in terms of how they could handle Tom's condition. But they all showed up at one time or another to be here and were mostly supportive."

The trip to Switzerland was in October, and while the treatment seemed to help, by February problems started surfacing again, and things began to get worse. Dennis tells of the changes. "Tommy wasn't able to go out much. To some extent he was mobile, so we would go out to the movies. But he was starting to lose weight again, and his appetite was gone. He had a pick-line inserted, and on one particular day he decided to get up and take a Jacuzzi. While he was in it, the pickline had been pulled out partially. The nurse reinserted it, which was a mistake. Within a half hour an infection had set in, and we had to rush him to the emergency room. When they admitted him there, his lungs filled up. They did not expect him to live, and that is when we first called all the family together. They flew out, and Tommy was given last rites, which was just devastating. In a way, part of me was hoping he would go then. I didn't want him to suffer, and I knew if he survived this, the road was going to be very, very rough. I was petrified at the idea of his dying at home. If he was going to die, I wanted it to be in the hospital. I didn't want it to be at home because I was frightened of being home alone with his death. So I had a lot of mixed emotions."

But Tommy pulled through. After five weeks in the hospital, Dennis brought him home, where there were also nurses around the clock. Dennis had stopped working for four months. All of his efforts and energy were going to Tommy. He reflects on a poignant moment when he was observing the change in Tommy.

"To backtrack a bit, one of the saddest things I ever saw was what had been this beautiful kid of twenty-eight getting out of bed now and trying to go toward the kitchen. I was sitting at the pool, and I saw him walk by the door. His face was so filled with pain, and he looked like an eighty-year-old man scrunched over, barely able to move. It was just devastating. Around that time he started talking about ending his life, and he asked me to get books from the Hemlock Society. He said, 'I can't go through this. I want you to promise that you won't let me suffer,' and we talked about that. His attitude changed later."

Dennis describes some startling inspirational moments that helped him cope with the crisis. "Two small miracles happened. Prior to that I'd had very little faith. I was not raised religiously. I had next to no spirituality at all, and when Tommy was expected to die I felt I was losing everything. I didn't know which way to turn. Nothing was relieving the pain. Nothing was helping. I went downstairs in the hospital and started praying. Tommy was comatose at the time. I was praying because there was absolutely nothing else to do. It was like everything had been stripped away. I prayed for God to be with us, to let me know that He was present. As I was doing this, I heard a voice—very clearly—in my head. It said simply, 'I am here.' I got chills up my spine. It was as if my prayer had been answered. Once everything had been stripped away there was room for God to come in. It changed my attitude on how to deal with the crisis at the moment."

Shortly thereafter the time came when Dennis had to decide whether to keep Tom medicated or not, whether to keep him on the antibiotics. "Since I had power of attorney, it was my decision to take him off the medication or leave him on it. I was so torn. Tommy was unconscious in his bed. I went downstairs and prayed again. I said to God, 'You have to give me a sign of what to do—and please don't make it abstract! Make it as clear as You can.' I went back upstairs, and just as I walked in front of his room, Tommy got up and called out to me. I went into the room and closed the door. I said, 'Honey, you have to tell me what you want me to do.' I explained the situation to him. 'Do you want to live, or do you want me to take you off all this?' He quickly said, 'I want to live.' We embraced, and we both cried. Then I said, 'You've got it.' I went right out to the doctors and told them to keep Tommy on the medication. Then I went back into the room, and he was asleep again. But his getting up at that moment had been a sign—a very clear sign—that Tommy had been enabled to communicate his wishes to me, and I was not left to flounder about what to do. Tommy really wanted to live. Although earlier he had said he wanted to commit suicide because of the pain, Tommy never lost his spirituality. Up to the last moment he still had the idea that this was just the beginning of something and not the end. And I grew to believe that. By the time he died, I knew he was going to a better place."

Tommy was brought home from the hospital, but Dennis could see the deterioration daily. "The nurses continued to be here around the clock, but I was in there with them, changing diapers, packing him in ice, staying there as much as I could. I tried to sleep in the room, although it was very hard because of all the machines that were on. Then his family came out, and there were two more visits to the hospital. The last one was for just two or three days, and we brought him home again. Then it became a deathwatch. He lingered for two weeks—longer than the nurses thought he would. He was fighting valiantly to live. The doctors kept him plied with morphine, and he had other drugs that would have put out an elephant. One day it looked like he was ready to die, and the next day he woke up and said, 'I want to go to the Huntington Gardens.' So we got the wheelchair out, and with the nurse and his sister, we drove him out to the gardens. We spent about two hours just strolling through the grounds, taking in all the roses that were blooming and everything else. Then we brought him home. He was extremely weak. About four days later he passed away."

On the night Tommy died, Dennis's son, Sean, was with him. "My son was incredibly supportive. He was a rock for me, just unbelievable. Tommy's mother, Sean, and I stayed up all that night. I was holding Tommy's hand and stroking his head. I was reminded of a scene in *Longtime Companion* in which Bruce Davison is sitting by the bedside of someone who is dying, and he is urging him to let go. Davison says over and over again, 'It's all right. You can just let go.' That scene was very moving, but I'll tell you something—it does not even come close to what goes on in the end. The emotions were so incredible. Tommy was slipping away, and I was urging him to let go. I was talking about God and the warmth and the sunshine. I told him how much I loved him and what a difference he had made in my life. I kept telling him what he had meant to me and just continued to stroke him. His breaths started coming about one every thirty seconds, then forty-five seconds. I was sitting very close to him, and the nurse was taking his pulse as I was talking, talking, talking to him. Finally she said, 'He's gone.' It was absolutely devastating. I remember that as soon as he went my eyes automatically went to the ceiling of the room. I started calling out to him, telling him how much I loved him. It was like his soul was rising, and I kept calling out to him. Then I came out to the backyard by the pool and started yelling up to the sky that I loved him."

Dennis tells of the fears he had after Tommy's death and what helped him conquer his doubts. "One of the issues I faced when Tommy died, and one of my greatest fears, was that it was over and that when Tommy died he didn't have that moment of feeling warm and safe and happy. Instead it was only about the suffering. I remember sitting here for a couple of days and just praying to know that Tommy was all right. My son and I were talking about this, and it dawned on me that just praying wasn't going to help. I needed to do something about it. So Sean and I went to the bookstore, bought some books by Dr. Raymond Moody, and I started reading about life after life. Those stories and their similarity to our situation helped immeasurably. I began to feel better almost immediately. There is a corner in me that still has the doubts and fears, but for the most part I feel confident that Tommy knows absolute joy now. And that has helped."

Talking about Tommy's death was an important avenue of relief for Dennis. "I have a great deal of support at the Twelve Step program. A lot of people there keep in close contact, and that helps me. One thing I know from the program is that you can't push things down. You can't try to hold them off until a later date. So I try to face it, and when I feel the grief, I let it happen. The pain scares me sometimes because it is so overwhelming. But I go through it and then I pick up the phone and talk to people. I don't feel ready for a bereavement group right now. My feeling is that I'm in touch with people who care, I continue to share at the Twelve Step meetings, and I can have people to my house immediately if I need them. I know a lot of people who have lost their friends, so they understand and empathize. In a way, that's like a bereavement support group without an actual meeting. Just talking helps. Isolation is the worst thing."

Dennis had been concerned about upcoming holidays and what effect they would have on him. They were not as difficult as he had anticipated. "Actually, Thanksgiving was a better day than I thought it was going to be. I went to dinner at three different places, to friends' houses. It turned out to be a relatively nice holiday. In December, I chose to leave the city and go to Sante Fe and spend Christmas with my son. Obviously there were moments of remembering Tommy, lighting a candle for him at the local church, toasting him at dinner, always wishing he were with me. But the pain was not as deep. Being away from home and familiar surroundings made it easier. There were many fresh places to go to, things to do and share with Sean. We kept busy and out of harm's way."

Dennis describes his life after Tommy. "I can only say it's been a roller coaster. At times I've wanted to jump off and end it all. But those feelings pass. Sometimes there's serenity, a kind of acceptance. But this is frequently replaced with feelings of panic, incredible grief and anger, and thoughts of suicide.

Fortunately, through all this I've chosen not to drink, although the thought has crossed my mind on several occasions."

One indication of recovering, Dennis believes, is the fact that he has gone from ranting at God, from severe anger and blaming Him, to a point where frequently he thanks God for the blessing of having Tommy in his life for four years. "This has not been an easy transition," Dennis explains, "and sometimes I don't feel the gratitude. But more and more these days I thank God that Tommy and I were able to share a moment in our lives. Of course anger does creep in, and I have to remember that I'm only human and these are human emotions. I tend to beat myself up if I'm not perfect."

During one particularly difficult period Dennis called somebody who had gone through a similar loss and discovered a new purpose in life. "At one point I began getting extremely depressed. I just didn't want to go on living. I called a man who had lost his lover about six years ago. We met and had an illuminating talk. The thing that was most important to me was that he said he, too, had been suicidal about four or five months after his lover had died. He couldn't think of any purpose to life. But now, today, he said to me, 'It's six years later and I'm sitting across the table from you and I'm helping you! That alone shows a purpose. The purpose may not turn up immediately, but it will surface.' What he said to me was so profound, I thought. He had walked in my shoes six years ago, and he was now able to help me because I was in the place where he had once been. He was able to talk to me as he could because he had experienced the same thing. I hope that I can pass this along to others—to know you are not alone in your feelings and thoughts. Listening to this man and hearing about his experiences helped so much. I began to realize that regardless of what happened to Tommy, I had to be grateful for my life and not waste it. Once that sunk in, things started looking up, and I've been doing better ever since."

Dennis started going out again and tells of his anxieties and fears in that connection. "I am no longer dating the person I was seeing for the past few months. It ended amiably, and it has not sent me into a tailspin. Rather, I see those few months with him as a blessing, helping me through the grief and loneliness.

And I'm grateful for them. But when it ended, it did send me into panic—fear that I'll never have another loving relationship as I had with Tommy, fear that I'll be too old for someone to be attracted to me. And, of course, I fear dating. As recently as last night, I was crying over my loneliness and frustration. But that, too, passes. What I learned from Tommy is that I can have a nurturing, spiritual, physical, passionate relationship with someone, a relationship that grows with time and becomes deeper. What frightens me is the possibility that it will never happen again. If I can stay out of my own head, I'm better off."

Dennis believes that by sharing his feelings with others, and by continuing his therapy and writing about it, the intense grief has subsided into something approaching acceptance. "This acceptance doesn't stay with me all the time, but it's there often enough that it gives me some kind of vacation from the insanity. All in all, it's getting better. There are rocky moments, lots of turbulence, followed by moments of acceptance and serenity. Work helps me get through a great deal, and fortunately I've been very busy with my writing these past few months."

Dennis's therapist had suggested he write a letter to Tommy. "It was a very painful experience to go through, but I did write. I've been writing a lot of letters. One breakthrough came when I wrote a letter to Tommy and then my therapist suggested I write one from Tommy to me! That, too, was extremely painful, but it was part of the process, and it has helped a lot."

Two of the poignant and touching letters Dennis wrote to Tommy and from Tommy to himself are printed below in the hope that the reader will benefit in a cathartic way. They are love letters from the heart and express what many of us may feel we would want to say to our loved one. It should be stressed that before anyone attempts these kinds of letters, a therapist should be consulted. When Dennis wrote these letters, it was under his therapist's supervision, and when he read them aloud (which is of prime importance, Dennis states), his therapist was sitting with him, guiding him through his feelings. Let us now share these beautiful sentiments.

The following letter to Tommy was written at the pond where his ashes were spread. It was three months after Tommy died. In the letter Dennis refers to a note from Tommy that was written a couple of weeks before his death and left with his nurse, Scott, to give to Dennis afterward. Dennis started to read it the day Tommy died but collapsed in hysterics. He didn't read it again until this day at the pond three months later.

> *My dear, dear sweet Tommy:*
> *I'm sitting under a tree at the pond, looking over the water, and two swans are floating by. It's cloudy and cold, but it doesn't matter because I'm here with you. I've just read the last letter you wrote to me. The one you had Scott give me after you left. I couldn't read it until now, and I'm glad I waited till this moment, because it's so special. I, too, will love you forever, Tommy. I will never, ever forget how special you were and how special we were together. Words alone can't express my love for you. It's an indescribable feeling deep in my soul. Our love was hard fought, hard earned, and because of that, was deeply, truly felt. I seem very still at this moment, sitting here. It's a very strange calmness I didn't expect.*
> *I brought another letter with me. One you had written after one of our arguments. It's a beautiful letter, full of love and giving and understanding. Tommy, I pray and hope I gave as much to you as you have given to me. You grew so much. You were like a flower blossoming and growing more and more beautiful. You said in your last letter to me that I wouldn't be able to see you anymore but that you would be with me forever. Oh, God, Tommy, I hope so. I hope you're here now. I want you so much to be with me, to be sitting with me and holding my hand. I wish I could look into your eyes again and see that devilish smile of yours. Tommy, I wish we could have gone through life together.*
> *Jesus, Tommy, it's not fair not knowing you're all right, not knowing you can feel my love for you. Tommy, I ache with love for you. I hurt from missing you. I've brought three beautiful pale peach roses—one from me,*

one from Alfie, and one from Sparky.* I'm placing them in the water.

I'm going to read your letters again. Tommy, you're in the most beautiful spot on earth. It's everything you loved—the wonderful old cemetery, East Hampton, the swans, the grass. It's right where we walked, surrounded by the old houses we loved. In fact, right across the pond is one of the houses we saw when we were thinking of moving here. It's beautiful, and we loved it. I remember that day so well. I'll never forget any of our life together, and my prayer is that when I die I can be reunited with you. See how much you gave me? I want to spend eternity with you. Now how many people can say that?

How many times can I say I love you? What will it take for me to finally, truly, deeply believe, to know that you're alive in spirit, watching me, that you're happy and safe and warm? Of all the things in life, Tommy, I want that feeling inside of me. God, I pray to you, I have the willingness to believe. Please take my hand—please take me to where I know in my soul that Tommy lives. I ask nothing more and nothing less. You brought Tommy into my life, bring him back to me. Let me know his spirit lives with you, and that all his suffering led him to a world as beautiful and as loving as I've heard.

Tommy, you and I were a miracle together. I am so grateful to have had you in my life. I will never ever forget you. I will never ever stop loving you with all my heart and soul. You will always know that, Tommy. Please, please don't leave me. Always be part of my life and know that no matter what happens, you are in my heart forever. Your life did make a difference. You helped me grow, helped me learn about love and compassion. Through you, I learned what true love was all about. I will be forever grateful to you, forever in love with you, and I will always look forward to when we can be together again. Rest in peace, my love. You deserve all the happiness, love, and peace God has to offer.

*Our two dogs.

God, please take care of Tommy. If ever there was a special child of God, Tommy is that child. You created him. It's your responsibility, so damn it, you better take care of him! If God loves you half as much as I do, Tommy, you're in good hands.

God bless you, baby, and save a place for me!!!

All my love forever!!!

Buddha[†]

Dear Buddha:

Oh, God, I want to be there with you. I know you loved me. I've never, ever doubted it. You're the only one in my life who, the more he got to know me, the more he loved me. You have no idea how much you meant to me, how much you changed my life, Buddha. I could trust you. I never could trust anybody, but I trusted you with my life. You took care of me. You loved me. You cried for me. You took charge—nobody ever did that for me.

Don't you ever question whether I knew you loved me. I did. And what's great is that I grew to love you just as much. I love you now, Buddha, and it breaks my heart to see you in such pain. I would do anything to keep you out of pain. You just have to trust that I'm all right. I know you loved me and trust that I love you. I will always, always love you, Buddha. What we had was so special, but it's changed, and you have to move forward with your life. You have to have faith. You're doing everything you can, but you have to have faith. I promise I'll see you again. I promise I'll always love you. I miss you and the puppies, but now it's time to move on. Buddha, don't cry so much for me. Please. It makes me cry. Don't stop talking to me or writing to me, but the pain you feel can't go on like this. For me, Buddha, please have faith that everything's okay. I love you!

Tommy

[†] Tommy's nickname for me.

Writing, be it in the form of letters, poetry, or simply jotting down sentiments, provides many survivors a quiet place to store memories and air daily thoughts. Such was the case for Herb Schwartz.

Herb, now in his early sixties, and Dick Robinson, who was fifty-four when he died in 1992, were an older couple and had been together for sixteen years. Herb finds that writing in his diary and reflecting on events—the good times as well as the bad—provides a great sense of comfort to him.

"When Dick was sick, I didn't keep up with the diary, but now that he's gone, I try to write things down each day, the little things that happened between us. I write about what I remember—the way he buttered his English muffin in his own particular way, how he folded his newspaper, the kinds of specific things I will never forget. There were also rough times, but mostly I write about what we shared, like the trips we took, especially the ones to London and Italy."

Other entries in Herb's diary comment on things that bother him now—and bothered him then, prior to Dick's death. Especially troublesome to Herb was the fact that Dick would not talk about his impending death or his last wishes. His refusal to do so left Herb in a quandary in the end.

"There is one thing that still bothers me. Dick never talked about his imminent death. Even when we were well, we could never really broach the topic or talk about funeral arrangements. I would say that I wanted to be cremated and that I didn't want any kind of service. 'Just put my ashes in a pretty place,' I said. But I never got a response from Dick, like 'That's what I want, too' or 'No, I'd like this.' So I did for him what I would like done for myself and had him cremated."

Herb tells of his decision as to where to place Dick's ashes, given the fact that he had no clue from his lover about this issue. Five years earlier the couple took a trip to Vermont. Dick had special memories of vacationing there as a child with his grandparents. "One day," Herb remembers, "while walking through the woods there, we saw the most exquisite flowers and rushing streams. Suddenly we got off the trail and climbed over a stone wall. It was like the most perfect place in all the world, with beautiful grass and magnificent flowers, just the perfect place.

The image of that has stayed with me, and I shall never forget it. So when Dick died, I thought, This is where I can put his ashes. This was the perfect place. And Dick and I had talked about it being the perfect place, so I felt very good about putting his ashes there. As I did, I knew that was what I was going to do about myself."

Herb's therapist was concerned when he learned of the plans to scatter Dick's ashes—only because he felt Herb should not do this alone. Herb called upon Dick's cousin and her husband, and along with several other friends they drove up to the "perfect place." Herb recalls the peaceful day.

"There were eight of us. We walked up the trail. I said a few words and explained why I was leaving him in that place. Also I had found a beautiful poem among his papers. It was 'Dirge Without Music' by Edna St. Vincent Millay. So I read that. Then we put on a tape of Dick singing songs he had written, and I scattered the ashes. His cousin strewed some flowers over the ashes. I finished before the tape ended, so we stood around and listened as the tape played out. It was very beautiful, actually. The tape ended, and we wandered back down the trail."

Another issue that still troubles Herb revolves around his denial that his lover's health was declining. He had always considered himself to be a cool, calm, collected person. But when Dick developed CMV the stress took a toll on Herb.

"He started out with a terrific pain in his leg. His nervous system began to break down, especially in the spine. Then, for a long time the doctor was very positive and medicated us at home. The one thing I look back on that was awful was that I lost it a lot of times and I broke down. I couldn't bear to see him getting worse. If he couldn't do something that he had been able to do a few weeks before, I would insist, 'Oh, yes, you can do it!' And I would push him. It was a form of denial because I didn't want it to happen. I was hysterical most of the time. Every new thing threw me.

"Except for the doctors, no one knew that we had AIDS. Dick didn't want to tell anyone, and I didn't, either. I was being very protective of my mother. I didn't want her to know. Although I had outed myself with my mother, and she accepted my relationship with Dick, I don't know how much she wanted to hear about it. I couldn't hurt her by saying I had AIDS. I know she loves me, and I'm trying to be a good son."

After Dick's death, Herb went to see his doctor about the depression he was immersed in, hoping to find a way out of the morass. He also decided to seek out a support group and called the People with AIDS Coalition. He learned that help was just around the corner. "I spoke to a fellow recommended by PWAC and broke down on the phone. I told him that my lover had died, that I had AIDS, and that I needed an AIDS support group. He said, 'I think you need a bereavement group as well,' and told me about one I might join. Not only did it help me, but I'm still going, that's how great my experience with this group has been."

Herb likens his experience with the group to discovering a newfound family with whom he feels safe and secure. He tells of the warmth and affection generated in this haven of compassion. "You develop a kind of caring for the people in the group, and they become like family. You listen to their stories, and you feel safe enough to talk about your own experiences—about anything, revealing yourself in a very basic way. It's really wonderful, like reading a great novel or something, but more so because you're relating to real people who care about you, too. It's very moving and at the same time very helpful. I don't know why, but it works! I suppose it's the sharing that we do and the intimacy that you feel with the people in the group. You never fully recover from such a loss. The pain will always be there, but I have noticed definite changes for the better by being in the group. This was not the case earlier when I went to a couple of walk-in support groups run by another organization. I only went twice because they were very large groups and there were a lot of new people each time. I think you can lose yourself in such a large group."

Herb has found he is now able to resume some of the activities he pursued prior to his lover's death. "Recently I have gone to a couple of concerts. I went to one alone and to another with a friend. I've been going to the theater, and I'm beginning to do things again. I guess maybe I'm starting to accept the way things are."

* * *

Another surviving lover who found support groups of enormous help was Yoshua Eyal. He needed a place to vent his emotions. Yoshua was angry—angry at the AIDS plague and enraged at his lover of eighteen years. "Why did my lover have to go out and get AIDS from someone else? This was the question I asked myself. How dare he? We had what I thought was a caring and trusting relationship. Since I am HIV negative, I knew he didn't get it from me."

Yoshua was completely unaware of his lover's illness. "I didn't know that Paul had AIDS until he went to the hospital, where he was diagnosed with AIDS pneumonia. Six weeks later he was gone. He went so fast. He never talked about his disease to me. He talked about it to everyone else but me. He even asked his doctor not to talk to me about it. He didn't tell me anything concerning his illness, even at the end. When I finally found out the diagnosis, I did all the talking. 'You tell me how you got AIDS,' I said. 'Tell me, because I'm in the dark.' He didn't reply. Then he was at his sister's house for a few days, so I held off, preferring to talk to him about it at home. But he never got home. He never came back. It was an unfinished story, and I felt like shit."

Time has diminished Yoshua's anger. "I will love Paul forever. He was the whole world for me. Of course, I have forgiven him. At the time of his illness, I couldn't think clearly. I didn't understand what was going on. This was the first lover I was sure of and thought I knew. After I discovered he had AIDS, I didn't understand what had happened. Also, it was the first AIDS case in my life. I had heard of other people getting it and dying, but this was the first time I actually experienced it. Paul and I were involved with each other. We were not involved in the gay underground. I have friends from my early twenties and teens, and I have always kept them as friends. When I reflect on things, I believe that Paul was trying to spare me from pain and stress. He knew my nature and that I would have gone bananas, which I would have."

Yoshua takes comfort in believing he and Paul will be reunited. "Paul was a Puerto Rican Catholic, and I am a Jewish

Israeli. I believe in an afterlife and that we will meet again. I can feel his presence around me and know that our souls are one. I believe he is with my mother. She died fourteen months ahead of him."

On his lover's birthday, Yoshua went to the cemetery. A photographer by profession, he wanted to bring some of his photos from a special project on AIDS to his lover's grave. He wanted to make a statement. Yoshua tells what happened at the scene. "At first I was going to have someone else take my picture there. Then I decided to do it myself. I took a picture of me lying right over the gravesite, with my head by the plaque showing Paul's name. As I was lying there, I suddenly wanted to go straight down into the grave to be with him. I had to fight the feeling, yet I didn't want to fight it. If the ground had opened up and if I could have gone into the same box with him, I would have said, 'Okay, thank you, Jesus.' But the ground didn't open up, and I thought, I'm alive, and I'm going to do the best I can with it."

The theme of Yoshua's special photography exhibit was suggested by a friend who said to him, "Why don't you do a show of all the people who have lost someone to *this* holocaust—the *AIDS* holocaust?" Yoshua thought it was a splendid idea. "The show honored the caretakers of the people who died of AIDS and was shown on the second anniversary of Paul's death. You can see my pain in the photographs. In one, a man wearing a business suit is barefoot on the beach at Southampton, holding ashes in his hands. They are his lover's ashes. Another one portrays a dinner table, set for two people, but only one fellow is there. So it becomes a dinner for one. Opposite him is the chair with his dead lover's dinner jacket on it. This shows everything that's going on today."

As Yoshua approached the first anniversary of Paul's death, he contacted the Gay Men's Health Crisis, which referred him to a bereavement support group. Yoshua tells of the fears, the guilt, and the hopes shared at the meetings. He also stresses the importance of networking.

"I have created new friendships within the group. Whenever I go there, we keep saying, 'Network, network.' That's what it's all about. That's the only way you can survive. When I see newcomers, I tell them the same thing. I can feel their pain because I can relate it to mine, and you help yourself when you help others. You soon find you can relate to people who have been through your experience, who have walked in your shoes. You need the right people to talk to or they cannot relate. I want someone who will let me cry my head off if I feel like it.

"We shared many things at the meetings. I feel guilty that my lover had AIDS and I don't. He was the young one, not me. When I first met Paul, he was twenty-three. He died when he was forty-two. I don't know why, but a lot of gay men feel this way. A lot of us feel guilty for staying alive. But now I realize I've been given another chance in life, and I'm going to take it. It's important for me to survive. I also talked about our families. Paul was an abandoned child. His mother left him when he was two years old, and he was raised by an aunt. He had a very difficult childhood. When he was sixteen, his father denied him. 'Because you're gay,' he said. Other than one sister, he really had no support. I was his mother, father, brother, and main support. My own family is in Israel. My mother accepted it somewhat. My brothers would have nothing to do with us because they are homophobic. That is their problem. Inasmuch as my family is very Judaic, they can't accept my way of life."

Yoshua addresses a fear shared by many surviving lovers. "Everyone I talk to has the same fear—they are afraid to start up a relationship because of their loss. And now, at my age, which is fifty-one, it's like 'How can this work?' I feel I have to get on while I still have life left, and then I say to myself, Where are you, Paul? I feel I have the right to 'be' again, but guilty thoughts take over. Paul is dead, and I'm okay. How do you explain it? I've tried to get things going now. You don't want to start up again, but you know you must."

I N T H E above story, we heard a survivor tell how his lover made efforts to spare him pain and stress. In the following account, a young woman talks about similar efforts made by her loved one.

Even on the day he was dying, Nancy Miranda's lover tried to spare her pain. He had always been protective of Nancy, twenty-four, who was twenty years his junior. That desire to protect her didn't change when John was hospitalized. Nancy tells of his request that she leave his bedside.

"On this particular day, he was very weak and having trouble breathing. He said some very nice things and also told me there were so many things he wanted to do but couldn't. I imagine he was thinking about the fact that we were supposed to move to Florida, but we didn't get to do that. And we were going to be married, and we never got to do that. At the hospital, he said if I ever got tired, or if I couldn't take it anymore and wanted to leave, he wouldn't blame me in any way if I left. I told him I would never leave him, that I would stay with him until the end.

"Once before when he was in the hospital, John got angry with me for being there, insisting I had to live and that I shouldn't be spending all my time at the hospital with him. He kept pushing me away, and that really aggravated me. When he came home, he told me to go to my mother's house. I was very hurt. I didn't want him to be alone. But that's the way he was. He had to be strong and wanted to protect me from his illness, from seeing him so weak. I went to my mother's home as he wished, but I was only away for a couple of nights. I did so much talking to him on the telephone, eventually I convinced him that I should come back. And I did. He couldn't take my being away anymore, but he continued trying to spare me and never complained of his pain. His attitude of wanting to protect me didn't change when he went back into the hospital. On the day he died, he was adamant that I leave. I saw how upset he was in wanting to make sure I was not there to see him die. I had to respect what he was doing and what his wishes were. I had to let him have that final strength as a man, taking care of me by asking me to leave."

Two hours after Nancy left the hospital, the doctor called her to say that John had expired. "At first I did some screaming. Then I called my mother and father. I felt that my soul had been ripped out of me. My parents came and took me to the hospital so we could view the body and say good-bye to him. But it was horrible. I still get flashbacks of seeing him on the bed with no life. It's very hard to know he isn't here. We both believed in soul mates. When we first met, he said he felt our souls had met once before. I'm grieving for him now, and I miss him so much. I miss him physically. I miss holding on to his hand in the street. I miss talking to him. But my soul longs for him and to be with him in the other land that he's in."

After John's death, Nancy was angry with him. "When you grieve, you get angry with the person who died. I looked at his picture and would say, 'How could you do this to me? You left me in this world all by myself, and I'm afraid. You're not here to protect me anymore.'

"I knew John was HIV positive from the first day I met him. But when he went into the hospital, I was terrified. I felt so alone. I was very dependent on him. I wasn't working and was having a hard time finding a job. I had a job interview scheduled, but that was the day John landed in the hospital. John was very well educated and was an HIV educator as well as a substance abuse counselor. He was a volunteer with the People with Aids Coalition, and was on the Speakers Panel. He spoke about how he was living with AIDS. John and I went to see a therapist together to talk about our fears of dying. Everything seemed fine after our sessions, but later I was in an emotional turmoil. I wanted to be in his fight. I made a promise to him that when he died I would finish what he started. He fought and stood up for what he believed in, and that is one of my goals—to continue his work in helping people with AIDS and survivors like me. One of the first things I did to help myself was to try to bring comfort to people. I let friends know that he cared about them and loved them, and that he wanted the best for them. There were times when I would be strong and then other times when I needed someone to be strong for me. Although my parents and my friends were there for me, I wanted someone to slap me and wake me up—this nightmare was not happening to me!"

At one point in her life, Nancy felt that God had let her down and that going to church was for goody-goodies. She didn't believe that the church solved anything. Rather, she thought it made life move slower. "When I was an active addict, I felt that God had abandoned me. I'm a Catholic, so I grew up with religion. At one time I was very involved. But then I got into drugs, parties, and drinking and figured that was what life was all about."

After John's death, Nancy's views on God and going to church changed dramatically. "I no longer saw God as a punishing person. I realized that going back to church was the only way to salvation for me. My thought was, Go back to church, pray a little more, and ask God to help you. It was better than going to a bar and asking the bottle to help me. I feel that going to church and to therapy helps. I go to therapy once a week, and there's also a group at the church called BEREAVEMENT for people who have lost loved ones. There are times when I still get angry and yell. I spoke to a priest about this, and he said, 'If you have to yell at God and yell at John, then go ahead.' He added, 'It's okay for you to do that.' But I also light a candle for John every night. It makes me feel that he's at peace. For quite a while I really felt he wasn't at peace. I had also had that wishful thinking that maybe he was still in the hospital. Or, I imagined, maybe he had moved to Florida with his sister and was hiding over there. A lot of times I was tempted to call his sister and say, 'I know he's there. The jig is up.' "

Nancy shares an odd experience she had at church, one in which she sensed John's presence. "I had always told John, 'If you die, I want you to come back and tell me if there is a heaven.' He promised he would. When John died, I started questioning, Where are you? Please tell me that you're okay. I was worried about him. I've read that we, the ones who are left behind, do worry about them after they have died. We ask, 'Can you please just come back and tell me that you're okay?' At the church one morning, I had a weird experience. One particular priest never says the homily during the week because on those days the masses are only a half hour. The priest was standing at the pulpit when all of a sudden I saw a figure of John standing behind the priest! It almost seemed like the figure was imprinted in my mind and wasn't like he was literally there. And then he disappeared into the priest. Just after that, a curious thing happened. The priest said a homily, talking about heaven. That day at the church it was like John came to tell me, 'There is a heaven, and I'm fine.' I felt paralyzed with fear, and yet at the same time I felt peace. I couldn't get up to leave. I strongly felt his presence that day. It doesn't mean that I accept his death. I'm still in the process of trying to do that. I know it's going to take a while, not only for me, but for anyone who has lost a loved one. But now that the incident in the church happened, my fears are lessened, and I'm not afraid of death anymore like I used to be."

Realizing she has more work to do, Nancy is continuing in therapy and is moving in the direction John took. "It was John's most earnest wish to help people conquer their woes, and that's the route I am taking. I'm getting more involved with the People with Aids Coalition. Whenever I get the opportunity, I volunteer. I'm making it a point to learn more about AIDS and went to Albany for AIDS Awareness Day. I live on a day-to-day basis. I don't live in the past, and I don't live in the future. Like other survivors, I'm trying to make it without my loved one, and it's hard."

M ICHAEL DANILOWSKI also went through a phase when he lost his spirituality and subsequently regained it. He was struggling with the trauma of hiding his life-style. Michael went from being a hidden griever at his work place to that of an open advocate of sharing an AIDS loss with co-workers. He describes the events in his life that led to this extraordinary change.

"My life partner, Mark Bivens, was only twenty-six when he died. I'm nine years older, and we had been together over four years. Mark was never able to accept the disease as a reality, and it was very difficult to watch him in the end because he was in so much pain. I wanted to help him let go, but his anger was such that he struggled through the very last night that he lived. I have a house in Jersey City, and most of caring for him was just helping him with home stuff, cooking for him and things like that. The worst part was the diarrhea and helping to clean him up. It's amazing, but you never forget the look on somebody's face when that happens—it's such a humiliating thing to happen to an adult. During the time Mark was still home, we tried to lead as normal a life as possible, even when he got sicker.

We had people over for dinner and to visit, which he really enjoyed.

"Mark's family lived in Ohio. They visited us on a regular basis each summer. He came from a very large family, so his mother would rent a van and a bunch of his brothers and sisters would come with her and stay with us for two or three weeks. Generally Mark would go home for Thanksgiving and then stay in New Jersey with me for Christmas. For some reason that last year, he decided to do the reverse. He went with me to my family's for Thanksgiving and went home for Christmas. But I had an uneasy feeling about his trip and asked him, "Please come back." When he left for Ohio, he was fine. When he returned, I picked him up at the airport and he was in a wheelchair.

During the time Mark was ill, Michael found it very difficult to go to work, not because of his duties there, but because of the comments he heard associates make about people with AIDS. His lack of courage in facing such a barrage of negative remarks added to his stress. Michael describes the feelings he had during that painful period.

"The week that Mark was sick, I kept calling in every day and taking a vacation day. Then, when he died, I took more vacation time. I had to go back to work the day after the funeral and pretend that nothing had changed in my life. I hated going to work. It was really stupid because it was my own fault for not telling the truth about what was happening. The people who worked with me knew it was unusual for me to just call in on the spur of the moment and ask for a day off, so they asked if everything was okay. All I was able to tell them was that a very close friend of mine had died. But that wasn't the truth—my partner had died. I had to suppress a lot of anger in hiding that truth."

A newly established program at his company enabled Michael to come forward with the truth. "My company started a program to change the corporate image. Part of it was taking a course for personal growth. They wanted employees to facilitate the course. I applied and was accepted. I went to Philadelphia for training the week after Mark died. At first I was going to cancel, but it turned out to be one of the best experiences I ever had. During that time I was able to get rid of a lot of the anger I'd built up against my company because I couldn't tell them about my loss. There was a sense of trust and camaraderie growing among the group of people being trained to be facilitators. But it wasn't until the end of the second week that I was able to reveal my sorrow. They knew that someone in my life had died, but they didn't know the relationship. During those two weeks I would come to the course, and the people would talk about the fact that they had spoken to their wives last night, or to their husbands, or to their kids, and how great it was. That was eating inside of me to hear all of these comments because Mark had just died. Normally I would have shared all of this with him, and I couldn't. So at the end of that second week, I was in tears. I broke down and told them that every day they had been talking about their loved ones, it had been killing me. I told them Mark was my partner and the one I would have called to share all of this with. I explained who Mark was to me and that he had died of AIDS."

Michael was astonished at the support he received from his group of co-workers and found it to be a very healing experience. "Just being able to get that out in the open really helped me with my work because I didn't want to go back and pretend that life was still normal. And I felt a great sense of relief at the way everyone offered support to me. But my own medical problems curtailed my work soon afterward. I have AIDS myself. I got sick the year after Mark died. I had been HIV positive for nine years and had some problems about six years ago that Mark helped me through. About two months after Mark's death, I started having illnesses that got more serious as the year went on. I had pneumonia. I developed KS, which is the AIDS-related cancer. Actually, I continued to work longer than I should have."

Michael had a premise about continuing to work. He figured he had survived nine years with HIV and that if he just kept on working and being productive, he wouldn't die. "In my mind, I was equating stopping working with starting dying," Michael recalls. Although he had been on chemotherapy for almost a year, Michael was trying to hide his illness at work. Vision problems and a worsening situation forced him to take a week off at Christmas. It was then that Michael did some careful soul-searching. "I realized I was probably killing myself by remaining at work, so I went in the following week and talked to my boss about what was happening."

After he stopped work, Michael's life was a daily rotation of doctors and hospital visits, combined with evenings spent with his family and friends. He found there were many empty hours during the day and decided to do something constructive to fill them. "I missed the work environment contact—when you are with people—and I thought maybe I could be helpful to others like myself. So I called the People with Aids Coalition in New York and started working as a volunteer on their AIDS hot line. It has been extremely rewarding to me doing this."

In working the PWAC hot line, Michael made a startling discovery—one he hopes to help rectify. "I was shocked when I found out that there are so many people who are not anywhere near a place that can help them. When we live in a major metropolitan area, we take so much for granted. The other day, for example, a twenty-three-year-old woman from Arkansas called. She has AIDS and a three-year-old child. She just wanted to talk to somebody with AIDS. So I talked with her for a while. What we attempt to do for people out of the area is to find support services located near them. I couldn't find anything within two hundred miles of her, and I thought to myself, My God, what would I have done if I hadn't had the support groups that were available to me?"

Michael reflects back on the groups that helped him in the months after Mark died, as well as the ultimate support from his own family, who had initially found it difficult to accept his sexuality. They also found it hard to talk about Mark after his death, as did many of Michael's friends. Because of their reticence, Michael decided to let everybody know it was okay to speak Mark's name.

"When a person dies, people are very strange about not knowing whether to talk to you about it. I told everybody, 'Don't ever be afraid to talk to me.' I even got upset with my parents. During the first couple of months after Mark died, they never would bring up his name. I finally said to them, 'It won't upset me if you talk about him. It upsets me more if you don't, because it's almost as if you're denying the fact he ever existed.' They said, 'We wanted you to bring him up. We were afraid if we did, you would be upset.' I said, 'No, I would be comfortable with that because in some ways talking about him keeps Mark alive for me.' "

Initially, Michael's parents had difficulty in accepting his life-style. "When I was in my early twenties, I came out to my parents. They had a lot of trouble coming to grips with that fact. They are very strict Catholics, and their problem stemmed from what the church says about gay men. But I was very determined and didn't give up on them. I knew that they loved me, and I loved my parents. I just stuck with them to let them know I'm not a different person now that they knew I preferred to sleep with a man rather than a woman. Even when they got upset about it, I just stayed around. I didn't run away. I refused to accept their being unhappy with it. Over time, we got into some heavy arguments. Basically, I kept staying there because I knew that if you loved somebody, his sexuality wouldn't really matter because you loved who that person was inside.

"As soon as I met Mark I told my parents that I had found somebody special. There was an upcoming family function, and I told them I wanted Mark to be invited. I think my parents immediately recognized he made me very happy, so they welcomed him into the family and were really accepting. And after Mark's death, it meant a lot to me that my parents were willing to acknowledge that loss in my life as the equivalent of losing a spouse."

Michael describes the period when he lost his spirituality and offers hope to others by remembering when he regained it. "I was raised a Catholic, and I'm religious, too, but not in the traditional sense. I think I'm more spiritual. I don't believe in a lot of the dogma, but I do believe in God, and I believe in something beyond this life. But after Mark died, I went through a phase when I lost my spirituality and I stopped praying. It wasn't that I hated God. It was simply that I couldn't pray anymore because I didn't feel comfortable. But eventually that all came back again, and I saw something good that came out of all of this. I saw some changes in me, some understanding that I never had before about things. With that, my sense of spirituality returned."

The changes and understanding Michael mentioned above were brought about primarily through the growth and empowerment he experienced after becoming part of a bereavement support group. Michael recalls the strong desire he had to strangle the facilitator at the time.

"I can laugh about it now, but the first time I actually wanted to strangle a nun was during the first group I went to for bereavement counseling. It was at a Catholic hospital, and at the end of the fifth meeting, there was a lull in the group's conversation. The nun, who was the facilitator, asked us, 'Well, have you learned from this experience?' or, 'Have you grown or changed from this?' I nearly leaped out of my chair, ready to go for the jugular. I wanted to say, 'I don't think there is any lesson I could learn from this that's worth losing someone as special as Mark was to me.' *But I don't feel that way today. I know I have been changed by Mark's illness and by his death—changed in a positive way.* I would still rather have him back, of course, but through his death I have learned a lot about myself, a lot about him, and a lot about love. *I'm really a different person.*

"It's funny. When I talk to friends now, or new people who have suffered a loss, I want to tell them that it *does* get better and you *do* have a sense of change and growth. But I'm almost afraid to tell them that because it's something they have to learn on their own—I know when the sister said it to me, I was ready to throttle her. But now, two and a half years later, I feel differently. It took me about a year to start to realize that I did learn from the experience. I learned that I was there for Mark and found out through friends he had told that to. I have learned some nice things about myself and some not so nice things. I learned how in some ways I was selfish in a relationship. I learned about how important love is in your life because of the friends and family who stayed by us throughout Mark's illness and afterward when I was struggling with his loss. They understood I was in pain, and they were willing to listen to me. So I learned a lot about the kind of love you take for granted before a loss of this magnitude."

Michael conveys the sense of connection he felt by participating in a support group with people who had been through the same experience. "Although my friends and family were wonderful, in many ways they didn't really understand. I don't think it's ever possible to completely understand something you have never experienced yourself. In the support group, when you talk to someone who lost a lover or significant other, when they say things, it really strikes a chord. You say, 'Gee, I felt that way, too'—and you don't feel so crazy with some of your own thoughts."

Keeping a journal was also helpful to Michael and enabled him to observe changes in his feelings as time progressed. "Since Mark died, I found it to be very beneficial to write down my feelings. I don't do it that often, but every now and then I kind of look over earlier times. I see the distinct change in my feelings from the time he first died, the anger at the loss of someone so young, and I realize I'm not that bitter anymore. I think putting your thoughts down on paper is very therapeutic. In fact, I tell my friends that you have to get the stuff out in some way. If it's through writing, that's fine. If not, talk about things. Don't hold them in."

M OST SURVIVORS indicate the key to recovering is talking or "letting it all hang out" in writing. George Marentis did both.

George was assailed by overwhelming feelings of guilt surrounding his lover's death, manifested partly in his relentless struggle to convince himself that he had nothing to do with Philip's illness. He describes his torturous thoughts. "It was very painful from the start, and I've kept wondering and mulling it over in my mind as to where Philip got AIDS. I don't know if this is an issue for other gay men or not, but it is one that has driven me to distraction since 1985, when I also tested positive. I was in a state of turmoil, trying to come to terms with losing Philip, but also having to deal with feeling that I don't have the right to grieve for my lover because I might have been responsible for his death. Friends have tried to convince me it is absurd to think that way and although I realize how illogical it may sound, the feeling is still there, however small the percentage of possibility may be. People have said, 'There is also the possibility Philip gave it to you.' But, oddly enough, I would never consider sitting here and saying 'Philip, you did this to me' or blaming him in any way. When I met him I certainly wasn't a virgin, so there would be no basis for blaming him. Yet I've been able to blame myself and that's where the absurdity comes in. I feel this has blocked me from being able to mourn him fully. In a sense, it may be a way of not wanting to let go."

George was also tortured with the ostracism generated toward gays and tells of traumatic details. "AIDS is a disease that had to be hidden. I recall taking Philip out of our apartment on a stretcher to the hospital and cringing that people were looking at us. I always worried someone would say 'He has AIDS' and that we would be kicked out of our apartment or harassed. It wasn't bad enough that my lover was terminally ill; there was also the fear of being watched and scrutinized, of having to be under cover. It was a feeling of isolation and trying to brave the world alone. AIDS in the minds of many is still an unacceptable disease. Also the notion that Philip was gay, hence he had AIDS, was outrageous—as if he'd chosen it. And I go back in time to the sight of my lover—whose innocence and inner beauty I have both felt and witnessed—lying there dying, and he is not being allowed to feel total acceptance and compassion from others because he doesn't have the 'right' disease. So I do my best to ease his emotional pain and, in the end, feed him drugs to ease his physical suffering. I pray for some miracle, some happy ending, a spontaneous remission, perhaps. A shiny and new Philip. It doesn't come. He gets worse. I don't feel I have any right to complain, so I start taking his painkillers, too. They deaden my desire to scream, 'It isn't fair, it isn't fair. *Stop, stop, stop!*'"

Although friends offered to help care for Philip, George recalls that he took it upon himself to try to be Superman. "I tried to do everything, wanted to make everything right for Philip. As for Philip's family, his parents had died and his sisters were relatively nonsupportive. They called about once a month, and that was hard on him. It was hard for me with my family, too. I've never involved them in my life-style, so I couldn't convey to them that I was devastated over losing my lover. When my mother learned Philip was ill, she was nice in that she brought food to us at times, but it wasn't the same as if my brother-in-law were dying, and what a tragedy that would have been in the family. It was a totally different situation because it was not viewed as a spousal loss."

Although George and his family have always been on good terms, he found it difficult to be open with them. "As a gay person, there has always been the sense for me that I've been a disappointment to my family. I've never been fully embraced and accepted, particularly when I go to family functions. Nobody ever says, 'Oh, here's my son. He's gay.' It's more like, 'Oh, George isn't ready to get married yet.' Well, George is thirty-five years old, and it's not whether I'm ready to get married or not, it's that I'm gay. So I remain someone rarely spoken about. I'm kept hidden to a degree, and that's kind of insulting when I think about it.

"I've never really pressed it, because it's a difficult issue. I've never demanded that I be accepted as a gay man and that it be acknowledged within family circles. I've always rationalized and said, 'Well, I'm tolerated, and we have a good relationship. It doesn't need to be spoken.' But now, with all that's gone on with the AIDS issue and losing people I love and seeing friends sick, it makes everything else seem so terribly insignificant. There is the temptation to tell relatives that I'm gay. I mean, they always ask me, 'Who are you dating?' and stuff like that. Obviously I'm not dating anybody female. So it's weird in a way to remain closeted, and yet I still feel an intense desire to scream and shout out somehow. My mother knows I'm gay, and to see her go to all lengths not to mention it kind of hurts me. It's as if I were born with blue eyes and she put brown-eyed contacts on for my whole life because they were an embarrassment of sorts."

George elaborates on how he has managed to cope with some of his obsessive thoughts about having killed someone— Philip—and how therapy helped him pull through this painful period. "It was torture going through his illness and toying with the horrible idea that I caused Philip's death. My therapist has gotten me to the point where I can actually say to myself, Yes, this is a possibility. Yes, this makes me feel very sad. Yes, this makes me feel awful, but it doesn't necessarily make me a bad person. And that's worked, believe it or not, which is incredible because this is something I have agonized over for eight years—morning, noon, and night."

What also eased George's distress was being able to express his thoughts and fears not only with his therapist, but also at support group meetings and to friends. One hurtful episode in particular haunts George. "Every time I recount it, I cry, but then I experience relief talking about it. Philip's doctor at Sloan-Kettering had prescribed morphine pills to eliminate his pain. That evening, while I was in the bathroom, I heard a thud and came running out to see what was going on. There was Philip on the floor. He had fallen off the bed and was smiling. He said, 'I just got up. I forgot I couldn't walk.' He looked so sweet and innocent. If only I could unlock his legs, I wished, and make him walk again. If only I could free him from the nightmare of AIDS. If there is any consolation to be derived from all this, it would be that Philip is at peace, free from his suffering, and that before he died he felt my unconditional love for him."

George had difficulties trying to shake the mental images of AIDS and believes the route to survival is to tell the truth about all of the emotional pain suffered, the feelings of helplessness, the desperation. "Just keep talking about it until it becomes less overwhelming," he urges. "I know it sounds trite, but time is really the healer. Time distanced me from some of the nightmares—of what Philip's legs looked like and things like that. I was totally consumed and would sit around and move my legs and feet as if I had the same affliction on my body. But somehow time and talking about it did help, and those horrible feelings subsided."

Only recently, George found himself reminiscing about happier days with Philip. "I thought to myself: 'Rather than think of Philip in sadness, let me think of him at all his funny times.' I began to recount all the cute things he used to do, and I actually started smiling. It was tinged with a kind of longing, but it was helping to recall those moments."

Four years after his lover died, George found it cathartic to write about Philip. His poignant words follow.

• *p h i l i p* •

Four years and four months after he was diagnosed with AIDS, Philip lay in a hospital bed at Sloan-Kettering. His doctor admitted him on January 20, 1989. I knew how sick he was. Oddly I didn't know at first that he wouldn't be coming home. I had prepared myself for his death, but then he'd looked a little better and I thought, "Well, maybe he'll be okay for a while." I guess he knew because he'd signed a form stating that he should not be kept on life support and he'd asked that a priest give him his last rites. I slept on the floor in the corner of his room—on a mat— and it felt good just to be near him and to know that my presence brought him comfort. He wasn't bitter. In some ways, he seemed relieved. He held my hand and said, "I can't believe you stayed with me," and he said, "The only thing that matters is love." How I wished that love could heal his physical disease—rid him of AIDS. We would walk out of the hospital together and do all the things he'd wanted to do—simple things like see Cybill Shepherd return to the movie screen in Chances Are. *He loved Cybill Shepherd at a time when others would look at him and say, "Cybill Shepherd, are you kidding? What a no-talent has-been." Then came "Moonlighting" and Cybill's return to popular acceptance and he was so excited. Just like a little kid. His childlike qualities—his innocence and his playful nature—made him so lovable. People who knew Philip would automatically know he was a big Cybill Shepherd and Burt Reynolds fan. For a long time after his death, I could look at neither of the two without wanting to scream, "It just isn't fair. He should be here to see them!"*
The essence of Philip was love and kindness. What words cannot translate is his Philipness—all the stuff that made him uniquely Philip. I mean the funny and silly things he would do at home—things that if anyone saw them, he would die of embarrassment. Or his displays of

kindness toward others. Not to be able to re-create Philip hurts. The void is there. I could speak of Philip until I'm blue in the face and still not accurately describe him. After he died, his aunt Gloria said, "He lives on in my heart." And I immediately thought to myself, I don't want him in your heart. I want him back. Alive. The way he was. I just managed to mutter that I thought he might be coming back. This thought sustained me for a while. The thought of Philip actually returning vibrant and alive. He called me Chickpea. And I called him Foozie. He would knock on the door: "Surprise, Chickpea, I'm okay." "Oh, my God, Foozie, my sweetheart, I can't believe it, it's a miracle. I'll call your sisters, I'll call Aunt Gloria, I'll call Aunt Chickie, wait until Ed hears . . . "

Philip died on February 16, 1989. It was about 3:30 in the morning. I woke up and looked at him and didn't see the sheets going up and down with his breaths. I climbed into his bed and lay next to him and put his arm over me. His face looked so peaceful and beautiful. I said, "Where'd you go, my Foozie?" After a few minutes I buzzed the nurses' station. "I think Philip is dead." The nurse came and checked his vital signs and determined that indeed he was. "Are you sure?" I asked. She nodded. I felt numb. "He was only twenty-nine," I said. And tears filled the nurse's eyes.

It's been almost four years since Philip died and sometimes I feel like it doesn't hurt anymore. Then something brings Philip's Philipness to mind and all the sadness comes back.

I love you, Foozie.
Chickpea

''O N E day, he was lying there swatting at something in the air. I asked him, 'What do you see? A fly?' 'No,' he replied. 'There are these big brown bats attacking me!' So I helped him swat them."

Michael Jalbert was coping with a catch-22 situation because of the course AIDS was taking with his lover, but his primary concern was trying to keep Willy calm. "I wanted to do anything and everything to keep Willy from being upset. I knew the disease had affected his mind. It began to affect mine, too. It was so scary. I tried to calm him down. I knew if he became aware that his mind was messing up, it would freak him out. So I had to pretend it was normal. Usually I just sat there in the chair next to him. I would read something or talk to him. But on the day he was fighting off the bats, I almost lost it when I began to swat along with him."

Although Michael describes the relationship he and Willy had with their families as basically good, he also tells of his feelings concerning the lack of caregiving support. "He had two brothers in Idaho. Willy and I used to live in San Francisco, and they lived in Oakland. Both of Willy's parents had died—his mother five years ago and his father ten years ago. I knew his family for the nine years we were lovers. We never hid anything from them. They knew about our relationship, and that was fine with them. The same was true with my family. But to really get in there and deal with his illness was a different story. They didn't help with that, and it fell on me alone to take care of him. I feel ambivalent about that because although that's the way I suppose I would have wanted it, I also would have liked to have some kind of day-by-day support in taking care of him. However, I know of many cases where the lovers are cut right out of the picture, where families just come and grab their sons and take them home. That stuff really does happen. We were lucky in that respect because no one tried to do anything like that. I felt it was my duty, anyway. But in retrospect, I think it would have been nice if the family, both his and mine, had been a little more supportive through the illness because they knew what was happening from the word *go*."

Michael had a lot of anger that he had to set aside in order to concentrate on taking care of Willy. "When I started to think about our families' limitations and what they could have done but didn't do, there was a lot of anger about that. At one point, when I didn't think he was going to pull through, I called his brothers. At my encouragement, they came to New York to see him. It meant the world to Willy that they were there. Shortly before he died, my folks came down to visit Willy in the hospital.

Every time he was in the hospital, which was a lot, they would send flowers and cards and those kinds of things. I think the reality of AIDS was pretty frightening for them, and the stigma kept everyone at a distance. It was too scary for all of them, including my brothers and sisters. Even some of our friends backed away. Just the word *AIDS* will do that. You can sense their discomfort by some of the things they say. For example, when you talk to people, they will comment, 'this terrible disease' or use some other euphemism for AIDS."

Trying to find a bereavement group after Willy's death presented some unexpected problems for Michael. "When I first tried to go to a group, I called, but unfortunately they only form these groups after they get a certain amount of people. I tried to get into the group a couple of weeks after Willy died. It took them a few weeks to call me back. By that time I had joined another group because I didn't want to wait on them. I needed help *now*. It was good just to be with other people who had also suffered a loss. At first it was very hard to go because it was during the holidays. I got very depressed. I didn't go to the second meeting because I couldn't get myself out the door. When I did go back, people talked about the different things that bothered them. Some were more talkative than others."

One of the issues that Michael was now able to face was the residual anger. "One of the things that came up at the bereavement group was to express your anger. Because my priority had been taking care of Willy, I suppressed a lot of anger. At first I didn't feel angry at all, but it was too early for me to feel that. I just felt numb and was experiencing the shock and sadness of early grief. But in the group, my anger really surfaced. I realized I had been making excuses for what everybody *didn't* do—like the family for not coming out to visit more. And all those times that our friends, who knew Willy was sick, didn't do anything to help us. Even with his close friends, I would have to get on their tails to get them to come to the hospital. People are afraid to go to hospitals. It depresses them, and that would be the excuse. 'It's so depressing' or 'I don't like hospitals' or some other lame excuse that made me crazy. When someone is fighting for his life, he needs support. Willy was so generous to his friends. If he had a friend who was ill, he would go to visit them in the hospital every single day, even if it was on the other side of town. Willy never gave excuses, much less puny ones. That gets me angry because people didn't give him the kind of support that he needed and that he deserved. Maybe I had very high standards of what I wanted people to give him. I will never forget the pain and suffering he went through and that those who could have helped him were not there. I was also angry at the disease. We were in our early thirties and just building our lives. Now it's all gone."

Guilt was another problem area Michael had to grapple with in the group. "I felt a lot of guilt. I tried to think of everything I could do to keep Willy alive. Ultimately, I knew that I was not able to do that. I knew it was not within my power to keep him alive. Now I feel very guilty about the petty fights we had before he got sick. It all seems so foolish, such wasted time. After an argument we wouldn't speak for a week sometimes, and I feel guilty about that lost time. At least, when he got sick, we were both aware of making every moment count."

Michael tried escaping from the pain, if only for a few hours, by going to dinner and visiting with mutual friends. "I'm not a going-out person, but that seemed to help for the moment. But ultimately I ended up right back in the same place—pain. No matter what you do, you still have to go through the pain. There is no answer to death that is going to take it away, and nothing is going to make it easier to accept. But, after the six-month mark, I started to feel relieved and was able to let go of a lot of the negative feelings."

A very curious thing happened one day on the subway when Michael found himself engaged in conversation with a stranger. "It wasn't the most private of places, but we got to talking. It turned out he had lost his lover a month ago. When he found out that I had lost my lover, he asked me, 'Does it get any better?' I was amazed to hear myself saying, 'Yes, it does. Over time, you do start to improve and get better.' And I meant it!"

E D   M A R L A T T ' S mother had been his pillar of strength during his lover's illness. She tucked Jimmy and Ed under her wing and nurtured them. It was a heartwarming sight to see this trio, so immersed in love and concern for each other. But, similar to events in Agatha Christie's story "Ten Little Indians," murderous villains (named AIDS and cancer) entered the scene, and soon that number dimininished to one.

When his mother went into the hospital for tests, Ed was concerned. It was thought she might have kidney stones. Two weeks later she was in the operating room for over four hours. Although Jimmy was also very sick, down in weight to less than one hundred pounds, he insisted on going with Ed to the hospital. As Ed sat waiting in the recovery room with his dying lover, the doctor came in and announced that Ed's mother had terminal cancer. Soon after the surgery, however, Ed's mother improved remarkably and started radiation treatment. In fact, Ed remembers, the diagnosis became much more positive. It was almost as if his mother wouldn't allow herself to die before she could complete her mission to help her son see Jimmy through his death.

As painful as it was for Ed to fathom that he was going to lose the two people he loved most, some positive things came out of the experience. Ed explains, "When you are taking care of someone who is dying, the caregiving and the intimacy, along with the time spent together, gives you the chance to discuss so many things. I felt it was important with both of them to talk about the good times we had shared and also to talk about an afterlife. Jimmy and I had been together for seventeen years. I was thirty-eight when he died, so there were many memories. With my mother, a lot of stuff resurfaced in our talks. As she lay dying and I was grieving for her, the loss of my father came up. I had never really grieved for him.

"My father had died of cancer, a slow death. It had been very helpful to us that my father was put into a hospice, and my mother suggested we do that to help with Jimmy's needs toward the end. He went to the Cabrini Hospice in Manhattan. He was at home until the last three weeks. My mother's illness was taking a toll. Jimmy's sister stayed with him during the day, and I would spend all night. I was with him the moment he died. It was very early in the morning. The sun was shining in the window, and for a few minutes I felt that the world had stopped. That was my sense, that everything had stopped. I realized that our physical life together was over."

Another trial for Ed was delivering Jimmy's eulogy while his mother was present. But, once past that, his mother reinforced her support by bonding with Ed's friends. "I was eulogizing my lover, and in the front row was my mother, who was also dying. That was very rough. But that night my mother sat in my living room with twelve of our gay friends, and I realized how totally she had accepted me for who I was and how warmly she had embraced my partner in life. I appreciated that, and it's a fond memory."

Following Jimmy's death, Ed's mother spent the first two nights with her son, but she encouraged him to resume living alone. "She said to me, 'You know, Ed, the sooner you get back to staying alone in the apartment, the better it will be for you.' I was leery about that but agreed to try it. The first night was very rough, then it got less and less difficult. I reached out and developed a telephone network with so many people. Also, a month later I got a pet, a cat named Hector. It's been wonderful. I'd never had a pet before, and this was a big help to me."

Work was a big factor in helping Ed cope. He works with children who have hearing problems. Currently he is on sabbatical and is attending Gallaudet University in Washington, D.C. Ed also found other ways of helping himself. "The most important thing that helped me was the Caregivers Group, which was run by the Brooklyn AIDS Task Force. There were six of us. It was run by a psychologist whose husband was a hemophiliac and had died of AIDS. There were five of us in the group besides her. Four of us were gay and had lovers, and another was a woman whose brother had AIDS. As time passed, we all lost our loved ones. I was the third in line, so to speak, and I saw how the first two dealt with their loss. I used them as 'role models.' That support group was extremely helpful to all of us. After that, I went to the bereavement group at the Gay Men's Health Crisis, and that was also very helpful. I went there two weeks after Jimmy died and continued for about six months. Then, about a year later I went to a special bereavement group at St. Vincent's Hospital developed specifically for HIV positive partners who had lost a lover to AIDS. We were not only grieving, but we also had the same virus that killed our lovers.

"I have also been involved in a group called Body Positive. It's for people who are HIV positive who have not yet developed AIDS. They offer orientation and seminars and twelve-week support groups. I facilitated one myself about two years ago. Then I felt I was burning out on groups. When my lover was dying, he was at a support group at GMHC, and that was very helpful to him. He also had an AIDS 'buddy' who was very helpful to me because my lover's family had a tough time with AIDS and the gay issue and dying."

Ed found it comforting to go to the cemetery to visit his mother and Jimmy. "At the gravesites, I would have conversations. It was important to me, and I have no qualms about that. I felt my lover's presence, and whether real or imagined, that was helpful."

Ed was also given other opportunities to memorialize his lover. "On the year anniversary of his death, I donated money to the Brooklyn Botanic Garden. They put a bench in with his name on it as a memorial. There was also an opportunity for me to speak about him on World AIDS Day."

When Ed was alone and not with the support groups, he found other routes to help him get through his pain. "In the house, I used meditation, which helped to calm me. I called a lot of people when I had an intense grief period, or I would go to the gym, and that helped me get through very difficult days. I prefer to mark their birthdays rather than their death days, so on Jimmy's birthdays as well as my mother's I have flowers put in the church. I have done a lot to get through the rough stuff. And my friends have been enormously supportive. Also, traveling, reading, and different activities have all helped."

In Washington, D.C., Ed became involved in an intimacy and relationship group for gay men. "I'm the only person who's lost a lover to AIDS, but the group has been very helpful. I think the major issue for me was grief and letting go, and then my own HIV positive status. I'm about ready to start dating again. I haven't dated for nineteen years. I was thirty-eight when Jimmy died, and I really never had a roommate of any kind, only my lover. I think that the end of a major grief is finding a new relationship, when you reach the point where you feel you can go out again and can let go of the grief. I know a lot of people in my bereavement group who started dating right away. Sometimes I thought, Oh, gee, I'm falling behind! There's something wrong with me! Then I realized a lot of them had only been together for a short time, so they picked up fast. Or perhaps they did it because they were desperate to find someone else. I don't know, but I gave myself a lot of time. I'm just getting my life back. I'm working on my Ph.D. and hoping for a new relationship. So I'm not focusing on other issues. With my HIV, I'm very healthy still, and it's been seven years since I was diagnosed. The only issue I have with HIV is disclosure with other people, dating, and stuff like that. But I think you should tell about your HIV positive early on, because it starts to build."

Today Ed feels he is doing very well but recognizes there is a sense of loneliness. "Right now I'm proud of the fact that I learned how to reach out. Sometimes I really feel the sense of loneliness because I travel alone a lot and I see the empty chair at the dinner table. I don't think it really has to be like that, and hopefully a new person will appear in my life. I'm grateful, though, for the terrific support I had. I don't know how I would have made it without the groups and my friends. If I can help someone who is going through this, that is the reason for participating in this book. Maybe this will pass some of it along."

I N   T H E preceding testimony, we heard from a survivor who had suffered two losses—his mother and his lover. In the following accounts, we hear from survivors, Michael Zients and Bill Davidson, both of whom suffered the loss of two lovers.

Michael Zients was concerned that he hadn't mourned properly for his first lover and was determined to chase away all the ghosts. He set out to find ways of insuring he had put both losses to rest and explains the course he decided to take. "This time, I have attacked bereavement with a vengeance because I was worried that I hadn't really done it right the last time. I wasn't sure that I had said good-bye to Bruce [who died in 1986], and now I am facing the acceptance of the death of my second lover, Don."

Because Michael felt he had kept postponing his grief, he is cautious about repeating his former reluctance to deal with the issue. "I had always felt I wanted more time to heal after my first lover's death. I kept thinking time would make it easier. I wanted to make sure that wasn't the case after my second loss. I don't think simply waiting makes it any better. I'm never sure whether the feelings I'm experiencing are grieving or bereavement or whether they are just feelings I would have anyway. Now I've been much more aggressive in trying to work this through. I go to a drop-in group at GMHC and also to another bereavement group for AIDS survivors."

Initially, Michael felt put off because he had to wait six months to get into the bereavement group. As a result, he is in a group with participants who have suffered more recent deaths. He explains how both groups have been beneficial in different ways.

"The group at GMHC has been more helpful than I expected. At first I was reluctant to join a drop-in group. I thought that the weekly change in people would be difficult, but in some ways it's better. My prejudice was that it would be easier to relate to the same group of ten people for eight weeks because you would get to know them and feel more comfortable. But, actually, I found that you overcome the discomfort of talking in either situation. In some ways it's helpful to listen to different people's experiences and their reactions and then bounce your own responses off them. When you have the same people, everyone has a position. When the people change, there is a difference. In the drop-in group, people are at different stages. There is more of a variety. I'm also in individual therapy. The Gay and Lesbian Community Center has bereavement intervention counseling. Also, I find that reading provides me with insights that have been helpful. There was one book about a woman who lost her husband in a car accident when she was in her thirties. Her book was just anecdotal about her own feelings and responses. It was different, but the experiences were similar. Some of the other books are simply too clinical and psychology-oriented to be helpful to me.

"Now, I'm actually feeling that I'm starting to taper down. I'm planning to go hiking in the Tetons in Wyoming for

Memorial Day, and I've got a bicycle trip planned to Seattle for the Fourth of July. I don't feel I need the bereavement groups as much. I seem to be getting along okay. For a while at work, I had a lot of trouble concentrating. But I feel a lot better about things generally, not just work. I'm somewhat reluctant to say I feel normal, because I don't trust that feeling. It might go away again. Once before I felt that I was there, and I wasn't. But now I think I'm functional and back to life. I feel a little guilt about that because it's been only seven months, and that doesn't seem quite long enough. Nevertheless, I do feel better."

Many survivors have come to understand that recovering doesn't mean they have to forget. Nor does it mean they may not have occasional setbacks. While there may be many good days, there may also be some difficult ones. Time allows people to ventilate their emotions, and those bad days will occur with less frequency. Some survivors believe extended bereavement is necessary as a tribute to the deceased loved one. Often they rationalize that the longer they grieve, the longer they are symbolizing their love. But this is an impairment to recovering. Loved ones will always be missed, but no one has to serve a lifetime sentence to prove it. There are many different feelings the bereaved experience in the grief process, and each person's temperament and makeup determines those emotions.

O N N E W Year's Eve, a time when most people are celebrating and anticipating the countdown to one minute past midnight, Bill Davidson was left with the passing of the old year and the death of his lover. Many survivors facing traumatic anniversaries because of specific holiday dates—New Year's, Christmas, Thanksgiving, Valentine's Day—find that even if they want to forget those dates, the newspapers, television, and radio are constant reminders.

When it comes to holidays, birthdays, and anniversaries, what *can* ease the pain and loneliness on these days? Grief therapists suggest there are ways in which the bereaved can try to survive the difficult dates. They also indicate that the anticipation may be worse than the actual day. All anniversaries stir within us a conflict of past joys and present pain. What may be right for someone else to do on those special days may not work for you at all.

Do things that are very special or important to you. Don't feel locked in to continuing to do things in a traditional manner—and that pertains to friends, co-workers, and family members as well. Although they may sincerely want you to be part of their activities, don't be fearful of saying "no" to invitations or accepting on a tentative basis.

If you don't feel comfortable in having a Christmas tree or a Hanukkah menorah, try compromising with a bowl of ornaments or a bowl of fruit on the table. Similarly, in any given situation, whatever is uncomfortable should be altered. Moreover, don't be surprised if resentment, guilt, anger, and sadness are intensified around holidays and anniversaries.

While it may help to do things a bit differently, bear in mind that just because you choose to do something one way the first year after your loss does not mean it's written in stone. You don't *have* to do it the same way next year. The rule of thumb is if it feels right for you, go for it; if it feels wrong, forget it.

In Bill Davidson's case, initially he found that the holidays were the roughest time for him, but later he discovered that the pain diminished as each progressive holiday passed. "After you've lost a loved one," Bill explains, "the first year is the most difficult. During birthdays or anniversaries, there are times when you passionately wish the person were there. I spent this last New Year's Eve by myself. It's kind of a blur. I know I went to church and then spent the rest of the hours by myself listening to some quiet music, and I cried. But it gets easier as time goes on. Although you realize he is no longer here, you have good memories of being together."

Remembering his lover's last Christmas just days before he died, Bill poignantly describes those last precious moments. "Christmas was Mikel's favorite holiday, and it had always been a big event for me since I was a kid. Mikel and I collected antique Christmas ornaments all year long. The whole house would be done over for the holiday, and it was such fun going to get the tree and bringing it home. It was such a wonderful time for both of us. I'm thankful to God that Mikel was able to appreciate his last Christmas. I got him into the shower and dressed him a little bit. I persuaded him to try to open his presents. He made it to opening one gift—it was a stuffed animal. I helped him with opening it, and then he held on to it so lovingly. The other gifts remained unopened. Christmas lasted maybe fifteen minutes before I had to put him back into his bed. It still brings tears to my eyes. It wasn't until a year later that I could take the gifts I had purchased for him and open them—and then I put them away."

Bill lost two lovers to AIDS. His first loss was his companion of nine years, Ronald, who died at a time when no one really knew what AIDS was all about. Bill describes the tumultuous period. "People had started getting strange illnesses and were dying, but no labels were attached. I was so confused because I didn't know what we were dealing with. Ron had a case of shingles, then a respiratory infection that was hanging on like a flu that wouldn't go away. I'm talking about somebody who was an exercise fanatic—great body, good health, and no history of illness. So this was all strange. Today we would immediately know that these were symptoms leading toward AIDS. Ron went into the hospital and seven days later he was dead. I was even more devastated because the day before he died, the hospital staff had urged me to go home and get some sleep. They'd assured me that Ron was responding beautifully. At two-thirty in the morning, the phone rang and I was told that he had passed away. I was totally unprepared for that news."

Two years later Bill experienced a happiness he never thought to see again. "I was very fortunate that I met Mikel a couple of years later. We started up a relationship, which I never thought would happen again in my life. After we were one year into that relationship, Mikel became ill. Five years later he passed away—the way we had *planned* it, beautifully, with dignity, and at home. He wanted no life support. We talked about all of this from the onset of his illness. When his mind was no longer clear and he couldn't make any decisions, I was capable of taking care of him and making the decisions we had discussed at an earlier point. That is something I think more couples should do, and it's one of the things we talk about in our group. You have to be very involved as a couple in dealing with the illness, being very open. You must ask questions of your doctor and ask questions of each other—things like what forms of service do you want, how far will you go, whom do you want to be contacted, and what do you want to be done."

Bill tells of some difficult moments he and Mikel shared in their discussions about the illness and the effects on their lives. "We not only discussed his pain, we discussed my sorrow. He was very upset that he would no longer be with me and that all the dreams we had planned as a couple would never be realized. Any terminal disease robs you of your future, and all couples, whether heterosexual or homosexual, plan for a future."

Bill addresses many issues that survivors face—their own health issues, prejudice even within their own circles, and the fear of loneliness. "After the first bereavement group, which focuses on the grief after your lover has died, you may be left to deal with your own health crisis. You may be HIV positive yourself and feel tainted by society's outlook even within your own gay world. You're dealing with your grief, but you are also trying to handle your own health care problems, possibly wondering if you will be left all alone when you become sick. I was in the midst of this when I received a letter indicating that a new group called Beyond Bereavement was being started. The group was targeted to men who had lost their partners and who were also HIV positive. I joined, and it's now been a year that we have been meeting. We go for ten weeks, then take a couple of weeks' respite. Some people drop out, most remain, some new people come in from other bereavement groups and continue on with us. It's been a wonderful experience—like being an 'Old Man of the Sea,' so to speak. You are able to give hope to other people who are very fresh to their loss. Much of this sounds very trite, but later on a lot of the pain goes away and then wonderful memories fill your heart when you think of that person. The loved one never leaves your life. We're also looking death square in the eye, determined to make the rest of our lives easier and meaningful."

Having lost two lovers, Bill believes his presence in the group offers hope to others that it is possible to have someone new enter their lives. Although Bill is not seeking another relationship himself, he derives comfort from offering that hopeful outlet to others. "I consider myself a widower, and I'm very comfortable with that. There is another fellow in the group who has also lost two lovers, and he is hoping for another liaison, which I think is great. It is a matter of personal choice. But I think it's so important for the younger people in the group who have just gone through their loss to hear our stories. It shows them that there is hope and they can form another relationship for whatever time that they have left. They don't have to face the world alone. If they choose to live without another partner, at least they have friends they have developed within this group—friends who will help them as they get progressively sicker. I also discovered I have a parenting complex of my own. I've been using my experience to help others who have been sick, helping them go through their illness and their death, which, unfortunately, happens too often. Being able to help someone live the last part of their life with as much dignity as possible, and to die with dignity, has made me a better person. That is something very few people will have the opportunity to experience."

Bill believes his desire to help others is an outgrowth of many influences in his life. "I am also extremely religious. That was my mainstay all the way through Mikel's illness. I have a strong belief in God. I don't understand some things. I know the disease, AIDS, exists. It is not a gay plague. It affects everyone and, unfortunately, will affect many, many more people. Mikel and I went to a Catholic church on major holidays, and we often stopped in just to pray periodically. The parish was in a gay neighborhood, and the priests were all very helpful. They have also been very responsive and helpful to other friends of mine. I believe in an all-forgiving God, so my idea of Catholicism does not fit into mainstream, textbook Church dogma. But the church has been a major support for me. I gather my own strength from it, even though we differ. Although Mikel attended my church, he wasn't a Catholic. However, religion was a very strong part of his background and was a comfort to him throughout his illness."

Family and friends also played a major role in seeing Bill and Mikel through the difficult times. "I was connected with the Gay Men's Health Crisis in a Care Partners support group throughout Mikel's illness. Most of us had lost all of our friends, so our group became a network of friends and family. When Mikel passed away, I was on the phone at once to let them know, and three of them came over to me within twenty minutes. All of us have worked to prepare others for the same situation. To this day, we are still doing that. I was also very thankful because Mikel's family was phenomenally supportive throughout our entire relationship and Mikel's illness. His mother and two sisters are nurses, so all three of them had firsthand experience. One of them specialized in an AIDS ward for a period of time. Although I was the primary caretaker, when I had to go away on a business trip, they would fly in from Seattle, stay, and do what they could. They went back and forth so Mikel could spend as much time with them as possible. We are still close, and I consider them my family, too, which is wonderful. In fact, Mikel's family thanked me for having kept him alive as long as I did."

With all that he has endured, the loss of two lovers, his own HIV status, and the loss of so many friends, Bill still considers himself very lucky. "I truly am thankful for all the wonderful people who have been in my life. And I consider myself fortunate to have the good memories. Life becomes very precious when you realize it can be shortened so quickly."

I N T H E passages above, we read how Bill Davidson spent his first New Year's alone. In the next story, Peter Newman tells of spending holidays with his family as well as his lover's, as they had done in the past. Richard Greene was not only Peter's lover, he was also his business partner. "Richard was fashion editor for *GQ* and for the *Daily News Record* and was fairly well known. We were in business together and had seven men's stores. When he was diagnosed, things started to change very quickly. We got out of our businesses and started living for today."

Although Peter and Richard came from different worlds, they hit it off from the beginning. Peter comments on their previous life-styles. "I was married for eleven years and came from a Jewish background in New York City. Richard had a Catholic background, was from New Jersey, and was a man about town for many years. I was not. I came out about a year before I met Richard, and then, in many respects, Richard became a mentor for me. When my wife and I got divorced, my family was very concerned. They were upset for both of us. Once we got through the divorce and the anger, we decided it was easier to be friends."

Richard's diagnosis came the week of his fiftieth birthday. Peter describes the events that led to a blowup with the hospital surgeon after Richard was rushed in for an emergency. "Richard wasn't that sick. Up to almost the very end, he was able to take care of himself. He had a bout with spinal meningitis and was in the hospital for five weeks with intravenous twelve hours a day, but he came through that fairly well. Then he became strong again. That was a year after his diagnosis. His illness started when we were up at our house in the Berkshires, near Albany, on Christmas vacation. So he remained there and got excellent care.

"In August, I went to Las Vegas on business, and Richard nearly collapsed while I was away. His sister took him to the hospital because he was in such pain. He was diagnosed with MAI and given antibiotics. He seemed to get better and was then released from the hospital. The next month a similar situation occurred, and my parents got him to the hospital. Richard's doctor was waiting there and took X rays. A hole was found in his intestines. The next thing I knew, the doctor consulted with some specialists and then said, 'The story is he's got another three days.' I went absolutely bananas. I called everybody I could think of and was hysterical for about a day and a half. His family flew in from California. Everybody rallied around."

Peter now comes to the surgeon who caused him such unhappiness. "Richard had been in a VA hospital in Albany, and they were absolutely wonderful. At the hospital in New York, Richard also had a great attending physician, who was my own doctor as well. The surgeon was a different story. He was against surgery, said there was very little chance that Richard would survive it, and that he would not leave the hospital alive. I will never forget the scene or what was said there. I was across from Richard's bed when the surgeon turned to Richard and said, 'Well, you know you're going to die anyway, so it really doesn't matter.' I became so enraged, I absolutely lost it. I charged over to Richard's attending physician and said to him, 'If that man ever comes within one foot of me again, he will die! I do not want to see this man again—ever! You had told us in your own way what was happening. Richard knew what was going on, and so did I. Richard didn't need this brute to come in and say what he did in such a way. We didn't need to hear that.' There are a lot of insensitive people out there. On the other hand, the social worker was terrific. He came to see me and Richard two and three times a day."

After Richard's memorial service, Peter flew to Mexico to get away for a time. He then tackled the upcoming holidays. Richard died on October 30. "Our families had always spent holidays together. Richard's family, for example, was always part of my family's seder at the Passover holiday. We celebrated every holiday together, both the Jewish holidays and the Christian ones. I spent Christmastime with Richard's sister and her family in Connecticut. My parents were supportive throughout. At New Year's I was with friends in the Berkshires, although it was very difficult to go up there. I'm not alone in my circle of friends. We've all been through this many, many times now, and I've lived through it with people who have been going through the same thing. We hug and cry, then have a glass of wine and cry some more. Sometimes tears come out of nowhere. I can be having dinner and all of a sudden a smell, a word, a sound, something, and tears come to my eyes."

Peter marvels at the fact that he made it as far as he has and tells what helped him. "It's been six months now. I never thought I'd make it past the first two weeks. I never thought I'd make it through the day. I must say the bereavement group I attended was very helpful. I was able to share experiences. I realized I was not 'losing it' because of the things that were going on in my mind. There were other people who felt exactly the same way I did—confused about going on with life. Trying to establish ourselves as oneness instead of twoness. We discussed that in the group and the fact that people meeting us for the first time know us only as ourselves and not as a couple. And that's very difficult. The other thing that the group helped me sort out was that everything sad that happens to me is not all related to Richard's death. I have to disinvolve the sadness from work and the sadness from other things in life. I've just got to realize that for the rest of my life there will be other things that make me sad or upset, and I've got to learn to understand that on a broader level. I hope time will take care of that."

There will always be memories, Peter acknowledges. One in particular comes to mind. "Richard must have sensed it was going to be his last year. I believe that because of something he said to my mother when he presented her with a gift. Richard had also been in the antique business. He had a beautiful antique diamond-and-pearl pendant that he had gotten for the shop. But my mother was turning seventy this year, and he decided to give it to her, saying, 'I don't know if I'll be here for your seventieth birthday. I want you to have this now.' When my mother wears it, I get a little nuts, remembering that occasion and what Richard said. I'm happy she has it, but it's a tough memory."

Peter also recalls the peaceful surroundings at Richard's burial place. "Richard was buried up in Valhalla. It's a nondenominational cemetery, a beautiful place. He would have loved the magnificent setting. It's very old and woody. We had a nonreligious service. He did not want to be cremated, so he was buried in a pine box. It brings me comfort to know he is in such a lovely spot."

There is a message Peter wants to impart to those who have lost a loved one to AIDS. "The one thing I want to stress to others is that *it helps to talk about it.* Find somebody with an open heart and an ear, someone who is a good listener and who is supportive of you. You have got to keep talking about it. If you don't have someone like that, there are support groups all over the country that have hot line numbers. If you can't find anyone in your vicinity, call one of the hot lines just to talk. Gay Men's Health Crisis is very important. In almost every major city, there are AIDS awareness support groups and hot lines that you can call for some moral support—just for an ear. *Reach out and find one!*"

Note: For information on various groups and hot-line numbers, see the last section of the book, "Helping Hands."

chapter 2

●

PARENTS

• *First our son told us he was gay. Then he told us he had
AIDS. We not only had to get used to the idea that our son was
a homosexual, we had to face the fact that he was dying.*

• *When the doctor told me my daughter had AIDS, I could feel
my life's blood being drained away. She was my only child.*

• *People were afraid to be around us. Even our best friends
were fearful we were contagious, and they thought they could
get AIDS from us.*

• *It's only recently that my husband and I have been able to
talk to each other about our son's death. It's been over three
years, but we both grieved in different ways.*

• *We didn't know what to tell people. In a small town like
ours, there is such gossip. We told everyone he died of
leukemia.*

> • *My mother died three months after my son, but I couldn't grieve for her. There was no room for any more pain.*

> • *I went back to work right after my son's death, but it was too soon. One morning I broke down in tears and collapsed. My supervisor came running over to see what was wrong. I told her, "I think I just realized that my son died."*

As Pat Fuller sat in the pew of her church for Sunday services, she was greeted with a blistering attack from the pulpit. The woman was dumbstruck. Only days before, she had sought refuge in her church, confiding in her minister that her son, Ken, twenty-six, had died of AIDS. She had tearfully told him of the pain and heartache she had endured and how her son had been cremated in Florida against her wishes. Now, as she sat in the fourth row of the church, the minister continued his scathing sermon on those who had died of AIDS. Pat recalls the deafening words.

" 'Those who have sinned will all burn in hell,' he shouted. He looked straight at me as he continued to say the terrible things that would happen to my son. How could he talk of burning in hell when I had just bared my soul to him? I came to my church for help. Instead I was left with more pain. Where was the compassion? Where was the understanding?"

Although family and friends were around her, Pat knew they could not understand her loss. When she attempted to speak about her son, they withdrew. "For the most part, everybody left me alone. They didn't say anything. That was the hardest thing because I really wanted to talk about it. But if I said anything about my son, everyone would get real quiet. They backed away. I live in a very small town in Alabama, so the attitude is 'Well, let's not talk about this. I'm afraid somebody will hear me talking about it.' I went to a counselor, but she was a single woman who had never been married and never had children. While she was very sympathetic and listened, I felt I needed to talk to a mother, someone who knew the pain of a mother who had lost her child. I needed to talk to someone who could understand how I felt about the cremation, having no real funeral, having no body to bury, no casket, just coming back to my hometown to have a semblance of a funeral service. Even with the people who have lost children, it's not the same as an AIDS death. Their kids didn't have to be cremated!"

Pat harks back to her daughter's wedding, Pat was horrified when she saw her son. "AIDS was like Greek to me. I didn't know anything about it. I didn't even know Ken was sick until a month before he died. When he came home for her wedding, I took one look at him and knew that he was dying, but it still didn't register with me. I guess it wasn't a thought I could accept in my mind. I had seen him a few months before, and although he had lost some weight, I didn't think too much of it. It was not unusual for him to lose or gain a little weight, as he had a rheumatic heart. He'd always had some health problems. After the wedding, he went back to Florida, where he lived. About two weeks later I got a call that he was in the hospital. I went there immediately. When I arrived, the doctor took me aside and told me my son was dying of AIDS. He died two weeks later."

Anger ate away at Pat—anger at Ken for getting the disease, anger at God for letting the tragedy happen, and anger at Ken's father, who Pat felt had abandoned her son at a difficult time in his life. "Ken's father knew that his son had a gay lifestyle. When we were divorced, he practically abandoned him and had nothing to do with him for about thirteen years. I don't know how she did it, but my sister-in-law finally convinced him that Ken was dying. She brought him to the hospital about three hours before our son died. That was wonderful because all Ken had talked about for two weeks was, 'God, if I could just see my dad, if he would just tell me he loved me, I could die.' The man walked in that morning at eight-thirty and the first thing he said was, 'I love you, Ken.' And that allowed my son to die in peace. But it didn't take away my anger that his dad had refused to be a father to him.

"I was also angry at my husband. I had remarried, and this was not Ken's father. When I was in Florida and knew that Ken was dying, I called my husband and begged him to come and stay with me. I kept telling him that my son was dying. He refused to believe it and said, 'You're crazy. He's not dying.' The last time I called was the night before Ken died. I pleaded with my husband again, 'Ken's dying.' And his reply again was, 'No, he's not, and besides that, I don't have time to come down there.' Ken died the morning after that last phone call. To this day I don't know who notified my husband to tell him what had happened. I assumed it was someone in my family. When I flew back to Montgomery and got off the plane, he was there. I remember looking at him and thinking, I hate you, and wondering why he was there now. We drove home to Alexander City in silence. Three months later we broke up."

After the death of her son Pat went right back to work, but her return was premature. "About two weeks after Ken died, I was just standing there and I broke down and started to cry. I hadn't really cried before. My supervisor grabbed me and said, 'Are you okay? Has anybody said anything to you?' From her question, I gathered she thought someone might have offended me by something they had said. In a small town like ours, I'm sure word about Ken's death had gotten out. But I said, 'No, nobody said anything to me. I think I just realized that my son died.' She took me aside and led me to her office. 'Come in here and sit down. Rest for a while,' she said. Then she and a couple of the other ladies at work sat down and prayed with me. They got me calmed down and then took me home. Later I asked for a couple of weeks off, which they granted. I knew I needed that time."

Pat began to block a lot of things out of her mind. If she wasn't thinking about her loss, she surmised, she didn't have to deal with it. Like many survivors, she began to develop physical ailments. "It was the only way I could handle the pain, blocking it out and trying to forget it. I just held things in, but as a result I began to get physically sick. First I had pains in my chest and I'd be sent to the hospital because they thought I was having a heart attack. They took EKGs. Then, later, they did an ultrasound test and found a problem with my gallbladder. They removed it. After that I began to develop every kind of allergy you can think of. My sinuses got progressively worse. My arthritis got worse. I know that stress caused these physical illnesses, and that's why I knew I had to find a way to get my feelings out and talk about them."

It is not uncommon to see physical illness beset parents of

a child who has died. At the top of the list are complaints of arthritis, loss of appetite, headaches, insomnia, heart palpitations, ulcerated colitis, muscular aches, pains, and minor accidents. Surviving brothers and sisters often suffer similar ailments.

Incredibly, it was not until seven years after her son died that a group for bereaved parents formed in Pat's area. "I went to a meeting. I didn't mention that Ken had died of AIDS because all of the parents there were talking about other kinds of deaths. When I left the meeting, someone handed me a copy of *Thanatos* magazine. I was very angry at this. I didn't want to *read* anything. I wanted to *talk* to somebody. When I got home, I was so mad I threw the magazine on the floor. Later I picked it up, and as I did, it was opened to an article that blew my mind away. It was about a mother who had lost a child to AIDS. I couldn't believe I was actually seeing something about this subject, a parent who was talking openly about AIDS. Through that article I was able to make contact with the author, Katherine Fair Donnelly, and she networked me onto several other bereaved parents."

Pat told her newfound friends about her seven-year nightmare. "I opened up all the feelings I'd closed off for so long. They gushed out of my mouth: 'Do you feel this way, too?' 'Do you wonder if you are going crazy?' One parent said, 'You lost your child—not your mind.' These parents really helped me through some very rough patches. It was the first time I felt there was hope for me, and that maybe I could be helped, too."

It was during a conversation with one mother in particular that Pat had an incredible awakening about similar experiences. "I shared something with a mother because her son had been cremated, too. I knew she would understand how I felt. I told her how I had held Ken's ashes in my lap on the flight home. It was like 'Oh, God, he's my baby again.' I could feel him sinking into me and my arms. The other mother said, 'Yes, I remember feeling that way when I flew home on the plane and I was holding his ashes.' And then she added something that took my breath away. 'It was like I was putting him from my arms back into my womb.' When she said that, I gasped. 'What is it?' she asked me in a concerned voice. 'What's wrong?' I had to compose myself for the minute, I was so shocked. Then I said, 'I never thought I would ever hear anyone else say that, but that is exactly what happened to me on the plane. That is just the way I felt—like my son was returning to my womb!' "

Pat was also able to talk to the other mothers about the funeral directors in Florida who had refused to accept her son's body unless cremation was allowed. "You should have seen me the weekend after my son's funeral service. I was beside myself. My sister said to me, 'Pat, do you know how angry you were?' I replied, 'Wouldn't you be? Walking into funeral homes and hearing them say, 'We can't take your son. He has to be cremated.' I felt I was cheated because I didn't have my son's body to bury. I thought it was some kind of law that they were talking about when they said he had to be cremated. They said because of his blood and the handling of his body, cremation was our only choice. When we got back to Alabama, we had a service at a chapel in the funeral home there. We put the urn with the ashes into a large bronze container, and we had a picture of Ken set on top of that. Then we had a short service. I wanted to have *something*. Then we went to the cemetery and had a gravesite burial. I had to have somewhere to go to visit my son."

Another issue Pat was able to talk about now was the treatment she and Ken received when he was hospitalized in Florida. "Ken was the first AIDS patient they'd had. We were treated horribly. They stuck us off in a room and quarantined us! Most of the doctors and nurses refused to come into the room. A couple of them did, but most wouldn't come near us. They made us put on masks, gowns, gloves, everything. I would walk down the hall and I could see people move away from me. They would look at me as if they were thinking, Oh, my gosh, she has AIDS! I know it was fear. They were scared to death. I could see it in their eyes. There was one doctor who had some previous experience with AIDS patients, and he was very understanding. But other than this doctor, nobody would come near us. It was very hard with no one helping us, nobody to work with us, nobody to lend us support. It was real hard."

Today Pat knows she has a lot of catching up to do in sharing and talking. "I will never be able to give myself back seven years of loneliness and isolation, but I am so grateful to have the new friends I've made with parents who have lost children to AIDS. They have been wonderful. Just listening to me talk, sharing their feelings and experiences with me, and in general just being there. That is a miracle in itself—to have somebody you can call whenever you feel like it—somebody who isn't afraid to mention your son's name."

J OE CALCATERRA , father of five and a widower for twenty-four years, is surely every child's dream parent—kind, caring, nonjudgmental, interested, and, most of all, concerned.

Like many parents, Joe was surprised when he learned of his son's life-style. He describes the thoughts that ran through his mind in those first few moments, as well as the feelings he had after ruminating a bit. "Jon was nineteen when he told me that he was gay. My initial reaction was, Gee, I wonder if I did something wrong. I asked Jon if he'd ever had any contact with a girl. He said yes, but he just didn't like it. My son answered me honestly, and I had to appreciate his choice. After that discussion, I started reading everything I could get my hands on about homosexuality, and I came to the conclusion that God made each of us the way we are. You either are born gay or you aren't. Of course, it's just my personal opinion, but I believe from the beginning Jon's orientation was preordained."

Joe offers some words of caution to parents who may be struggling with the gay issue. "I want to make one point clear to anyone who is homophobic, and particularly to parents whose sons are gay. If you don't accept your son and associate with him now, you will have missed one of the greatest opportunities in your life. If I had abandoned Jon and driven him away from the house, I would have missed a precious chance to know my son and to have him for ten more years. The fact that he was gay never altered my love for him."

Joe was at work when he received the heartbreaking news that his son had tested HIV positive. "As soon as Jon got the results, he called me. We were both crying on the telephone. I told him that he shouldn't despair, that there was always hope. For the next two years, Jon's health was pretty good. Then his T cell count started going down and the doctor put him on AZT.

However, he didn't respond well to the drug, and it affected him adversely. I had retired by the time he developed more symptoms and was able to take care of my son at home."

Taking care of his children was nothing new to Joe, having raised five children alone after his wife died, but the tasks required in seeing to Jon's medical needs were new to him. "Jon had the pneumonia that people with AIDS get, and we had to get a respirator to alleviate the condition. A nurse was sent to show me how to put the chemicals in and how to take them out of a bottle with a syringe. We had him on that machine for a few days, but he got worse and finally was admitted to the hospital. By this time the virus had hit his brain, and he was speaking incoherently. My son died six days after he went into the hospital."

Joe was grateful to a number of people for their help and concern. "The social workers in the hospital were great. They counseled the parents or the lovers or whoever was grieving, and with such compassion and understanding. I also found great support and compassion in the gay community among my son's friends. There was such a warm camaraderie. I could spend hours talking to them, and they listened and understood how I felt. They knew just what to say. A couple of Jon's friends were priests. When Jon died, I called one of them and asked if he would officiate at the funeral service, and he was happy that I called."

After his son's death, Joe felt the need to join a bereavement support group in his vicinity. Although his friends and family were of help to him, Joe found himself struggling with his grief. "Jon and I were more than father and son. We were good friends, and we did a lot of things together. We traveled extensively, went to Europe twice, and even took a couple of cruises to the Caribbean. I was having trouble with all the memories and the tears, so my daughter and I went to a bereavement group called the Wellness Network here in Michigan. It caters to people who are HIV positive, to those who have AIDS, and to their families. It's a great organization, and I wanted somehow to assist them in their wonderful work, so I went through a training program for volunteers, learning to help others. Then I went on to an AIDS hot line. Now I answer calls from all over

Michigan from people who have questions about HIV testing, AIDS, safe sex, and anything else they want to discuss. It gives me a good feeling to know I am helping others."

Joe tells of maintaining old friendships and at the same time establishing new ones. "My friends were all sympathetic. None of them shied away when they found out why Jon died. I've met people at my bereavement group and through volunteering on the hot line. We interact and have dinner at each other's houses. That's what you want to do because it helps you a lot. These people are just so understanding. I don't know how to describe the outpouring of warmth that you feel. The whole key is being able to talk to others."

In a way, Joe has literally remained a father to all of his son's friends, offering them love and acceptance. Joe tells of the strong bond he has maintained with his newfound friends. "All of these kids, who are my son's age, have kept in contact with me since Jon died three years ago. We do a lot of things together, have dinner, go to the movies. They have enhanced my life immeasurably. My son's friends are some of the nicest people I ever met."

Another experience that brought Joe great comfort and an incredible sense of closeness and bonding was his visit to the AIDS Memorial Quilt Project in Washington. "The entire quilt was displayed, and we saw the panel we made for Jon. The sight of all the panels and the throngs of people was like nothing I had ever seen. There were hundreds of thousands of people, a sea of humanity, and all such nice people. I could have gone up to anyone and had a good conversation. On Jon's panel, we had put a picture of his pet, a black cat. Also, Jon loved to cook. He had a chef's hat, so we sewed that on top of the quilt, too. A portion of the panel contained some of the beautiful words from the eulogy given by one of Jon's best friends: "Deep in everyone's heart, there is a special corner saved for a special person. We are here today because Jon filled that special corner in our hearts. He brought great happiness to us all. A happiness that can never be forgotten."

Joe talks about the impact of Jon's death on his other children. "My kids are surviving Jon's death pretty well. I know each of them mourned him in their own way. My youngest daughter misses him terribly because they were very close. When Jon was sick, he used to go over there and lie on her couch just to be near her. They had a very good relationship, and her husband was also very sympathetic. My daughter never worried about her brother being gay. She showed her love, and his lifestyle didn't matter. I think I've been very fortunate to have such nice kids. They are all grown now. My oldest child is forty-two and married. My other daughter is married, lives in Chicago, and has one boy. Another son, also married, lives around the corner from my house. This son was very close to Jon and at one time was absolutely homophobic. I always called him my redneck son. But he's a neat kid, too, and it was this same son and his wife who accompanied me to Washington to see Jon's quilt."

Joe explains that he has good days and bad ones, but for the most part, he says, he has learned to live with his loss. "After Jon died, I didn't have anger. What I felt was a great deal of sorrow. I really missed the kid, and I still do. If I think of Jon during the day, tears can roll down my face. However, I'm happy to be able to think of him because I don't want to ever forget him. I feel he's still with me as long as I can bring him to mind."

I N T H E above story, we have witnessed the loving concern displayed by a surviving father. In the following scathing diatribe issued by Florence Rush to the parents of her dead son's lover, she sends a powerful message to those who are shamefully lacking in such compassion.

AN OPEN LETTER TO THE PARENTS OF MY SON'S LOVER
by Florence Rush

Ron, my son's lover, died of AIDS at the age of 31 in June 1990. My son Matthew, age 39, died of the same disease six weeks later. Ron's parents, whose lives are guided by an upstate fundamentalist Bible church, never accepted Ron's homosexuality or the fact that Matt and Ron were devoted companions and lovers for almost eight years.

This letter could never have been written while Ron was

alive. He was so anxious for his parents' love and approval that any expression of my anger would have disturbed him deeply. Now, more than a year after his death, I am free to say what I feel about his "religious" parents and, for that matter, what I feel about all parents, family members, relatives, and so-called friends and acquaintances whose homophobia, ignorance, and prejudice have achieved a cruel victory over compassion: nor do I ignore all those who stand in judgment and dare to throw the first stone.

To the Parents of my Son's Lover, Ron, Whom He Called Mom and Dad:

Neither of you, Mom and Dad, were there for your son's long, tormented illness. You turned your back on him. Dad, you once said to me that, after all, he chose this life-style—meaning, of course, that AIDS was the deserved punishment for Ron's homosexuality. That Ron chose to be gay is debatable; many feel that sexual preference is inborn. But that AIDS was his punishment . . . never! The agonies he suffered were no more ordained than the agonies you suffered as the result of your painful spinal affliction. What Ron consciously did choose was to love my son. In a Valentine's Day card he wrote to Matthew:

This is a message of my love for you. These trials and tribulations will soon pass and we can go on enjoying life together. You have fulfilled my life and given me strength. I love you.

Ron.

It's a pity neither of you were there to bask in their love; to see them skillfully maneuver their sailboat, to share their pleasure in the home they cherished, to enjoy the slides taken of their travels and laugh with them as they sparked conversations with humor. Pity you never took pride in Ron's passion for art, his kindness to others, his creativity, and his capacity to amuse and evoke the love of children. And, it most certainly is a pity that you were not there to see your son, a Christian, and my son, a Jew, celebrate Hanukkah, Christmas, Easter, and Passover together in perfect harmony.

Where were you when your son, in terror, learned that he had AIDS; when he was hospitalized with a rare form of pneumonia, when his body was racked with violent chills, with fever of over 104 and 105, with throbbing headaches; when he had to tolerate painful biopsies, a surgically inserted catheter, and intravenous medication to prevent blindness?

I was there.

I was there to hold him tight when spasms threatened to throw him out of bed, to apply ice packs to his burning body, to get him to and from doctors and hospitals and to arrange for someone to care for him when I had to attend to my own sick son. I was there to get his tax form completed, to help him pay his bills, fill out insurance claims, and deal with other necessary chores at a time when he could barely hold up his head.

Ron once said to me, "Florence, you have been more of a mother to me than my own mother." But, it was you, Mom, that he yearned for. You didn't hear, you didn't come, and, for all he knew, you didn't care. I don't regret one moment of my involvement, but it was you he wanted and your rejection of him was almost as painful as his illness.

Then, suddenly, three weeks before he died, you both appeared. You came when he was helplessly paralyzed from the waist down. The moment he saw you he cried with wrenching sobs. Neither of you shed a tear, you talked cheerfully of traffic problems, blooming azaleas, your new mobile home, and grandchildren. Later when I asked for help, you, Dad, explained that although retired, you had household tasks like cutting the grass and you, Mom, declined because you were looking after your elderly mother who, incidentally, is about my age. When I described the difficulty in caring for two sick men, you, Dad, suggested that Ron be put in the hospital. But Ron hated the hospital and begged to be allowed to die at home. "Would you," I asked, "have the heart to put your son in a hospital to die among strangers?" You didn't answer so I pressed for at least some financial assistance. This time you responded quickly and conveniently recognized, for the first time, the relationship between our children. "Matthew is financially responsible for Ron because they are like a married couple," you said.

Why did you show up at all during the last days of Ron's life? You rejected him from the moment he told you he was gay, ignored him when he became ill and appeared only when he was dying. You arrived, of course, at his deathbed to save his soul for Jesus.

Ron always identified himself as a Christian and asked for a Christian family burial. Matthew respected his wish, notified you of his death, you sent for his body, arranged for his funeral, and Matthew, sick as he was, mustered up whatever strength he had to attend Ron's funeral. His wonderful nurse, Kathy, packed his IV pole, his nutrition pump (he had stopped eating), the various medications which barely kept him alive, and drove us upstate for the funeral. The trip was a nightmare. Matthew was so weak, so frail, but we had to help him say his last goodbye.

The pastor you selected to conduct the service knew nothing about Ron, cared less, and the best he said about the man we knew and loved was that he was "neat." Neither of you bothered to instruct him to recognize Ron's artistic talent, that he had put himself through a graduate school of art and design, that he held a respected and well-paid job in a prestigious advertising firm and that he had many friends and working associates who loved him dearly. Before the service, Matthew asked the pastor to acknowledge his love for Ron, their long relationship, and his loss, but this man of God would not even mention his name. His contempt for your dead son and my dying son was hardly disguised when he crassly requested of those in attendance, "You who wish to be saved by Jesus raise your hand." He used Ron's funeral to recruit for his church and Jesus. I later learned that although you arranged for the funeral, it was Ron's devoted twin sister who paid the costs. You gave nothing to your son while he was alive and your inability to love or give followed him to his grave.

Matthew was too weak to go to the cemetery but as we prepared for the trip home, this pastor who had earlier ignored him now eagerly approached with a pitch designed to convert him to his brand of Christianity. I wanted to scream! Who is this man and who are these people without any feeling for Matthew's grief? But Matthew looked the man straight in the face and said in a strong voice, "I am of the Jewish faith and have no intention of changing. Ron was of the Christian and he never had any intention of changing. This was never a problem between us. I don't understand why it should be a problem for you." Bravo, Matthew!

Soon after Ron's funeral you sent Matthew a note. It said:

> *Just a note to say hi and we're praying for you. It was a hot weekend and all the children and grandchildren were here swimming. I am including a DAILY BREAD booklet that we all read every day and I thought you might join us. The Lord will give you strength. I know nothing would make Ron happier than for you to accept Jesus as your savior so that you could be with him in heaven and with all of us. If Ron could talk to you he would say to you that Jesus is the answer and the provider we all need.*

It was signed "Mom and Dad" with a circle picture of a happy smiling face.

But when Ron was alive he never asked Matthew to accept Jesus as his savior or to read your fundamentalist booklet with quotes from the scriptures. What's more, Matthew was never welcomed in your earthly home, so why this invitation to have him join you in heaven? The answer is obvious. You were never able to turn Ron away from Matthew when he was alive but when he was dead and his will, conviction, and strength were no longer a barrier, you arrived to save his soul. You preferred Ron's lifeless body to your living, courageous son. Only in death could you claim him, and while at it, you attempted to add Matthew to your collection.

Tell me, Mom and Dad, how many souls have you saved this week, this month, this year? And if you score the right number do you get a gold star, go to the head of the class, and are you sure that if you accumulate the proper amount you will have a place in heaven? I don't think so. Remember that Jesus was a healer on earth with love and compassion for the sick and dying. Remember that Jesus, just as Matthew and Ron, loved other men, he was always surrounded by his beloved disciples; and that Jesus, just as Matthew and Ron, never married and never had children. Remember that Ron never, never hurt anyone, but that you, his parents, sinned when you turned your back on him at a time when he most needed you. Jesus said, "Judge not that ye may not be judged. For with that judgment, ye shall be judged and with what measure ye mete, it shall be measured to you again" (Matthew 7:2).

How will you, Mom and Dad, meet your maker? Will you be forgiven for the way you judged and abandoned your son? Jesus said, "With what measure ye mete, it shall be measured to you again." Where there is a heaven there is also a hell, and frankly, I am not sure where either of you will eventually be located.

> The Mother of Your Son's Lover,
> Florence Rush

IN THE preceding letter, we read of the insensitivity of some bereaved parents. That was hardly the case with Arlene and Jerry Binkowitz, who, like Florence Rush and all of the other parents in this chapter, were immediately there to help their child in any and every way possible, offering their love and their support.

Arlene and Jerry Binkowitz's son, Barry, died when he was only twenty-eight years old. Barry was always very close to Arlene's mother and knew his grandmother would not survive his death. He was right; she died three months later. Arlene then had an experience not uncommon to bereaved parents: she was unable to grieve for her mother's death.

"Under normal circumstances, I would have certainly grieved for my mother. You expect your parents to go. Yes, it's sad and it's a terrible loss, but that's the way it's supposed to be—a natural progression of life. And you live on. But losing a child is *not* natural, *not* the way it is supposed to be. You are supposed to die before your children, not after. They are supposed to bury you. You are not supposed to bury your children. I couldn't even deal with my mother's death. I had no room because it was so soon after Barry died. But unless you have walked in those shoes, you cannot understand that."

Reflecting back on when her son confided that he was gay, Arlene tells of her reactions. "When Barry got into medical school, we were flying—my son, the doctor. A Jewish mother's dream! All this time I did not know my son was gay. He had many friends, also many girlfriends. After the first year at school, he came home and told us that he was gay. I couldn't believe it. My first words were, 'Barry, was there something I did wrong?' He laughed and said, 'Mom, it's nothing you did. It's the way I am.' I didn't know any homosexuals or anything about homosexuality. Even though I was working and supposedly a woman of the world, I still didn't know anything about this subject. So I started to read books. My husband and I became very accepting. We loved our son. He was brilliant, he was loving, he was wonderful. But there was no such thing as AIDS. We were coping with his being gay—never dreaming there could be anything like AIDS in our lives."

After their son died, Arlene and Jerry went to a bereavement counselor who helped them recognize their coping abilities. Arlene tells of their experience. "We had a magnificent bereavement counseler, Rosemarie Ampela, who saved our lives. In many aspects, she came to know our son better than we did. We came to see what type of person he was and the courage he had. All this helped us to cope. I guess we had the coping ability within us anyway."

Following their sessions in therapy, Arlene was asked to speak at the Board of Rabbis in New York. "It was the first time I had spoken to anyone, and they were overwhelmed—I was a

Jewish mother and had a son who was a doctor who died of AIDS. In their world, it didn't happen to our kind of people. From that, we did a television program on the Jewish response to AIDS. One thing led to another, and we became immersed in events happening in New York. We decided to contact a rabbi we had heard about in our neighborhood, in Oceanside, Long Island. We did not belong to a temple. We are far from Conservative. If anything, we are Reform. My son was Bar Mitzvahed, but after that we never joined a temple. I called and introduced myself to the rabbi. 'My husband and I lost our son, who was gay. We live in Oceanside. Is there something we can do to raise the consciousness of the people in our community?' He was very understanding and interested. He called us in, and we had several two-hour sessions with him. He wanted to know everything about the subject, to learn everything we were involved in, everything I wrote, the therapist who led the group, the people in my son's life. He wanted to find the common thread."

That summer, the rabbi asked Arlene to speak at the temple. "He asked me to speak at Selichot services, which are given late at night about ten days before Rosh Hashanah. I thought to myself, Who is going to come and listen to anything about AIDS at a ten o'clock service on a Saturday night? Well, over one hundred people came to the temple. I was shocked and couldn't believe how many came. After that, the rabbi suggested forming a support group in Oceanside. I said, 'Who's going to come to a support group in a little suburb like Oceanside?' He said, 'If we have to sit here and just wait, we will do that.' Little by little, the group was formed. One woman came, and the next week a couple came, then another person and another. And then it became several couples. We all met in the rabbi's study every week. This was only for parents. Gradually we started to become known. We sent flyers to various groups on Long Island. We put out more announcements, and more people began to hear of us. I was just asked to be on the advisory committee of the Elder Care Group in Brooklyn. They want to form a support care system for HIV positive and care partners who are fifty-five and older. Because we are caregivers, many people have learned about us and they call. The group in Oceanside was initiated primarily for parents who had living children who were HIV positive. As people began to have losses, the need arose for a separate group—a bereavement group."

Arlene expounds on some of the many issues parents have to handle. Empowered with knowledge about AIDS that they had absorbed in the group, the parents were able to fend off problems. "They now have learned how to deal with friends. They have learned how to deal with doctors and how to deal with insurance, with Medicaid. They have learned how to deal with their feelings, with their children, with the anger that they had, and with their guilt. They've learned to share."

The work that Arlene and Jerry are doing provides a ripple effect for new people who come into the group. Arlene explains: "Now that the present group members have become enlightened, when new people come into the group, they know how to handle them to best help them. They remember how uninformed they were when they first came. They know how to talk to people through their own experiences. They are each living through this and helping the next one. That's the whole point of our group. Even if they have the support of their families and friends, it doesn't help in the same way as the caregivers who are in the group."

One of the other important aspects of the group is that men have been participating and discovering it's all right to cry, all right to let their feelings out. Arlene describes the warmth she and her husband have experienced when men came to the group meetings. "We have a diversified group. Of course there are widows, some people who are divorced, but we also have men. They come with their wives—and they speak. It's been a wonderful experience to see men, who don't usually talk about their feelings, come to our group and become part of what's happening. They talk, they cry, and they show the love you don't see too often in men. My husband is there, which is a great help because he is a very sensitive and compassionate man."

At the meetings, Jerry Binkowitz tells other men about his feelings. He talks about his son, and he listens to what fathers say about their children—with compassion and a caring heart. A red flag for Jerry is the lack of understanding by parents about gay children.

"When Barry told me he was gay, I simply thought, Well, he is and I'm not, but we're both human beings. What I don't comprehend is the lack of understanding and lack of caring that some parents display when they find out their child is gay. We have seen TV programs where parents have talked about throwing their kids out of the house when they discovered their son or daughter was gay. Who the hell are they? These kids are individuals. Who has the right to tell another person that this is the way you ought to be? And parents are no exception. You can't tell someone to be this way or you're going to be in trouble or whatever. A person is that way because he is born gay, not because he chooses to be gay. You have to accept your child for what he is. You can't put yourself above God."

Jerry acknowledges that the group helped him, even though it was formed several years after Barry died. "The private counseling we had beforehand helped a lot, but coming into this group and listening to all of these guys helped me as much as it helped them. When they shared their thoughts, it helped me to know that I'm not alone. We also talked about the bravery of our children. The kids who are facing and have faced this disease have more courage and guts than anyone I know. And the people who really started this whole movement was the gay community. I was with my son at the very beginning when they first had the underground drugs. I was also there when they had conferences in the Village and decided on what to do and how to get together. The gay community is incredible. They're not taking anything from anybody. They did their own thing to help spur AIDS education, and those are the people who really deserve everything. If it wasn't for them and their incredible courage, they'd be back to zero. Even to come out and say that you are gay is incredible—and now every two days you read something about it in the paper. People are now aware of things they would not have known if it had not been for this early group and for the groups that are continuing to educate people. It shows a lot of strength, and I think it is wonderful that they do this. Another thing that I find is that along with incredible courage, young people with AIDS also have an extraordinary sense of humor, given the fact that they are facing a fatal disease."

At Christmastime, Arlene and Jerry volunteer at the Nassau

County Medical Center. "We bring the people with AIDS down to the party. If they can't attend, we go upstairs and give them food, a nice dinner. The people upstairs may be too weak to come downstairs, but to see them with the spirit, the humor, and the acceptance is unbelievably uplifting. Part of lasting longer is humor. These are mostly young kids who have been told they have a fatal disease—and the way they are handling their lives is incredible."

Although Jerry knows couples who have grown distant after the death of their child, he believes he and his wife are not part of that milieu and have remained as they were before— protective of each other. "We talk about Barry, but we try not to bring up the bad stuff—his illness. We are trying to look forward instead of backward. We have a daughter who is terrific, and she won't stand for anything else. She's a bright kid, and we love her very much."

There are still painful moments, and Jerry tells what can set these off. "The thing that gets to me more than anything else is if I happen to hear beautiful music that I know Barry would appreciate. I get a little too watery. There are certain things that are connected. Music is my weak spot. I'm a music lover, and so was Barry. He was also a good piano player. We have a beautiful piano in our home that my father had in his home. Barry loved to sit down and play it. I used to play it quite a bit when I was a kid, but I can't bring myself to do that now."

Jerry comments about the anniversary date of their son's death. "That day is not that bad for us because every day we think about Barry. We adored him. So it's not like one day is different from any other. But his birthday is special for us. From the first year he died, and which we will continue to do, we have a special time for Barry. We take his best friends—Johnny, Carl, Lonnie, and Susan—out to dinner. Sometimes there are five or six of his friends, and we go to a different restaurant every year. We make a toast to Barry and have a nice dinner together. We learn to take it one day at a time."

Arlene believes that parents who get involved helping others after their children die do so because they are inspired by their children and want to make others aware of what is happening. "I hope we have done that in our way. I can't say that we will ever be happy the way we were before our son died. A part of us is missing. He was such a joy. There is a void in our life that will never be filled. But the fact that so many people know of our son now is something that helps us survive."

A N O T H E R   B E R E A V E D   father confides how he let his hair down at a support group meeting for bereaved parents. He had been trying to maintain control of his temper, but his anger was building. One evening he exploded and let his complaints be known. "For several months I was at this self-help group. We met once a month, and the group consisted of parents who had lost a child to various causes. At each meeting, as I listened, I got madder and madder. Finally I blew up. One guy was saying how his kid was so great and how he was always so proud of everything his son did. I guess I have a short fuse these days because I laced into this guy. I told him it was bad enough he had to deal with losing his child, but that it was a terrible thing to lose your child and *not* be proud of everything he did.

"All my life I was brought up by my parents to believe I should grow up, get married, have a family, and raise my kids, and that they should grow up and have children, that we should enjoy our grandchildren. Of all the other deaths in the group, my wife and I were the only ones whose child died of AIDS. We didn't deny it. But it's a question of trying to deal with two kinds of deaths: the death of our son and the death of the son we had hoped he would be. If someone else in a family dies, a parent, a husband or wife, for example, the issue of their sexual habits or personal life-style never enters the picture. But if someone in the family dies of AIDS, all of a sudden a magnifying glass comes out. Everyone wants to examine when they went to bed, with whom they went to bed, how many times, and on and on. I guess what I'm saying is that many AIDS parents are dealing with a full deck and one extra card—one they don't know how to handle sometimes."

S E E K I N G   O U T   help was something both of the following couples did. Edwin and Barbara Koski's son Paul was found to be HIV positive while being treated for severe psoriasis. Ed and Barbara share their experience of losing a beloved son to AIDS and tell how they have subsequently tried to cope.

"Soon after Paul was diagnosed, he could no longer work in Chicago as a restaurant manager, so he came back home to the Detroit area to live with us. HIV then turned into full-blown AIDS, and he commuted from home to hospital and back several times. Pneumonia was the first battle and toxoplasmosis the last, which he lost at age thirty-six.

"We were grateful that we could care for him, being able-bodied and retired. We applied daily warm, wet wraps for the psoriasis and kept track of the many medications, though we were somewhat apprehensive when we gave him IVs. Helping psychologically was the whole-hearted support of the immediate family. There were no critical or sarcastic comments that we later found to be common in other situations."

After Paul died in 1990, Ed and Barbara faced the future without him. They tell the ways they were helped. "The things that helped us recover were the two of us being there, being able to care for him, and sharing that responsibility for the three and a half years of his illness; the continuing support of the family; the spiritual help of our two parish priests; and going to PFLAG [Parents and Friends of Lesbians and Gays] meetings."

Talking about Paul was a cathartic experience. "An important part of recovery has been the opening up to other people of Paul's illness. A certain cleansing process happens. So much seems to be necessarily suppressed concerning AIDS. We have been guarded in revealing his illness, but we realize suppressing it is not healthy. We are now able to talk about Paul in our everyday conversation. Keeping his memory submerged and nonvocalized is wrong, we think. We feel it has helped us to attain some degree of recovery, and hope that our experience can be helpful to others who have suffered the loss of a loved one to AIDS."

N ANCY HESLER put on a stoic cloak and tried to hide from her pain after the death of her son, Christian, in 1989. He was thirty-three. Nancy ran away from the reality by masking her sorrow and putting up a noble front. This running is a familiar experience to many bereaved parents. If you run fast enough, you won't have time to remember. The trick, they think, is to make the time go faster. Nancy theorized that if she kept up her frantic pace of speaking engagements and other activities, it would offer some relief. She hoped that moving, moving, moving, would in some way not allow time to freeze in the agonizing present—that somehow moving would enable the clock to be pushed forward to some future time void of thoughts of a dead son.

Even in her work place, a school for the blind, Nancy hid from her grief by taking on the problems of everyone around her. But her emotions were bursting to be released, and her penetrable armor was no longer able to offer protection. She explains what happened when the dam broke. "Everything came crashing down on me. I had been suppressing my own feelings too long, trying to handle everyone else's troubles. I have a wonderful boss, and he is the one who said to me, 'You just have to quit doing this, taking on everybody's load. You have to allow yourself to grieve.' "

Nancy took her boss's advice and sought help. "I went to the 'Home for the Bewildered' for a while. That's what I dubbed the stress center I went to. I named it that from something I read in Barbara Johnson's *Pain Is Inevitable, But Misery Is Optional, So Stick a Geranium in Your Hat*. I went there for ten days. We were in meetings and did a lot of talking. We found out how other people handled their problems, especially with AIDS. We learned that people need to realize they are being too stoic and how important it is to talk about the things that are bothering you."

Christian died in his parents' home in Carmel, Indiana. Nancy recalls how her younger son, Scott, bonded with his brother during that terrible time. She also remembers the incredible kindness of Christian's friends during his hospital stay in Atlanta, where he was living when he became ill. "My husband, Glen, and I were amazed at the care and consideration of Chris's friends while he was in the hospital. Each hour a friend would come in and rub his legs. They knew something we didn't—AIDS patients ache."

Once Christian returned to Carmel, Nancy and Glen couldn't bear to send him to a hospital. They wanted to help their son in any way they could, and caring for him was their last opportunity to do that.

"AIDS is a horrible disease and Chris had it all. He was incontinent, lost his ability to write or speak, he went blind, and he had to be given morphine for his pain. A nurse came in twice a week to help. We had set up a bed for him in the living room where he could look out the window and listen to music. But even with all the misery, some wonderful things happened. There had always been some sibling rivalry between Chris and our younger son. But when Chris became sick, Scott was right there to help his brother and to lend a hand. We could see the bonding taking place between them. Chris also had a very good friend here whom he knew from high school. He was right here to help through the whole thing."

Currently Nancy and her husband are still involved with the Damien Society, an active AIDS group in Indianapolis for people with AIDS and their families. "It's been a help to the newly bereaved to see us there. And this has really helped my husband, too. He and I have grieved separately, and we are just now getting to where we can talk to each other about Chris. Glen still goes to the meetings. I more or less work one on one with those who have lost someone to AIDS. The churches in Hamilton County are also forming an AIDS group for families who have just found out about their children. We are not going to be facilitators of the group, but we will be part of it."

Nancy assesses where she is in her grief now. "Today I believe I'm doing just fine in my grief, and I think my husband is, too. Of course, Chris is never out of our minds, and we miss him very, very much. No matter how many years go by, certain things will always bother us, whether it's a birthday or just hearing or seeing something that reminds us of Chris. You can't do everything the way you used to do it, but that doesn't mean you are not adjusting. And by helping others, if we can help someone else survive, we can make it, too."

●

chapter 3

HUSBANDS/WIVES

● *We had such a normal family. Three kids. My husband had a good job. What went wrong? Why did he need drugs in his life? I had no idea he was using them. He died just weeks after I found out he had AIDS.*

● *After my wife died, I went to a support group meeting for widows and widowers. When I mentioned the word AIDS, it was as if a time bomb went off. Everyone moved away from me. I became an untouchable.*

● *When my husband told his employer he had AIDS, they tried to get rid of him. Not only was he fighting for his life, he had to fight to keep his job as well.*

● *I never had a clue that my husband was bisexual. He never gave any sign. But after he died, I found a lot of things in his closet, hidden in a box. Now I have to worry if I will test positive.*

> • *Our kids don't want to see anybody. They've been through such traumas, having everyone ask if their father had AIDS. We've all had to lie and say it was pneumonia, because I've been petrified I'll lose my job if we say anything else.*

Amid a flurry of publicity, Maria and David Hefner were married in St. Patrick's Cathedral in New York. Both prior to and after their wedding, newspapers such as *The New York Times,* the *Daily News,* the *Village Voice,* and many others had headlines that blared out the controversy: Because he had AIDS, David and Maria could not be married in the church, even though their initial request to do so had been granted. That situation was soon corrected.

The couple, who were married in a civil ceremony several years earlier, had obtained approval for a Valentine's Day wedding at the cathedral from an associate pastor. Maria tells what happened after that.

"During our appointment with the priest, we told him the truth about everything that had happened with David's illness. He asked David, 'How did you get AIDS?' David responded, 'I used to be a homosexual.' That was the only thing David could figure, but we really don't know. Who could prove that? A few days later the priest called me and said, 'Maria, I don't know how to tell you this, but I can't marry you and David.' I thought it was a joke, but it wasn't. The reason he gave was because David had AIDS."

Following her conversation with the priest, Maria was reluctant to tell David of the refusal but knew she had to do so. "It was very painful for me to relay that news to him. He was already very sick and suffering from AIDS, and I had to add to that with such a harsh rejection. We were very upset and told a friend of ours, who said, 'Let's get publicity, and I'm sure you will have your rights.' *The New York Times* was notified and wrote an article about the situation. The rector had issued a statement expressing concern over a person with a communicable disease passing it on to a spouse or child and stating that a couple in such a situation should seek premarital counseling in their own parish, where they are better known."

The decision not to marry the couple brought cries of protest from civil rights groups and Protestant and Catholic clergy, several of whom invited the Hefners to be married at their churches. However, there was no need. A few days later, John Cardinal O'Connor, the Archbishop of New York, reversed the decision and permitted the marriage sacrament in the cathedral. The wedding took place as scheduled on February 14, and the ceremony was attended by the cardinal.

Maria tells of earlier events that led to their Valentine's Day wedding. "David and I wanted to get married in church. I was a Catholic and he was a Protestant, but he knew how much it would please me. Originally we had hoped to be married in Brazil, where my family lives and where I was from. David was from Texas. But because of his hectic work schedule—he was a hairdresser—it was too hard to get away for two weeks. When I realized how sick he was, I said, 'David, we've got to do it. We are married spiritually and emotionally, but I can't watch you die without marrying you in a church.' I wanted to walk in church with the man I loved and get a blessing. Not by the cardinal or the church. The church is a house. The cardinal is a person like you or me. I wanted God's blessing."

When they first met, Maria was twenty-nine and David thirty-five. The relationship blossomed, and until AIDS, the pair enjoyed a wonderful life together. Maria describes the unusual thoughtfulness of her husband.

"He used to surprise me with so many things. He wanted to celebrate everything—the first day we met, the first time we made love, the first day we went out for dinner, the first day we went to the beach. Everything was a first-day event. So in 365 days, we had over 200 days of celebration. He would put surprises under the pillow for me. If I didn't notice at first, he was like an excited kid and would say, 'There's something wrong with this pillow,' until finally I would find his gift. It didn't matter what it was. It could be a dollar gift or some little toy. He could never come home without bringing me a flower, or my favorite candy bar, or something to make me smile. He was such an unusual person, so thoughtful. I was happy for the first time in my life, and David was happy for the last few years of his."

In February of 1985, Maria and David went out to dinner, but David was not himself and could scarcely eat or drink. The next day the couple went to two doctors. The first was unable to offer any indication of what was wrong with David. Through friends they called another doctor, who suggested David check into a hospital for tests. A few days later the results revealed that David had AIDS.

"I was very shaken. I loved David and knew we had to face this situation together. I decided, I'm his doctor, I'm his nurse. But the day they inserted his Hickman [a catheter positioned in the chest that enables the patient to receive an IV more easily], I felt like walking to a bridge somewhere and jumping off. But I said to myself, I can't think of me now. Let me take care of David first. Then I will think about Maria. Some of my friends kept in touch and called all the time. If I had to come home from the hospital, they would stay with him. Two friends offered to pay for a private nurse because they thought I was doing too much. I told them I appreciated that and would love them for the rest of my life for their kindness and caring, but I said, 'You've got to understand that I want to spend every second with him.' "

After David died, Maria decided she didn't want to work. Instead she went back to school. "I went to Columbia University for about a year and took some English courses. I felt I wanted to speak English correctly. David always motivated me toward that. To keep busy, I went to concerts, shows, and the ballet. There were many times when I would be associating things that had to do with my life with David. That would make me like the concert or the performance better, or enjoy the music more. It's hard to describe. If you take a pencil and write something down, you can erase it. But you can't do that with your feelings. They are imprinted permanently in your heart and mind."

Maria cautions about the necessity of grieving and also offers some constructive suggestions to those who have lost a loved one. "Eight years after David died, I discovered I hadn't really been able to grieve his death. I went for therapy to help me tackle that grief. What I would say to a person who is feeling isolated, with no help nearby, is to try to do constructive things. If you like to dance, go out dancing, or go to school, or write. Do what you want, as long as you know it is not destructive. It's very simple to go out there and just get drunk or do something nasty or be promiscuous. The next day you will feel shitty. You will feel angry at yourself if it's destructive. It's a temptation we all have because we have both good and evil in us, and it's up to you, unless you are sick or are losing control. Meditation is a help, I know. I've been there. Then you have some peace of mind. Also, in helping others, you help yourself. If you think about the other person, you build a kind of strength from that."

I N T H E preceding story, we read of a wife who knew well in advance of her husband's illness and was able to care for him during that time. The following account is from a wife who was taken completely by surprise—not only by the unexpected death of her child, but by her husband's death as well.

Theresa Rodriguez had suffered many losses. Her mother had died the previous year, and shortly before that two of her cousins and a favorite aunt passed away. But it was the loss of her year-old daughter, Kimberly, that took her totally unaware. The child was given a penicillin injection that sent her into cardiac arrest. She died in the doctor's office. In a tragic turn of events, Theresa was also left unprepared for her husband's death from AIDS. She tells of the day her husband was caught using drugs at his job and of subsequent events.

"In August of 1984," Theresa remembers, "the post office where my husband worked called and said my husband had been arrested for using drugs. I was in shock. I had no idea. It couldn't have been consistent because he kept a steady job and there were no traces of it in our home. During the following months, he kept getting sick and losing weight, but because no one could find anything wrong, we chalked it up to stress. In June of 1985 the doctor told me my husband had something chronic and that we had to get him into a hospital. He was admitted on June 12, and by July 21 he was dead. When they told me he had AIDS, my first reaction was, 'Do I have it, too?' I was frightened for my three kids. Although I'd tested negative, I lived in fear. I made a pact with God that He should give me at least ten years until my children grew up."

In the beginning, Theresa blamed herself for her husband's death, thinking if she had been a better wife, he wouldn't have turned to drugs. "You get all kinds of ideas in your head. I was very angry when Jimmy died, but I also knew I wasn't a perfect wife. I wondered if things I had done had caused him to turn to drugs. I also realized my husband had been a tormented and angry man because of prejudices. I am Italian and he was Spanish. In the sixties, when we started seeing each other, there was a lot of flak about a Puerto Rican and an Italian dating."

Theresa ran into other prejudices and injustices from the moment her husband died. "At the funeral parlor, I was told they would not embalm Jimmy. I was told he had to be cremated, but I refused. I felt there was no reason why my husband shouldn't get the type of burial I wanted for him. For an extra five hundred dollars, they agreed. Jimmy had been in the service, so I had an American flag draped over the coffin."

Two days after her husband's funeral, Theresa flew to Michigan to stay with her sisters. During her two-week visit, she went to the local church for solace but instead received a harsh rebuke. "At the church, the parish priest was far from comforting. He said to me, 'Your husband lived in sin and he had to die in sin.' I was furious. In another incident in Michigan, a couple of nuns were in a car and stopped to ask me for directions. I told them I wasn't from Michigan. One thing led to another, and we started talking. I told them why I was visiting and that my husband had died of AIDS. I was absolutely floored when, in the middle of the conversation, they rolled up their windows and drove off! This made me very bitter and angry."

Theresa was even more outraged and hurt by prejudices closer to home. She made attempts to rationalize them to herself and her children. "I went to visit a girlfriend, and she served my food to me on a paper plate. I thought to myself, 'She's never served us with paper plates. I can't believe she's so afraid.' I kept trying to excuse people and make allowances for their behavior. I tried to put myself in their shoes. But the fears and injustices carried over to my kids. For example, my daughter's best friend said to her, 'My mother told me not to share my candy or anything else with you.' This would be devastating for any child, but Dawn was in junior high school and at a very sensitive age. My children and I were outcasts. We were treated like we had leprosy."

At her work place, Theresa was also painfully aware of the

fears the word *AIDS* generated. "While my children were in school, I worked at a bank. I can't tell you how badly I was treated there. I had told my boss what had happened, and then it began. One day I asked an officer for a pen. She had a drawerful of pens, but she closed the drawer and said, 'I'm sorry, I don't have one.' She was so afraid I might touch her pen. After my husband died, they were going to give me a month off but said in order to come back I would have to take a physical to make sure I didn't have the AIDS virus."

Theresa chose not to return to the bank. Instead she got a job with the board of education and decided to go back to school. "I went to a college for human services that was established for returning housewives, although men can go there as well. It took me two years and nine months to get a bachelor's degree in human services. Somehow I managed to achieve that. At present I'm in the second year of my master's at Fordham University, and all three of my children are in college. I have said a lot of prayers and shed a lot of tears, but I can also say, 'Thank God, we've made it.' "

Theresa stresses the point that she was and still is a very active parishioner at her church, where she received a great deal of support from her circle of friends. "Although I had to endure a lot, I was blessed with a support system from my community at St. Mary's Church and one priest in particular, Father Paul Keenen." She also credits therapy and joining a support group for helping her get through difficult times.

"The children and I went to family therapy with a therapist suggested by a friend. She was very helpful in opening up communication. In the beginning, the kids said they couldn't talk about their father. But little by little, the therapist helped us wedge the door open, and the kids began to talk. They were angry at their father for dying and for having used drugs that led to the AIDS that killed him. But they also missed him and cried. On Father's Day it was rough, especially in the beginning. It was hard for them to see friends with their fathers. Even today, with so many single-parent homes, the children among our friends still have their fathers. At Christmas we went to my husband's family, but when it came time for my brother-in-law to hand out the presents to the children, my kids said, 'Mommy, let's go, let's go.' This was something they had done with their father. He had always handed out their presents. We hadn't spent Christmas at home for three years. Finally I said to myself, I've got to get this together and carry on tradition in my own home. So I made Christmas at home. On Thanksgiving we go to my brother's because I can't handle that holiday. My husband used to make Thanksgiving dinner. I don't know how to make a turkey."

Theresa points out an important case of misdirected anger to one of her children and how she learned of discriminatory action on her part. "My son Jimmy looked so much like my husband, was so much like him, and bore his name. My therapist brought out that I used to take things out on him more than the other children. With Jimmy in the room with us, she said, 'Why is it that every time Jimmy does something, you seem to be more angry than with Keith or Dawn?' Thank God she asked me that question and brought it to my attention. I was not aware that I was hurting him by my misdirected anger. I leave communication open with all of my children, and that's been a great help. Today my children and I have a very strong relationship."

At the bereavement support group, Theresa was able to air all the thoughts she'd had about her husband and his illness. "When I was in the group, I heard other people's stories and I thought, Gee, I'm not alone. That gave me an uplifting feeling. I had felt lost for months, wondering if our entire family was infected. I listened to what everyone else said and felt their pain. I gained a lot of support from that group. We all owe a big debt of gratitude to Sister Patrice Murphy, who ran the groups. I admired her from day one. What was so interesting was that the group I was in was mixed—there was a mother who had lost a child, two of us who had lost husbands, and a woman who had lost brothers. We also had a prayer service with another group, which consisted of gay men who had lost lovers. We meshed very well and touched each other's lives in such a positive way."

D R . M E L I N D A Broman Ockey speaks from her own personal tragedy after her husband, a hemophiliac, died as a result of an HIV-infected blood factor transfusion. "Victor found out he was positive in 1985, and he went on to develop AIDS in 1986. He lived for two more years and died in 1988. We got married after he was diagnosed. We'd had a long relationship before that and had dated for many years. When someone has AIDS, I think the grieving process really begins before the person dies, because you pretty much know they are going to die. I had some hope that there would be a cure. We both had that hope, but we were not greatly optimistic. Also, it was clear my husband was deteriorating very noticeably, rather dramatically, right from the time he had his first serious illness. That was in 1986, when he was diagnosed with PCP [Pneumocystis cerinii pneumonia]. I was losing him all through that period."

Victor was open about his illness, Melinda states. "A lot of people in our community knew about it. Our neighbors knew and virtually all of our close friends. During the time he was still alive, I did not tell my colleagues that my husband had AIDS. I was tested after Victor died, and I was negative, but during the period that I didn't know my HIV status, I was concerned about my career and what might happen. So I didn't tell my co-workers, which was very hard for me. Fortunately, my family as well as my friends knew about Victor's illness, so I got support from them."

Although Melinda chose not to discuss the issue at work, Victor was of a different mind. At his job, he told his boss that he had AIDS. After his first episode of PCP, Victor felt he had to speak up because he couldn't go to work as often. He had to spend a lot of time at home. Some days he couldn't get out of bed. He was a management consultant, and his job involved a great deal of traveling to other cities, but while he was recovering from the pneumonia, he could no longer continue to do that. Melinda tells of the aftermath of Victor's decision to inform his employers of his physical status.

"He went to his boss and said, 'I've been ill and haven't been coming in because I have AIDS.' Very quickly they tried to get him to go on disability. To make a long story short, they tried to get rid of him and put a lot of pressure on him to leave. At his job, as in many other places, there was a fear of AIDS. They just didn't want him around. So Victor had to fight to hold on to his job. He loved working, so it was important to him to keep going to work to the extent that he could. Finally he was able to get the attention of somebody who was in a high-level position at his firm, and this individual made sure that he kept his job. He continued to go to work almost up to the time he died. That was very good for him to do rather than stay at home and brood about his illness. That's the sort of thing that happens to many people who have AIDS. A lot of people end up quitting earlier and going on disability."

Melinda explains that everyone who loses someone to AIDS has something in common—AIDS itself. "It is different from other terminal illnesses. It's a plague, and there is a lot of misinformation and discrimination attached to it. So anyone who loses a loved one to AIDS is probably suffering from feelings of isolation and discrimination or fears of discrimination. I think that is the biggest element in those people getting the support they need, whether it is through the death, through the period of bereavement, or prior to that, during the period of taking care of someone who is ill. That makes it different from cancer or other terminal illnesses. I experienced that isolation and discrimination. Anybody who goes through this experiences it. The gays experience it the most because they are already a group that is discriminated against. If you are a hemophiliac family, you're not coping so much with that element. But there is still a lot of isolation and discrimination within that community."

Melinda has friends who have gone through their bereavement and have had a much harder time coping with the loss of their loved ones. She explains her reasoning for this. "I have a different psychology from some other people. My experience may not really be like the ones other people have. Everybody goes through it in their own way. To some extent, what I would say is an old cliché: 'Over time, things get better.' For myself, what has worked is being active as a volunteer and activist in my church and profession and within the hemophiliac and gay communities. That's been very helpful for me, and the fact that today I can be open about AIDS. I can come into my office and raise money for the New York AIDS Walk (sponsored by GMHC) and I can ask my colleagues, 'Will you make a donation to the Gay Men's Health Crisis? They were very helpful to my husband when he was coping with AIDS.' It makes me feel good that I can do that. When Victor was dealing with AIDS, he was the only straight guy in a support group at GMHC. He became very close to the other men, who were gay. He was on the Speakers Panel at GMHC and joined with other individuals who had AIDS to give speaking engagements to educate people."

The main message Melinda wants to get across to people going through bereavement from AIDS is that the most helpful route is getting together with others who are going through the same thing. "The isolation and the discrimination adds a big psychological burden on top of all the medical issues, which are tremendous burdens in themselves. The psychological overlay is very difficult. I think the best way to cope with that is to be with people who are going through similar things. There is a strength in numbers that helps you to cope with both the psychological and social problems. It's tragic that so many people are going through this so quietly and silently. It's really sad when there are ways to break out of the isolation."

A B O V E , W E heard of the lack of compassion displayed by an employer to an employee who had AIDS. In the next story, we learn more of human nature, but in a place one would least expect to encounter ostracism. Fred was shattered when his forty-six-year-old wife, Connie, died of AIDS. "God, she was so wonderful about her illness. When she contracted AIDS, she never complained. She was so cheerful, to listen to her talk you would never know she was dying. I miss hearing her voice. In fact, one thing that frightens me is that I might forget what her voice sounds like."

Shortly after Connie's funeral, Fred noticed that many of their friends seemed to be drifting away. They didn't call him as much. He didn't see them often. He soon became aware that he was considered a pariah, that because he had lived with Connie and had taken care of her, he must therefore be "contagious." Fred was outraged and felt a need to air his feelings.

"I went to see our minister. He told me of a group for widows and widowers. Although I was reluctant to go, I decided to see what it was like. I took a deep breath, got into the car, and drove over to the meeting. Although it was a group for those who had lost a spouse, I began to feel I was not welcome there. It wasn't just a general feeling. It was very apparent in the attitudes of the others as soon as I announced how my wife died. That is what you do at the meeting—each person tells what his story is. I was the only one whose spouse had died of AIDS. And after the meeting, everyone was having coffee and cake and socializing to some extent. It was very obvious that they considered me to be some kind of contaminated creature. No one shook my hand to say good-bye, as they did to others. No one said to me 'See you next week,' as they did to others in the group."

Fred left the group disheartened and very angry. "My first impulse was to tell them all to go to hell. Then I thought better of it and decided I just wouldn't go back. I live in a small town in Missouri. My sister, who lives in the nearby state of Kansas, was furious at the treatment I received at the meeting and decided to check out resources in her area. I received a telephone call from a volunteer who was a telephone contact for people who couldn't get to their group meetings. We talked once a week for a while. Later I managed to get to a meeting every other month. But I thank my sister for being so determined because she really did help me by making this contact for me. It's good to be able to talk to other people who know what I have been through and what I am going through now that Connie is gone."

I N T H E following account, we hear from another segment of the population—a wife who learned her husband had been unfaithful. "Surely I will never be touched by AIDS," was Marlene's belief. She had been married to the same man for nineteen years. They had never used drugs, had always been faithful to each other. Or so she thought.

"We were a middle-class couple, played golf a lot, and tennis. We have three wonderful children in their teens. We've been the Little League and PTA route and are active in our church. We had what I truly believed was an ideal family. That ideal was shattered when I learned that my husband had AIDS. I then learned that I, too, had to be tested, and it was discovered that I was HIV positive. My first thoughts were intense rage, bordering on hatred of my husband that he had allowed this to happen. His assurances that he loved me and that this happened as a result of a onetime encounter at an out-of-town seminar were small comfort in the face of AIDS. I could hardly say the word! AIDS! In my life? Never! But here it was, and there wasn't a damned thing I could do to change it. It struck terror in my heart when I suddenly realized the ramifications for us— and for our children. How long would my husband live? What then was my future? Would my children soon be without both of their parents? And how to tell the children? What do we say to them? They have to know ultimately."

Marlene's husband died seven months after his diagnosis. She has learned to take one day at a time and is involved with a support group for wives whose husbands have contracted AIDS. "It seems a lot of men have had homosexual activities even though they are married to women. Some men have sex at bachelor parties, where a lot of crazy high jinks go on. Some men also may have gotten AIDS from available women who were prostitutes or may have been drug users. All of the women in the group I am part of had husbands who were unfaithful. So that was another kind of death to deal with."

Marlene is but one of a fast-growing number of female survivors who have learned that their husbands or lovers are either bisexual or promiscuous heterosexuals. An eye-opening fact was revealed on "Dr. Dean," an NBC television show, when a researcher from Seattle, Washington, shared some findings with viewers. In a recent survey conducted in that city, it was discovered that among one thousand bisexual men, over five hundred were currently engaged in primary relationships with women—women who were unaware that the men were bisexual. A female guest on the program told of her shock when, after her husband's death from AIDS, she opened a locked closet in their home and found nude photographs of seductive males and other revelations confirming that her husband was bisexual. The woman, who now has AIDS, told the television audience that she is trying to help herself by appearing on programs. In so doing, she believes she can help other women who may be in danger.

•

chapter 4

BROTHERS/SISTERS

• *When I went to a support group, the people there didn't seem to think my loss was as valid as theirs. They felt I had only lost a brother.*

• *My parents were so worried about what we would tell everybody. They didn't want anyone to know what my brother died of. When I put the word AIDS in his obituary, my parents freaked out.*

• *My brother's lover was always there to help. Now he's worried about who is going to take care of him. I keep telling him I will be there, and I will.*

• *I've not only lost my brother, I've lost my parents. No matter how I try to help them, I know I can't take my brother's place. It really hurts me to see my father cry. I've never seen him cry before.*

● *He was my only brother, but as close as we were, he didn't trust me enough to tell me he was HIV positive. Why did he wait until he was in a hospital? It was very unfair. I wanted to help, but by then it was too late.*

● *I had planned to visit him at Christmastime. We lived two hundred miles apart, but I had two small children and it wasn't easy to get away earlier. He died in October, and I'm heartbroken I wasn't there.*

"You only lost a brother!"

That was the outcry from many of the participants at a group support meeting where Judith Phillips had gone to receive help in her bereavement. Surviving siblings often encounter a condescending attitude from other grievers. Judith describes when the issue of "your pain can't possibly approach my pain" surfaced.

"As a sibling, the loss of my brother Robert was not considered as valid as the loss of a husband, a parent, or a child. People in the group got into things like 'Well, I lost a husband and you just lost a brother.' My response was, 'You can hate a husband and you can really love a brother. It depends on the relationship.' But some in the group were vehement and insisted my pain was less than theirs because I had only lost a brother! How could they measure my pain? Doesn't it also depend on how close you were? It may be that the people who said these things to me were not very close to their siblings. You get much more support if your mother dies. But if a brother dies, it's amazing how your grief is looked down upon and not recognized as significant by comparison."

Not only did Judith have to grapple with the abrasive comments of the support group, she was also reeling after hearing derogatory remarks by her colleagues at the school where she taught. "Instinct told me not to mention my brother's illness at school. I was so right. After he died, we were being shown a lot of video programs focusing on AIDS. I was stunned to hear the teachers saying things like 'They should be thrown into concentration camps.' Or 'They should take a gun and blow their heads off.' It's incomprehensible that supposedly educated and intelligent people could show such little understanding or compassion. There is so much hatred against gay men, it's unbelievable.

"I didn't tell certain friends, and others I did. But I didn't get any of the extraordinary negativity and horror I experienced at school. The friends I did confide in were very supportive. They didn't shun me even though AIDS was just coming into people's awareness and many were filled with fear. Even at the hospital, the fear was very obvious and interfered with the care of my brother."

Judith did not expect to encounter fear at the hospital and was appalled by the behavior of the nurses. The treatment of her brother at this facility caused her later to write a strong letter criticizing the hospital and its practices with regard to AIDS patients.

"The nurses were terrible. They were fearful of getting AIDS, and they would say that to us. It was a horrible period. For example, the beeper on my brother's bed was broken. No matter how many times we reported it, the beeper was never repaired. In fact, every time my brother went into the hospital, the beeper was broken. Same hospital, different rooms. My brother wasn't even able to call a nurse. If he couldn't call, obviously they wouldn't have to go into his room. When the nurses had to go into his room, they would run in and out. There were plenty of times when my brother had diarrhea. I would tell the nurses, and a hand would come in the door with a bedpan extended. His care was actually given over to the family."

The refusal to tend to her brother's needs was not limited to nurses, Judith states. "When Robert was out of the hospital, he had to go for chemotherapy and needed an ambulette. But not one would come. I called so many ambulette services, and they all refused. So after I finished teaching for the day, I had to take him. Even the television guy wouldn't come into Robert's hospital room for his check. I had to give it to him outside. He wouldn't take it from my brother. Another area of distress was the sloppiness of the doctors in the hospital. They had extracted bloody fluid by the quart from his lungs. When I would walk into the room, they would have the bags on top of my brother's breakfast table. The bags would leak all over the floor and his pillows. No one would come to clean up. I mean no one! So my husband and I had to clean up his room. After my brother's death, I wrote a fifteen-page letter to the hospital administrators to let them know my grievances. The letter was forwarded to the president of the hospital, who was outraged at what I cited. He called several meetings and quoted from the letter about my brother's treatment. I was glad to see that action was being taken to correct things."

Holidays are not easy for Judith, and this has been compounded by the loss of her mother. She tells of her sadness and shares the unique way she decided to celebrate Christmas. "I have a tremendous sense of the loss of my family. I have two surviving brothers, but there are no other family members. No aunts, no uncles. All of my mother's family has died, and we are not close to my father's family. And I have no children—none of us did. This past year was the first time that I celebrated Christmas since Robert's death. I guess I thought it was time to do that. Christmas was my brother's favorite holiday, and that's why it was so difficult. It took me so many years because it was too painful that he wasn't here. Whereas in the past I always had a traditional tree, this year I decided to make a Victorian Christmas tree. I made little houses out of tissue boxes. Then I made a Victorian facade with plaques. I built a room in the back and made little miniature furniture. I took pictures of my brother and mother and turned them into little people and put them into this little house. It gave me a measure of comfort while I was doing it. I guess it's somewhat like having a photograph album, only done in this manner. It made me feel very good."

Judith has no regrets about the care she gave to her brother. "When we learned of Robert's diagnosis, his doctor said, 'Your brother is going to need a lot of support.' I said, 'You don't think we're going to abandon him because he has AIDS, do you?' He replied, 'A lot of families do.' I quickly responded, 'Well, not us.' We were a small family, but we were there for my brother—my husband, my mother, my two brothers, and my sister-in-law. When I first heard he had AIDS, I didn't know where to turn. What is this disease? It seemed there wasn't any place to find relief. That's when I heard about the bereavement support group, and I went there for eight weeks."

Judith also has no regrets about going to the support group. "Even though some of the group members didn't accept my grief, it was still helpful to me being in the group and hearing others talk about the pain of losing a loved one to AIDS."

W E   H A V E read in the preceding pages about the insensitivity of people in almost every walk of life—all stemming from fear of AIDS. In the following accounts, surviving siblings talk about their anger at the lack of compassion, the lack of understanding. Siblings are often the "forgotten grievers"; when compounded by unthinking remarks, grief is made all the harder for these mourners. We now hear from a sister whose life goal is to make up for some of the judgmental and uncaring remarks made by nurses.

' ' H O W   C O U L D all of this have been over so quickly?" Kelly Coady Gonzalez wondered. Her brother, Bill, was at work on Friday, hospitalized Sunday, and was dead on Thursday. His death was as sudden as if he had been killed in an accident. The death certificate stated the immediate cause of Bill's death was progressive multifocal leukencephalopathy (PML), a rare brain disease related to AIDS.

When Kelly's brother first told her that he was HIV positive, she didn't know what to expect. At a time when AIDS awareness was just surfacing, Kelly was filled with apprehension. She shares some of the concerns she had.

"Everything about AIDS was so new to me that it was hard for me to think about what all of this meant for my brother. Bill told me he felt fine and was ready to fight this horrible disease. I supported him through everything and prayed that a cure would be found. Although my brother was strong, the reports of deaths caused by AIDS continued to skyrocket. I knew in my heart that it would take a lot more than my brother's will to live to fight a disease that had no cure."

Throughout the five years he was HIV positive, Bill had repeated blood tests to check his T cell level. Sometimes the level was high, while at other times it had dropped. Kelly never quite understood all the medical terminology, but she listened carefully to the news reports and read articles about AIDS. "I wanted to gain a better understanding of what was happening inside my brother's body. He always called me after his frequent doctor visits, and our unique sense of humor that we mutually shared was a big part of our phone conversations."

However, in 1991 Bill's health began slowly to decline. He was still able to work, but he seemed to be in and out of hospitals for more tests. Kelly describes the developments that led to a barrage of tests.

"Aside from being HIV positive, there was something else wrong with Bill, but no one could seem to find out what it was. He endured bone marrow tests, blood transfusions, and endless other blood tests. Finally, after about three months of this, his doctor discovered that my brother was suffering from tuberculosis, not in his lungs, but in his bone marrow. Medication was prescribed, and my brother was hopeful that it would cure the TB. Unfortunately the TB was determined to be AIDS related. So after five years of being HIV positive, my brother now had AIDS."

Kelly reflects on the day she learned this tragic news. "I remember that dreadful phone call so vividly. All the humor in the world couldn't take away my devastation. Even though I was aware he could have developed AIDS at any time, I always remained hopeful that a cure would be found and this moment would never arrive. I felt helpless. There wasn't a single thing I could do for my brother, not even to be with him. He lived in Los Angeles and I lived in Idaho. It wasn't as if I could just drive over to his house and hold his hand and hug him endlessly. I quietly tried to accept this fate as my brother and I made plans to visit each other sometime during the year—maybe during the summer or at Christmas. After all, we both figured, AIDS patients can live up to two or three years. There was still time for visits and phone calls."

Sadly, their timing was off. Six weeks after Bill was diagnosed with AIDS, he suffered seizures and was admitted into the hospital. Because his condition was critical, he was placed in ICU. Kelly immediately flew to Los Angeles to be with her brother. She describes her anguish at seeing Bill's condition.

"I was horrified at the sight of a thin, frail-looking man with several tubes and machines connected to every part of his body. I wanted to cry, but I was numb. I just sat with him and held his hand. He was very happy to see me, and we shared a few silly jokes. I spent the night with him in the hospital. The next morning, while he was sleeping, I left to go to his apartment. I was his beneficiary, and since we had talked beforehand about what needed to be done, I began making the phone calls— funeral homes, obituary information, his job, and so on."

After completing her tasks at the apartment, Kelly returned to the hospital. She shares her last poignant moments with her brother. "He was sleeping, and all the machines had been disconnected because he did not wish to be resuscitated. He appeared so peaceful, not restless like the day before. I sat with him some more and decided to put some lotion on his arms. His skin was terribly dry. As I applied the warm, moist cream on his arms and softly spoke to him, he suddenly took two peaceful, deep breaths, and then he was gone. My brother was dead. I sat there and finally cried—a cry that came from so deep inside, it hurt. After spending an hour with him, I said my good-byes and returned to his very empty apartment."

Although Kelly was grateful that her brother didn't suffer for endless weeks, she felt somehow deprived at not being able to care for him in his last days. "When Bill told me he had AIDS, I remember how helpless I felt not being able to be with him at such a tragic time, but I comforted myself by mentally promising and planning on how I would definitely be with him when he no longer could care for himself. Yes, I was there with him at the end, but his sudden death has left a void in my heart. I had pictured us being absolutely ridiculous and sarcastic with each other, even in the midst of the inevitable, because that's the way we were with each other. It was a coping skill we learned as children. I pictured holding him, reading to him, feeding him, watching over him to make sure he would never be alone. These plans were all stripped away only six weeks after his diagnosis. I guess I'm being selfish, because I know his dying without months of suffering is what he would have preferred and my need to have taken care of him really is irrelevant. Even though I was able to take care of him for only two and a half days, I do feel a great sense of peace."

Kelly lambasts the nurses who were on duty at the time of her brother's illness and is working eagerly toward her own nursing degree. "I want to take what I have learned and put it to good use in the medical field. The nurses who worked with my brother were very cold, and it is something I will never forget. They acted as though they had prejudged my brother for the kind of disease he had. I found this attitude to be so with a lot of people, including those from my own church. So many people asked, 'Well, how did he get AIDS?' What difference does it make? Do people ask how someone gets cancer or heart disease? And what right did they have to judge my brother?"

Making a panel for the Names Project AIDS Memorial Quilt in memory of her brother was a source of comfort to Kelly. "I started making it on what would have been Bill's thirty-second birthday and finished it on the one-year anniversary of his death." Kelly also finds great satisfaction in following in her brother's footsteps by working on AIDS causes. She tells of her goals in this area.

"When I get my nursing degree, I want to care for AIDS patients, especially those who have been abandoned by their families and are all alone. I will be carrying my brother in my heart, and his strength and courage will shine through the work I have chosen to dedicate my life to. This is my tribute to my beloved brother, my best friend. I love you, Bill."

W E N O W read about a sibling who tells of her sadness in not being able to share the pain of her loss with her father.

After her brother died, Lisa Eltinge hoped she could talk to her only surviving parent, but she was sorely disappointed. "When Daniel died, I turned to my father, thinking he would be another person this loss would mean something to. But it was like banging my head against the wall. He added to my pain instead of lessening it. He doesn't want to talk about my brother very much. In general, my father doesn't like to express emotion.

As an adolescent, I always had to say 'I think' because the word *feel* was perceived as a weakness."

Lisa's mother died a year ago, followed by the death of her first cousin. "My cousin died of AIDS a few months before my brother's death. My cousin was constantly in and out of the hospital, was emaciated and down to seventy pounds. Because I had experienced the agony of that death and the slowness of it, I felt it was a foreshadowing of my brother's death. I found out that my brother was HIV positive about six months before my cousin died. But Daniel died quickly, exactly the opposite of my cousin. I thank God every day for that. He developed a breathing problem and had to have surgery on Christmas Eve. Although he had been HIV positive for a few years, that was the first time he had been hospitalized for anything. The diagnosis was lung cancer. He had been a heavy smoker for twenty years. He started smoking as a teenager and died when he was thirty-four. He had stopped smoking a year before, which was very difficult for him but he did it."

Although Daniel felt strong enough to go home a week after the operation, he soon started to experience difficulties. Lisa explains what happened and criticizes the doctor for his insensitivity. "Daniel had severe nausea and vertigo and was put back into the hospital. The doctor said the cancer had spread quite a bit. Two or three days later, my brother was diagnosed with meningitis. He died four days after that. Meningitis was given as the cause of death. The doctor made an unthinking remark to me—'His brain kind of blew up'—which I wish he hadn't said. I was also told that Daniel was awake—and alone. He also said this to my father."

Lisa believed she was doing fine until it suddenly hit her that her brother was really dead. "After the funeral, I thought I was all right. I was surprised that I was still okay a week or so later. Even after a couple of months I was getting along, because I was still in shock and had not faced the reality. But then three months after my brother's death, it kicked in again and I felt very desolate and alone. My oldest and closest friends are in California, where Daniel died. The friends here in New York are only professional ones. It was not like I could say to them, 'Get over here. I need you now.' Thank God there was my husband and my sixteen-month-old baby. Nonetheless, I was very lonely."

Some of Lisa's despair and loneliness was lessened by her special friends in California. "My friends Beth, Leslie, and Ron are extremely loving people. Leslie sent beautiful letters. She is very spiritual. A month after Daniel died, she sent a Valentine's note that said, 'Hope things are getting back to normal. What is normal without Daniel?' She loved us like a brother and sister. Beth sent me flowers out of the blue, and she is on a very limited budget, so that meant a lot to me, too. I was trying to learn to reach out to friends because my tendency is to get in bed and lie low. Beth would say, 'Thank you for calling me,' but I should have been thanking her because she was so gracious. There is just a loving aura, a gentleness, around Beth. She could feel my pain and distract me gently and not overtly. Ron, whose father died ten years ago, could share the experience with me. He sent me cartoons and stupid jokes that weren't funny, but just his attempt was funny. He was a savior for me. There was also a lovely mother whom I met in a nearby park. She called me regularly. This new acquaintance took the time to call and say, 'Hi, how's your baby?' and so forth. But one day she left flowers for me with my doorman. She had seen me earlier that day and could see that I was in pain."

Although Lisa and her husband have a very good rapport and he has been sensitive to her needs, there are difficult moments for both of them because of the continuing grief. Lisa explains how the anticipation of yet another death—her husband's mother—is affecting their relationship.

"My husband and son both forced me to keep going. My baby would come up to me with this huge smile, and even if you were in the middle of crying, you would smile back. My husband is a very caring man, but we still had to learn about each other and grief. There were times I didn't want to talk and times when it was better to let me feel bad. He's the kind who wants to make you feel better. However, he's learned that it's okay to let me experience my emotions. He is now in the process of losing his mother. We made funeral arrangements for her this week. It's hard for me to be there for him right now because I'm not on a full tank. I'm better than I was, but I'm still not myself."

Lisa began to feel overwhelmed by the ceaseless grief. "With the death of my mother, then the death of my cousin, then my brother, and now the upcoming death of my husband's mother, it's getting to be too much. I was just beginning to feel a little better. We're so tired of grief. I had made a mental adjustment, but now I'm scared. I know how upset and frightened I was after the other deaths, and I know what we are going to have to live through with another death. We pretty much rely on each other. My husband works at home, so it's right here all the time. So much under one roof."

Lisa explains that she was reluctant at first to explore a bereavement support group, but it turned out to be a saving grace. "At first I was apprehensive about going. I thought it might make me feel worse if I went. But it didn't. It made me feel better. Everybody in the group understood exactly what you were talking about, and they didn't try to change the subject. Other people got tired of hearing it, but no one in the group did. We all needed to talk about it. The group was a mixed bag, but we all seemed to work well together. It consisted of three guys who had lost their lovers, three who had lost their best friends, a mother who lost a son, and me—I was a sibling. After the group finished, we continued to meet once a month in each other's homes. Everyone in the group was very bright, and we meshed incredibly well. That had been another fear of mine about going into a group. I thought, What would I do if I didn't like the people? But I felt I owed it to myself to try, and it was the best thing I could have done."

W E H A V E heard above from a bereaved sibling whose father was unable to talk about the death of her brother. Often men find it difficult to talk about emotions, but just because a man does not cry outwardly doesn't mean he isn't crying inwardly. The images of John Wayne and Clint Eastwood are the stuff many men were brought up with, and those role models did not cry or show their hurt. It's been said that some men would rather suffer a heart attack than let their emotions show. However, many support group leaders say that men *will* share when they hear another man speak of a parallel experience. At meetings the raw emotion is so important for someone to hear. Translating that impact is impossible. One chapter leader of The Compassionate Friends, a self-help group for bereaved parents, says, "You have to see it. You have to sense it. You have to hear another father say, 'My son is dead and I'm hurting.' Then suddenly it hits them: 'There are other men who feel the same way I do.' And they realize this is normal. Most men cannot grieve because they don't realize how other men feel. Men who believe they must contain their emotions also believe that other men know how to handle difficult problems and that, surely, 'They must not be suffering the way I am.' It cannot be emphasized strongly enough that John Wayne and Clint Eastwood are actors—when you've lost a child, forget about acting! To siblings who want to help their fathers open up, try getting them to a TCF meeting. If they won't go on their own, ask them to drive you there. Many TCF chapters have meetings in which siblings participate. Try to get your father to come in with you and let him just listen to what the other men are saying."

Note: The address and telephone number for the national office of The Compassionate Friends is listed in the "Helping Hands" section at the end of the book.

I N T H E following account, Midge Anderson was able to talk to her mother but discovered the "shame syndrome" was a problem for her parent.

"After the death of my brother to AIDS had a chance to sink in, the issue with my mother has been 'What do you tell other people?' From the beginning I have told her if someone asks me how John died, I tell them that he had AIDS. I said I want people to be aware that he had AIDS. Then she asked, 'Well, isn't there some shame to that?' I replied, 'I guess it's all in what you think, Mom. I look at John and I don't think there is any shame in him.' After that she got quiet and hasn't talked about it much since. My mother is like that anyway—she doesn't dwell on bad things. She never did cry much. Many years ago she lost two children, ages four and seven, from illnesses that today would be cured by antibiotics. So she knows what it is like to lose a child. I've talked about that with her. I asked, 'How do you live through losing a child?' And she would reply, 'You just go on living. You have other children you have to live for. I just got busy and worked. I scrubbed the house from top to bottom. I worked day and night, and I got through it.' She can't do that now. She is eighty-five and an invalid, so now all she can do is sit and think. But my mother has a very strong faith, and I know that's why she can get through a lot of things. She has often said to me, 'Your children are on loan to you from God, and when He wants them back, He can have them.' "

Although Midge works in a hospital and is herself a nurse, her mind blocked out the possibility that her brother had AIDS. "I have six brothers, but I was always closest to John. We shared a lot. He was a biology teacher and president of the teachers union in his school district. The fact that he had AIDS never came out publicly in the school system and was never an issue. As far as they were concerned, he had cancer and they left it at that. But I'm sure the people who really knew John had to know it was AIDS. John didn't even tell me he had AIDS until a year and a half ago. I knew something was wrong. He'd lost weight and looked bad. But I would tell myself, Well, if he had something to tell me, he would surely do so. I just blocked it out of my mind. Then I would see some improvement and I would think, Gee, he looks better. I was wrong. In looking back, I can see there was such denial."

Midge explains that it was her husband of twenty-four years who was able to enlighten her about John's life-style. "John lived in Chicago, which is just fifty miles away, so we got to see each other often. He and his friend Tony were always with us on the holidays and birthdays. My kids were crazy about Uncle John and always looked forward to his being with us. In all that time, I guess I never really thought about the subject of homosexuality. My husband was also very close to John and is feeling his loss greatly. In fact, it was my husband who finally made me see that John certainly was a homosexual and that I was just kidding myself when I said maybe he wasn't. It wasn't anything John and I ever talked about. It wasn't ever discussed in our household with our parents. We come from a German Lutheran background. And according to my mother, who has made comments in the past, AIDS is God's wrath on homosexuals. So when your parents have that kind of attitude, you don't talk about it.

"When John finally told me he had AIDS, it was like all of a sudden now we were going to talk about the whole issue. Not only do you have to accept the AIDS, you also have to accept the homosexuality. And I accepted it—quietly. He was such a wonderful person. When I told my four sons that John had AIDS, we talked some more about the homosexual issue. Three of my sons are away at college. One of them, who is twenty-one and a junior, cried the day I told him John had AIDS. He said, 'We can't lose Uncle John, Mom, we can't lose him.' And I said, 'But we will lose him.' My son's unhappiness was very evident. 'There's so much I have to tell him. Mom, I want to tell Uncle John that I love him and accept him.' I said, 'Well, you have to let him know how you feel now. I don't know how much time we have.' My son then said to me, 'Mom, there are fags all over the campus. Uncle John is not a fag. He wasn't wearing earrings or dying his hair red or doing crazy things. He's an honest, caring person, and I love him.' My other brothers grieved and cried. They came home from all over the country. I also have a sister in Atlanta who came home as often as she could and was very supportive.

"John's friend Tony comes over almost every weekend. They lived together for seventeen years, and I promised John that we would never leave Tony, that we would always be there for him, and we will be. My kids love him, and he's been around most of their lives when he and John spent holidays with us. But I find being with Tony painful at times because it reminds me of John. But I also think it's helping me because I've noticed that every time I'm with him, it's a little easier. The only problems I've had are with my aunts and uncles, who are the same generation and faith as my mother. They have been cool and not easy to talk to. They also are very judgmental, and I have a hard time with that."

At the hospital, Midge found her boss to be extremely supportive. "She gave me the week off when John died. Every since I had learned of John's AIDS, I talked to her about it. She's cried with me, and she's been there when I needed to vent my feelings. She drove to Chicago for his memorial service, which touched me greatly. She had never even met him but said she felt that she knew him from our conversations. My friends were always there for me, too. They never put the issue down or said 'I don't want to talk about it.' They never said anything negative about the fact that he had AIDS. Most of my friends are in the health field, so they may be more understanding because of that."

Although Midge has thought about going to a bereavement group, she believes the support of family and friends have been enough help. "I honestly don't feel the need to go to a bereavement group. I believe I've been handling it. My support group has been my family. My husband has been wonderful, and when I want to break down and cry, I can do that. Lately I find that happening less frequently. Sometimes it does overwhelm you. Then you have to let go for a few minutes, and then you're better again. We've also gone through some 'firsts.' I had my birthday. Then my son had a birthday. And we cried about John's not being here to share them. I also help myself by talking when I feel the need to do so."

Midge has been concerned about Tony's grief and is helping to allay his fears for the future. "Tony is having a very hard time. He feels very alone and is also HIV positive. His family lives far away, and there have been times when he has broken down and asked, 'Who is going to take care of me?' I've reassured him that I will always be there for him, that he need have no fear of that. His grief is every bit the same as any spouse's would be. I've encouraged him to go to a support group, which he says he will do soon. Perhaps what he needs is for me to go with him, which I will. He is also volunteering with the AIDS clinics, and I know that is an avenue of comfort for him. I just want Tony to know that we will never let him down. We are all here for him now, and we will all be here for him when he needs us."

THERE WERE seven brothers and one sister in Doug's family, but Doug was closest to his brother Edward. A year apart in age, they were in the Cub Scouts together, went fishing together when their older brothers ignored them as big brothers often do, and they shared a secret hiding place—the place where Doug ultimately scattered Edward's ashes after his brother died of AIDS at age twenty-six.

Doug and Ed were both gay. None of their other siblings were, and this issue drove a wedge between the two younger brothers and the rest of their family. "My sister tended to look the other way, but she really didn't have much to do with us. My brothers were homophobic. It was only when Ed became so sick that most of them began to rally around. I guess the guilt got to them, and they were faced with the fact that Ed was dying. But even when Ed was in the hospital, they would call up for about two minutes. And when they came to visit him, they stayed for about five minutes. I know they were uncomfortable and afraid somebody would see them. Even though we live in a large city like Houston, the idea of being associated with someone with AIDS is still frightening for a lot of people."

Doug's mother died when he was eight years old. His father was a stern man, with strong religious views. "My mom was a dear soul, and no one ever had anything bad to say about her. I don't remember her too much, but I know she loved all of us. My father never lets us know if he feels any emotion. But he was always picking away at Edward and me about our lack of interest in rough sports. He was a big soccer fan, and he was very proud when some of my brothers made the football team. I never spoke to my father about my life-style, but I'm pretty sure he was aware of it. He didn't have much to say about our lives, because Edward and I rarely saw him except for Thanksgiving. My sister-in-law made a big dinner on that day, and the family got together. But it was always such a noisy affair, it didn't leave much room for any private conversations. Not that Ed or I wanted any particularly, but that's the way it was."

At Doug's office there were prejudice problems, and he still had not come out. "Our boss and a few of the other guys had a daily contest of who was able to make out in the office with any new female arrivals. My immediate superior was the biggest braggart. He was always talking about how macho he was, how big his biceps were, how good he was in bed, how every woman pleaded for more. He had a thing going with his secretary and a couple of others in the office as well. If he'd known I was gay, he would have fainted dead away! When Ed died, I only took off the three days allotted to employees for a death in the immediate family. Upon my return to work, someone in the office asked me what my brother died of and I told them it was cancer. That response was okay for them. That allowed them to nod their heads sympathetically and say, 'I'm so sorry.' I wonder what they would have said if I'd told them Ed had died of AIDS. I often think about what their reactions would have been. I really had to control my anger, but I knew if I told them the truth, my job would be in jeopardy. They would think I had AIDS, too. That was their mentality."

Fortunately, Doug's lover, Wally, provided a strong support system. When Doug finished work, he knew he had a safe place to retreat and mourn. "Wally loved to play the piano, and he knew how much I enjoyed his musical ability. Whenever I came home, right after dinner he would sit down and play some of the songs he knew I liked. It was so peaceful and quieting for me. I had been having nightmares, and Wally was trying to help reduce the stress I was under. I kept remembering the night my brother died. Many years ago we had gone to Japan, and after that visit Ed would never say 'good-bye.' Instead he would say 'sayonara.' Just before he died, he opened his eyes and we could see he was trying to say something. At first we thought he wanted water. Then we recognized the *s* sound, which was almost like a hissing, and understood he was saying, 'Sayonara.' Then, just like in the movies, my brother died."

Wally accompanied Doug when he set out to scatter Ed's ashes. "Wally wasn't about to let me go alone. I wanted to go fishing where Ed and I used to go. It was so cold, but I had to be there. So Wally came with me. I took him up to the secret hiding place. At first I wasn't sure I could bring the ashes. I wasn't sure I could scatter them and thought maybe I would just keep them in the house. But that thought petrified me because I didn't know how I would react to having his ashes and not him. So I decided the best thing was to leave his ashes at the hiding place. It wasn't really a cave, but it had the shape of what the outside of a cave might look like. We always called it the Ho-Ho Cave. Whenever we went there we would have a good belly laugh at the world and say, 'Ho-ho!' It gave us strength to be there together and laugh. When I put his ashes there, I felt a real sense of peace."

Another thing that gave Doug comfort was the support of close friends. "Many gay men draw closer together because we know we can count on each other. Whereas family might not always be there for us, we don't need to worry about that because we are family to each other. Our friends brought over food, took us to the movies and out to dinner. But the most important thing was that they were just there and listened."

' ' M Y B R O T H E R was a Buddhist, and when he died there was a Buddhist ceremony. They believe it is a celebration of life. You pass on to another level, so they don't want you to mourn. But I cried nonstop tears. I couldn't imagine Charles not being here and to know that when I went to Philadelphia I would no longer see my brother."

Stephanie Poindexter was home in nearby Williamsport, Pennsylvania, in bed, asleep. At 4:00 A.M. she sat bolt upright in bed, and her eyes went immediately to the clock. "I remember that morning so vividly. As the Lord is my witness, at four A.M. I saw the time and thought, What am I doing up at this hour of the morning? Then I went back to sleep. At four-thirty A.M. the phone rang. It was a friend of the family who told me that my brother had died. It was two days before his birthday. He was only thirty-one. I hung up the phone and looked out the window. It was snowing. I lay down and cried."

The hardest thing for Stephanie was not being able to share the present with her brother. "It took a while to swallow that we were not making new memories—no more holidays or any event. He was my only true friend, and we had an unconditional love. He was always there for me. Last Thanksgiving I wrote a poem in which I talked about my most memorable one. The day before that Thanksgiving, I caught a bus and on Thanksgiving Day I ate dinner with my brother in the hospital. To me, that's my memory of what Thanksgiving is all about. For a long time I would see someone who reminded me of Charles. I had a whole wall of pictures of him. It may sound morbid, but I didn't know how to let him go. This was my only brother. We were both gay and extremely close."

Stephanie tells how she went from grieving privately to being able to talk about her emotions at a recovery group. "I tried to get on with my life, but when I went to a recovery group, I attacked people. I told them how they needed to appreciate life, how short life is. I came down on everybody. I just couldn't get my life in order. I wasn't aware that I had to go through a grieving process. There are specific things you have to do. Regardless of how much progress I made, certain things held me back. For example, I have never gotten angry that Charles left me. That's a human thing. What I would do is use my intellect and say, 'Oh, I understand he had a disease. That's the way life goes.' But that was being internalized, and I wasn't expressing anger at anyone except myself. I would grieve only in private. I would not let anyone know that I was hurting. No one in my family talked about him. I guess it was too painful. So when I would go home, it wasn't cool to cry. It wasn't cool to talk about how much I missed him. I would hold all that stuff inside, and it would eat me up. I never got angry at God, and even today I'm not angry at Him. In the last two years I've had an aunt, a cousin, an uncle, and my brother *all* die of AIDS. Each of their deaths was different."

Stephanie urges those who have lost a loved one to AIDS to talk, to let someone know how they are feeling. "It blows me away how simple life can be and how I used to complicate it. I think the main thing is for people to talk, talk, talk. Speak about what's in your heart. You have to get your feelings out. Also, helping others helps you. My work in the AIDS Resource Center has been very rewarding for me. I'm a volunteer, and I work every single day with people who have AIDS. It's never easy, but it isn't as difficult as it used to be. I feel that God has a mission for me."

What helped Stephanie the most was going to see the AIDS Quilt in Washington. She was so touched by the experience that she wrote an essay, which was subsequently published in *Body Positive.* "When I went to view the quilt, en route I was afraid. But once I got there, I was like an excited child. I took my camera and carried an eight-by-ten picture of my brother. I walked around all of the people and the thousands of panels. As I continued walking, I cried. People would hug me and I would hug them. They didn't know me and I didn't know them. It didn't make any difference. I would stop and look up at the heavens and say to my brother, 'This is all for you.' He didn't have a quilt yet, but blank quilts were provided so we could write messages on them. I wrote my message: 'Charles, I came to meet your spirit today. Love, Stephanie.'

"At one point I needed to get away, but not too far. I went a little distance from the quilt and sat under a tree. I watched the motions of the people and the movement. I felt in awe of what was probably the largest memorial service in the world. I asked people to use my camera and take pictures of me and my brother's photograph beside me, with the quilt in the background. The organizers asked for help in putting away the quilts. Most people volunteered, and so did I. There was a caravan of quilts. The same way you fold the flag is the way we folded the quilts. Ever since that experience, I've been better in my recovery. I'm working again. I'm doing the things you would normally do in everyday life."

Stephanie has been pleased that through her writings she has formed a closer bond with her mother. "Since I began writing about HIV/AIDS and my brother, and finding a cause to stand firm for, the relationship between my mother and me has blossomed tremendously. She is very proud of me and is beginning a scrapbook of my writings and related material about my participation on various panels at colleges concerning HIV/AIDS education."

Currently Stephanie is taking classes to qualify as an HIV/AIDS instructor. She acknowledges the hard road she has traveled to reach where she is today. "This is a transitional time for me. By that I mean performing day by day as a recovering person coming back from an addiction and a long battle with grief concerning my brother Charles. I'm taking time that the Lord has allowed for regrouping of me and all that I'm not but yearn to be."

* * *

W E   W I L L now hear from two sisters who were angry—one because her family was not telling the truth about the cause of her brother's death and the other because her brother had not been open with her.

Kathy Eye was furious because those closest to her pretended that her brother had died of cancer. "I am very angry about the awful disease AIDS and how others treat people with AIDS. We have to stop pretending and start talking about it. We have to be sympathetic to those who have it and to the family members who survive it. Even my boyfriend told his parents that Richard died of cancer, which was very disappointing to me. We shouldn't be ashamed to discuss it."

Kathy's family was her biggest disappointment. "It infuriated me that they were telling people that Richard died of cancer. This was the same type of ignorance that led Richard to keep his disease a secret for so long. This ignorance and not wanting to talk about it robbed me of precious time with my brother. I refuse to do the same. I also get angry with some people's remarks. For example, they will preface a comment with some inference, such as 'You're almost getting over it.' I say, 'What you don't realize is that it's never over. You just get better at handling it.' When Richard comes up in a conversation, many people just change the subject."

Richard and Kathy were close in age, just fifteen months apart. The two siblings were also very close in their daily lives. "I'm thirty-two, and Richard was only thirty when he died. As we got older, we became closer. We both lived in northern Virginia and liked to do a lot of the same things socially. We had a great time together. We even went on several vacations together to Barbados and Cancún. With the exception of my grandmother, Richard was the only person in my family I really felt close to. That's what made his silence about his illness so puzzling to me."

Kathy began to suspect that Richard might have AIDS when he constantly had something wrong with him. "I was suspicious about all the different physical problems, but I was told by a member of my family that Richard had been tested and was negative. I now know that this was not the truth, but at the time I thought he was just depressed and that he would snap out of it. I was also certain that he would tell me if he knew that something was seriously wrong with him. The situation became even more strange when he started avoiding me. We didn't do as many things socially as before, and he didn't always return my calls. I believe now that he knew if we spent enough time together, I would figure out his secret."

During a family vacation to North Carolina, Kathy ran into more frustration. "It ended up being a terrible experience. Richard was very ill, but I couldn't get anyone, including him, to say what was wrong with him. I talked to friends in the medical field, and they agreed with me that they thought he was depressed. On the vacation, everyone was at each other's throats. Although we were at the beach, Richard was constantly lying on a couch watching TV. But there was no explanation. One day when I was out with my mother and grandmother picking up groceries, I asked them what was wrong with Richard and was greeted with dead silence. I asked why they wouldn't answer me, and my mother said she couldn't answer me because she didn't know. I ended up being very frustrated. I got into an argument with my family and left the beach early to go home by myself."

Several weeks later Kathy was still upset about her brother's illness and decided to write him a letter. "I wrote to Richard telling him that I could not help him if he was not open and honest with me. I said I didn't know what was wrong. I could guess, but I needed him to tell me. I told him that I loved him and that whatever it was, it didn't matter to me. Soon after, he called me but never discussed his illness. After that we talked several times before he went into a hospital in Frederick, Maryland, near where my grandmother lives. He had apparently been staying with my grandmother without my knowledge, since my mother and grandmother weren't speaking to me after the beach incident. Everyone in my family, including my sister, seemed to be afraid to say 'AIDS' but wanted me to assume that he had it. I visited Richard in the hospital and called him daily. He talked a lot to me now about his illness. He was concerned he might be unable to make decisions, and we spoke about that. I thought how unfair it was for someone who was only thirty years old—and my brother—to be worrying about whether he could make decisions. It nearly broke my heart."

At the hospital, the family rallied to form a united front. "During Richard's last weekend, the family really came together in the crisis to support each other. I discovered then that my mother had known that Richard had AIDS, but he had sworn her to secrecy. He didn't want people to know because he was afraid they would think he was a homosexual. My feelings were, So what if he was? It didn't make any difference to me. I didn't realize until later how many families turn their backs on someone because they find out that he or she is gay. It's hard to comprehend that they could abandon someone they care about at the time when they need them the most. I'm sure that this same thought crossed my brother's mind in his decision not to tell people. He had no idea how they would react. Later, many of his friends asked why he didn't tell them so they could have offered support to him. I told them I felt the same way, but I don't think Richard realized how many people would have been there for him. He was overwhelmed by the stigma of AIDS.

"All of us, family and friends, stood around Richard's hospital bed on Sunday night as he took his last breaths. I held his hand, and he squeezed it tight. I will never forget that, and I don't think I could ever do it again. It was so difficult, but I wanted to be with him. It was amazing to me that I was strong and calm until it was over. I know that I would have done anything for my brother. I also wished it could have been me and not him."

Kathy discerned a difference in the way friends responded to her grief. "The funeral was on the day before Thanksgiving. That was the beginning of many surprises and disappointments in my friends. I found out that a crisis can really show you who your true friends are. I know that people don't always know what to do or say, but I hated more than anything when they acted like nothing happened. Damn it, something had! And on top of it all, they really thought it was taboo to talk about it because Richard had died of AIDS. The people who were the greatest support called me, wrote cards, and were there to talk to me or just listen to me and let me cry. Those who couldn't handle it sent the most expensive flower arrangements to the funeral and didn't call for weeks."

The coordinator of the grief program in Springfield, Virginia, Helen Fitzgerald, offered a suggestion to the family to help ease the stress of the upcoming holidays. "We all missed Richard desperately. We did take one of Helen's recommendations and set off helium balloons with messages to Richard on Christmas Day. This helped us connect with him. Another time that was hard for me was December 30, my birthday. Richard is one of the few people who always tried to make it special for me. So many people, including my family, forget about it because it is so close to the holidays. Other days that were difficult were surprising to me because I wasn't expecting them to be so painful. For example, New Year's Eve and Valentine's Day."

Kathy finds that her days are like a seesaw: some of them are rotten and others are more on an upbeat note. "In January I started a new job and began traveling quite a bit. I found it very distracting to be away, but when I got home I was very depressed. It seems that when I was gone, I got a reprieve from the grief, but when I returned it came back with a vengeance. How I feel now is a day-by-day experience. There are many times when I wonder how I can go on living my life without Richard. He was such a part of my world, and I miss him daily. I also find that I have more good days where I feel happy, but I'm still not my 'old self.' Other days it's like I'm starting the grief process all over again. I find that many times I don't want to be around a lot of other people because they don't understand my feelings. As for guilt, I don't have much of that left. I wish I would have known sooner and that I had pushed harder to find out more. But I don't think it's productive to dwell on that. What I would rather do is see how I can change the future. I want to help others as well as heal myself. I have never felt such pain in my life, and I want to get beyond it to live with the happy memories. I also would like to make a difference in how others get through this process."

LISA LAHNER was angry with her brother for not admitting the truth to her about his life-style. "Before Steve moved to Chicago, I asked him, 'Are you gay?' He said, 'Of course not.' I didn't believe him and was angry that he wouldn't trust me with the truth. For the first time in our lives, we had a rough patch in our relationship. When we got closer again, we talked about that time and he said, 'You weren't ready and I wasn't, either.' I guess we had to play our cards the way they fell, but I wanted him to know how much I loved him. I wanted him to understand that it didn't make any difference to me, that I only wanted to know because I wanted to be able to share everything with him."

Lisa married and had a baby. With Steve in Chicago and six hours away by car, their visits were limited to telephone and writing. "Even though we couldn't see each other that often, we became very close in later years. When I was pregnant with my first baby, my husband and I went to see him and we had a lot of fun. After the baby was born, I got sick. At the time, neither Steve nor I had a dependable vehicle, so we spent a lot of time on the phone and corresponded frequently. My husband has always been my best friend, but Steve and I had a sense of when we needed one another. We were very much in tune and were only eighteen months apart in age. My husband, Rick, and I went to see him about a month before he died. That was very tough because he was in severe pain and was taking medications. He had just gotten out of the hospital. His partner, Larry, was taking care of him. It wasn't what we could call a 'visit' with Steven; it was just a matter of being close to him. I couldn't even touch him because it hurt him. He was in so much pain."

Two weeks after Lisa and Rick returned home, Steve called and he sounded wonderful, Lisa remembers. "There was a complete change in him. The pain was gone. He was happy and talkative. Now, in looking back, I realize he was getting things done prior to his death. He called a lot of people and said what he wanted to say to them. I think he knew he was going to die. He wanted to speak to me about something and asked me when I could come down. I said, 'Steve, I was just there two weeks ago.' He said, 'I know, but what about just you?' I thought that was strange, but I said, 'I'll try my best.' A week later he was no longer very verbal. He was still at home. When I got that call, my mom, my sister, and I went down to help Larry take care of Steve. My father and Steve had some hard times. My father used to write to him, but Steve and I thought the letters were judgmental. Who cares if sexuality is a choice or not? We're talking about life or death now, not choices. I was really mad, and I still have a lot of that left. I didn't want Steve to be upset, and I didn't know what my father might say, so I didn't extend an invitation for him to come with us. We stayed with Steve about three days. I got to say my good-byes, and then he died one week later, but he knew I had been there.

"Everyone freaked out when I wrote the obituary, put his picture in there, and said he'd died from complications of AIDS. Mom and I made a panel in Steve's name for the Names Project AIDS Quilt. I have the pin on my coat lapel. It says, 'The Quilt: See It and Understand.' When people see it they turn around and it's like 'What?' I have a big red ribbon under it, like 'How much more explanation do you need?' That really bugs me. You can't just say 'Well, the AIDS Quilt' and leave it like that. So I continue to wear it to educate people."

Lisa's friends try to be supportive, she explains, but they are cautious. "They don't know if they should talk about him or not. It's hard to talk to them, too. You want to say, 'God, I'm feeling crappy and I miss him so much. Nobody can take his place.' I tried to find support elsewhere but was unsuccessful. I went to the Healing Place Grief Support Center in Eau Claire, where I live, but as far as AIDS was concerned, no one had any knowledge or support available. And there is no reading material that really talks to me as a sister."

Lisa understands that her life has changed, and she has accepted things as they are. "I've gone through a lot of the grief stages. I know my life will never be the same as before Steve died. He's not part of my every moment anymore. In some ways it's a little scary, because I don't want to forget him. It's like you have to force yourself to stop and remember because your life is so busy and you're going and going. In my vicinity, there is nothing really supportive. A new group called NOWAP [Northern Wisconsin AIDS Project] has just come in. They take care of thirteen counties. I wanted to get involved, but they had just organized about a month after Steve died, so they were not there when I needed them. By the time they got an AIDS support group going, unfortunately it met on the night that I worked. Participating in this book is very important to me for that reason. I'm hoping it will help people like me who are in isolated areas with no place to go to talk, or who may feel they are alone and isolated from help. Maybe reading what others have said will be of comfort to them. They will know that people like me have gone through what they are going through and want to help.

"I want to help fight for PWA and their survivors, to give love and support and to share my story with others. My brother is gone, but the love and the memories are still strong. I still want to make him proud of me, and my involvement in this book is another way for me to do that."

I N T H E above account, we heard from a sibling who didn't extend an invitation to her father to visit her brother in the hospital. In the following story, another surviving sibling tells of her apprehensions about invitations to both her father and her brother to her upcoming wedding.

Shortly before their wedding in 1985, Karen Dillard and her fiancé went for premarital counseling at their church. Karen was concerned about interaction between her father and her brother Ken at the wedding. She was fearful something might happen to mar their happy day because her father and brother had not spoken to each other in over ten years.

At the last counseling session, Karen spoke of her concerns. "I told my preacher that I was apprehensive about the way the wedding might turn out because my father and my brother didn't get along. I had to unburden myself and told the preacher the whole story about Ken and his life-style and why he and my father didn't get along. He asked me, 'Have you ever thought about your brother contracting AIDS?' I said, 'No, I haven't.' And I hadn't. Most people were not really aware of it then."

Karen's parents were divorced, and both still lived in Alabama where the wedding took place. On that day, Karen was mortified at her brother's appearance but dismissed from her mind any thought of AIDS. "He looked so bad. I felt awful because he looked horrible. Of course, in my mind I still didn't connect it with AIDS. Ken had had some dental work and some hemorrhoid surgery. I knew he was having a real hard time recuperating from that, but I didn't put two and two together. After the wedding, Ronnie and I were living in Dalton, Georgia.

We had just been home from our honeymoon about a week when two of my aunts who lived in Chattanooga came down to see us. They told me that Ken was very sick and they thought he had AIDS. My mom had rushed to Florida, where Ken had been living with his friend, Ralph. She had called my aunts to come and tell me. I was devastated. I didn't know what to think."

Soon afterward Karen's mother called her daughter and told her the doctors thought Ken had a brain tumor. "My immediate thought was, Well, it's not AIDS. He has a brain tumor. But my mother quickly added, 'Karen, if you're coming, you'd better come now.' I came with my father, my stepmother, and her sister. My two aunts came in a separate car, and we got to Florida about seven o'clock in the morning, after driving all night. I went to Ken's house first to take a shower, and my father and his wife went to a motel. I had no sooner finished my shower when Ralph called me from the hospital and said we had better get over there."

When the family arrived at the hospital, Ken was having difficulty breathing, but Karen was able to talk to her brother briefly. However, she had to steady herself first. "The hospital had glass doors leading into the room. When I got ready to go in, I just fell to pieces, he looked so awful. Even though my mother had told me how much weight he had lost and how bad he looked, I was still unprepared and didn't expect him to look like that. I began to cry uncontrollably. It took me a while to calm down before I could go in. All of us were there, trying to take our turns being with him. But the doctors made us leave because they had to get him to ICU. They thought he had developed pneumonia overnight, and they wanted to run tests. We were told we could see Ken again in about two hours.

"After we returned, the doctor called us in and said he had to go over the X rays with us. When we went by his room, Kenny motioned for us to come over there. I turned to go to him, but the doctor stopped me, saying, 'Let me talk to you first, and then you can all go and see him.' So we went into a conference room with the doctor. I have no recollection of what he said to us, but just minutes later Kenny went into cardiac arrest. And, of course, that's when he died. So instead of being with Kenny as he had wanted, when he motioned to us to come, we were with the doctor."

After Karen returned home, she was reluctant to talk about Ken's illness. "We didn't tell anybody much of what happened except that Ken had a cardiac arrest. A couple of my friends who knew Kenny real well and were aware of his life-style were told, but they didn't talk much because they didn't know what to say. They felt just as uncomfortable as I did."

Karen felt left out of her mother's life after Ken's death and speaks about her hurt. "With my mother living in Alabama and my being in Georgia, I felt like everything was now focused on my younger brother, Jonathan. Even when she came to visit me, she would say 'Jonathan's got to have this' and 'Jonathan's got to have that.' It was as if she didn't have any other children. Now that Kenny was gone, there was just Jonathan. She was concentrating on her surviving son, and I understand that. I understood it even then. She had lost a son and was nurturing and holding on to the son she had left. Also, he was living with her. But I felt hurt then, and I still feel hurt today."

In an effort to move past the hurt, Karen reflects on the wisdom gained over the last few years. "Now that I'm older and have two kids of my own, I understand a lot of what my mother must have gone through. Before that, I would tell Ronnie, 'She's got to get over this. There's still life out there. She can't sit around and mope and feel sorry for herself. She's got to go on.' Now I realize that was a cruel statement. At the time, though, I didn't feel that way. But when I think about losing one of my children, I don't know that I could ever get over it. Someone said to me, 'Well, we're only human and we do the only thing we know how to do.' When you've never experienced anything like that, you don't know what to say or do, or how to act, even with your own mother. My dad was really pitiful there for a while. He didn't talk about his feelings, and he was trying to be strong for me. You could see the hurt in him, though. When I bring Ken's name up, he just changes the subject."

Karen is able to handle holidays and birthdays pretty well because she takes the time to psych herself up for them. But the "out-of-the-blue thing" causes the tears to flow. "Sometimes I might be driving down the road and have to stop for a funeral procession. Times like that really upset me, and I just start crying. My husband has been very helpful and kind. He is real sensitive to other people's needs, and fortunately our marriage has been very good. Ronnie has been comforting and was with me every step of the way. He would say things like 'I'm sorry. I wish I knew how to make you feel better' or 'I wish there was something I could do.' It made me feel good just knowing he was there for me."

Karen tells where she is today, seven years later. "I seem to be moving on in my life, but I worry that one day I might break down because I don't feel like I've completely dealt with it. I tend to put things on the back burner if they hurt too much. Maybe that's my way of surviving."

BEREAVED PARENTS are often so overwhelmed by their own grief that they are not always able to provide surviving children with the parenting that had formerly been given. In an earlier book I wrote to help surviving siblings, Judith Haimes, a bereaved parent, wrote "An Open Letter of Apology" to all bereaved siblings. Portions of it are given below in the hope that Judith's message will help open up communication between parents and surviving children.

Sometimes in my own pain, I did not see that you, too, were suffering for your lost brother. Forgive me if I have hurt you by not understanding. I never wanted you to feel, "Wait a minute, Mom. I lost a brother, too. I lost a sibling. You're not the only one." I want you to be able to come to me and say, "Mom, it hurts." I try to show you how much I love you, but I am only human. I am beginning to realize that you, too, are only human and my actions may have hurt you. I don't love any one of my children more than the other. I love each of you in a different way. If you ever thought otherwise, I ask your forgiveness because no one taught me about being a bereaved parent. No one knows how something like this is going to affect us. For all the times when I didn't want to talk about it and you did, and for all the times I needed to talk about it and you didn't want to hear, I'm sorry. But that was a thoughtlessness. I guess it's because none of us knew. You didn't know and I didn't know. It kind of works both ways. Maybe inadvertently you have hurt me by doing the same thing that I am apologizing for. It's all a part of our not being experienced in handling a tragedy like this. But whatever you are thinking about or what may be troubling you, please open up to me. Let me open up to you. Let's be honest about our feelings. If we can talk, we will never need to apologize to each other for the pain again. We can't undo what's happened and we can't undo the pain that's there. But we can try to prevent causing any more pain to each other or ourselves.

chapter 5

●

FRIENDS

• *We spoke every day and shared everything. Even when there
was nothing special to say, he left a message on my answering
machine. Now the machine seems to have lost its life, too.*

• *My neighbor and I were as close as sisters. When she died, I
couldn't sleep for weeks. I had thought I'd be able to handle it,
but I didn't realize it would hurt this much.*

• *He and I were soul mates. We knew our lives had touched
each other before. We had so many similar likes and dislikes.
People always thought we were brother and sister. The pain is
just awful.*

• *I was angry with many of our friends who rarely called or
came to see him in the hospital. "I can't bear to see him this
way," they'd say. Did they think it was easy for me to see him
wasting away?*

• *We always spent our birthdays together, since childhood. When his rolled around, I felt numb. I knew he was never going to be another year older, and the thought of that was devastating.*

• *Sometimes I wake up and think it's all been a bad dream and that all my friends aren't really dead. It's gotten to where I don't want to answer the phone. I don't want to hear that someone else has died.*

On his first day of school in the sixth grade, Dan Frambach made a lifelong friend. When Dan was only thirty-five, his beloved childhood buddy died of AIDS. "Jeff and I connected from the very start," Dan recalls. "In astrology, in our natal charts, his sun was exactly across the zodiac to the same degree of my sun. Jeff was quite an accomplished astrologer, and when he saw the configuration, he made note of it. It was not something you see often, but it's the kind of thing you would expect to coincide with compatibility or some sort of significant relationship."

Dan reminisces about his relationship with Jeff. "We were not lovers. He was my best friend. We were both outcasts in a way, outsiders growing up together. I think we were also drawn together because we were both gay, but we didn't acknowledge that until we had graduated from high school and moved away."

Later, Dan will describe the difference between the loss of this childhood friend and the loss of another newly made friend for whom he became the primary caretaker. For now, Dan explains that as close as he and Jeff were, his friend waited quite a long time before telling Dan of his illness.

"Jeff didn't even tell me he was HIV positive until he already knew it for a couple of years. At the time, he was living in Los Angeles and I lived in New York. For all the discussions we had in our lives, we never had any heart-to-heart talks about AIDS or his illness. He moved to North Carolina eventually to stay at his sister's house, and I know the rest of the family took good care of him. I had been telephoning him, but toward the end his sister asked me very nicely to stop calling because he had a lot of neurological complications with his handwriting and his speech. She said that telephone calls sort of put him on the spot because he wasn't up to them and it was upsetting to him. I began to send him a note or a letter every few weeks, something he could take his time with and savor. Oddly enough, my last note to him crossed in the mail with his last note to me. I had asked him earlier on for a photo because I didn't have one of him. So in his last note to me, prior to his receiving my note, he enclosed several photographs. At that point his handwriting was very wobbly, but he signed the note, 'Eternal love.' I took it to be his sign-off, and he died shortly thereafter."

Dan tells how Jeff's death changed his life. "I find myself at certain points feeling that I don't have any backup, like I don't have someone who would be there for me emotionally. Although I have a support network here, Jeff went farther back in my life than any of my friends. He knew my family and shared all of the kinds of intimate things from childhood that you can't explain to your adult friends. There have been glimpses every once in a while when I will think of something we shared, and I just feel I'm more on my own than before he died—somewhat abandoned. It's not to say that I don't have people in my life, but what I had with Jeff can't ever be replaced. A childhood friend is in a very special category."

Later, Dan decided to make a trip to Washington, D.C., to see the quilt project. Although Jeff's parents lived in Pennsylvania and his sister in North Carolina, it crossed Dan's mind that by some chance of fate he might see Jeff's family. The odds of his meeting them at that particular moment were astronomical. Indeed, as Dan walked over to Jeff's quilt, he was astonished to see Jeff's sister and her husband standing there. Twenty years had passed since Jeff's family had last seen Dan, and now, as Dan approached Jeff's sister, he had a weird experience.

"As I walked over to them, I realized they couldn't recognize me because when they last saw me I was twenty years younger. As I got nearer to his sister, I had the curious experience of being invisible to them. I thought, If I don't say anything, they will never know that I was here. It was such a strange moment, like being a ghost. I felt that I was among the dead and that these living people couldn't see me."

Dan tapped Jeff's sister on the shoulder and started to say

his name when she suddenly recognized him. "It was a very emotional moment. Then she announced, 'My parents are over there.' I looked up and saw Jeff's parents. When his mother realized who I was, she immediately started crying. Jeff's sister then began to cry, too. His father choked up and said, 'You don't look at all like you used to.' I was surprised, too, because they were twenty years older as well and were no longer the people I knew who were in their forties. They were very nice and were very glad to see me."

Dan had a sense that seeing Jeff's family was preordained. "I felt it was meant to be that I saw them, something like kismet. I had sent a note to both his parents and his sister when Jeff died. His sister responded, and I've continued to correspond with her. Tomorrow is Jeff's anniversary, and I'm putting a letter together to send to her."

Although there was a strong sense of appreciation of who Dan was in Jeff's life, this was not the case with the family of Dan's friend Adam, even though Dan had been Adam's primary caretaker. Dan describes the events surrounding Adam's death and the profound effect AIDS has had on him. "For many years there has not been a period in my life when I didn't have someone close to me who was either sick, in treatment, or dying. AIDS is now the central formative issue for me. It's the thing that shapes my life whether I like it or not. Obviously, I don't. When I first realized Adam was sick and dying, my life was completely shaken. But it had more to do with my feeling that the gay community was being invaded than it did with my own life being reshaped."

Dan and Adam had known each other for several years when Dan recognized that the friendship was blossoming. "It was very odd that the week before he told me he was infected I had been thinking, Gee, Adam and I have been talking quite a lot and spending a great deal of time together. I guess he and I are friends now." Dan reflects on the events that happened after he learned of Adam's illness. "One week I'm thinking that Adam and I are really good friends as opposed to being casual acquaintances, and the next week at lunch he tells me he is HIV positive."

From that moment until the moment Adam died, Dan's

primary role in life was being his care partner. "We were not lovers. We lived separately, but he was my first priority, and that was fine because it gave me a real sense of contributing, not only to Adam as my friend, but doing something concrete in the face of AIDS in the larger picture. It was a devastating loss, but it was also a fulfilling experience because I had made a commitment to him and I was with him to the end. After he died, I was allowed to stay with Adam even as his body was being wrapped, and they let me go down with Adam's body when they put it in the morgue."

Dan describes the thoughts that went through his mind during this incredible scene at the morgue. "It was such a strange thing, in some ways gruesome because I had never been in a morgue, but actually it was a serene experience, one that helped me. It was not like a coroner's morgue. It was just a large storage unit. What was so disturbing was that as you went in the door, to the left there were boxes full of specimen jars that had organs and biopsies and all these clippings from people. The thing that struck me at the time was that they were such potent symbols of the struggle that people are engaged in to be well and to stay alive. It was so different to have my friend totally enshrouded in plastic and have them rather cumbersomely move his body off onto this metal shelf to wait for the crematorium to pick him up—as opposed to the struggle that those specimens represented. There was nothing more that could be done for him or to him. But by the time he died he had had nine grueling weeks, not to mention three or four years of active treatment leading up to his death. It was a very dramatic contrast, too, in having seen him die, being with him then, and afterward witnessing the physical changes in his body, even the color changing."

Oddly enough, Dan experienced a comforting feeling while he was in the morgue. "When I saw him dead, it was very reassuring somehow to know that he was dead—and not just unconscious. It was just his body. To see a dead friend's body, to see it lifeless, somehow makes it clear what it is that animates a person. When that's gone, it's so apparent that the body remains but that the *person* has gone. It was a very moving and comforting experience, somehow, despite all the gore associated with it. When I think back on it, I have never felt as assured of fulfilling a commitment to someone as I did when I saw Adam to the morgue."

During Adam's stay in the hospital, Dan had some encounters with the nurses. He describes the attitude that prevailed. "There were times when I had to tiptoe around the nurses as well as Adam's family. The truth is I am still very resentful. I was very glad and privileged to do what I did for Adam, and nobody had the right to treat that with other than respect. If I had been his wife, they would have been opening doors for me. But there was a very dismissive kind of attitude, and I found that the nurses were great if I really kissed ass."

Dan credits support groups for helping him through many problematic periods. "After Adam's death, I would sob readily for weeks. There was a sense of disorientation that started the night he died because he had been my primary concern for so long—and then he was gone. I had nowhere to go, I had been so wrapped up in the caretaking role. In the bereavement support group, we talked about the stages of grief."

Dan reflects on where his focus is today. "We gays are in a wartime climate. Even though the rate of infection in the community has dropped way down because word got out, I don't think people give credit to the fact that gays began to change their behavior and to respond to AIDS before anyone else. The effect that the gay/AIDS community has had on the larger society is evident in the newly aggressive, highly effective activism that has developed around the issue of breast cancer, for instance.

"Still, as gay people in America, we are encouraged to believe that we are not a part of the society in which we live. Our existence as outcasts helps to define that society, of course, but in a real sense we are cut off from the comfort and support that a community offers. In order to successfully confront a challenge as horrible and unrelenting as this epidemic, each of us must remain strong. To do that, I think, it is essential to see ourselves as a part of something bigger than our individualities. We must cope as a community. For many years I defined myself largely as a member of the gay community. In the last decade I've come to add membership in the AIDS community. Without this perspective, my life to this point is unimaginable. My wish for anyone confronting AIDS, gay or not, is the realization that they already have a place in this community and no one can diminish it."

I N   T H E   preceding pages, we heard from a survivor who mourned the loss of a childhood schoolmate who was his long-standing friend. We now hear from a young woman who suffered deeply after the death of a college friend with whom she had become inseparable and learn how she was able to cope.

Terri Litz and her father had as close a relationship as a father and daughter could have. Yet when her friend Joseph died, Terri had a worse time of it than she did after her father's death. She explains why. "There was no other love like that in my life. My father loved me unconditionally, but it was a different kind of love. With Joseph, I was able to share intimate details of things that you could only tell your best friend."

With a dry sense of humor, Terri muses about all of the memories she and Joseph shared, as well as some of the plans that will never be. "We were supposed to grow old together, as buddies and friends, and sit on a beach in Long Island and cruise men in our eighties. We each had our own relationships, but still managed to maintain our friendship on a daily basis. We did so many things together—going on boat rides, drives, to the theater, jazz concerts, street fairs, art galleries. Joseph could call me at three o'clock in the morning and say, 'Want to go to Chinatown?' And we would go! When someone would see Joseph without me, they would ask, 'Where's Terri?' And when anyone saw me without Joseph, they would ask, 'Where's Joseph?' If I was having a bad relationship with a man, he would be there to buffer the pain. 'How could he do that to you?' he would wail in sympathy. We were always there to offer support to each other, and we were inseparable. AIDS changed all that."

Terri knew Joseph had gone to be tested, but he never went for the results. She was concerned because he was coughing, losing weight, and having trouble with his legs. Also, Joseph bore most of the burden of caring for his ailing father. "Joseph's father was a wonderful man, a Baptist minister in Oyster Bay. He was a revered man in the town, and I loved him, too. I thought he was terrific. When his father died, Joseph collapsed at the funeral from the physical and emotional fatigue and was rushed to a nearby hospital in Long Island."

Joseph's treatment at the hospital left much to be desired, and Terri was livid. "They treated him like dirt. The nurses wouldn't clean his room. They wouldn't even come near him. He was an untouchable. Not only wouldn't they touch him, they wouldn't even talk to him. They would throw needles and discarded tissues on the floor, and they wouldn't be swept up. No one came in to mop the floor. There was absolutely no confidentiality, either. It was written on his chart that he had AIDS, and the chart was thrown on the table for anyone to read. To this day I resent that hospital more than any other place on earth. Eventually we got Joseph transferred to a hospital in New York City, where he got incredible care. What a contrast in the nurses. Here they were loving and supportive."

The person Terri turned to after her friend's death was his sister, Cynthia. "Cynthia, who was younger than Joseph by one year, stopped her life in Atlanta, Georgia, and came up to take care of him. And she really took care of him—she never went back to Atlanta and has remained in New York to this day. In fact, she met a very nice, loving, and supportive man while Joseph was sick. One of the things that has helped me was that I was able to talk to Cynthia a lot. I'm also friendly with many of Joseph's friends. One of them, Billy, did a lot of things with Joseph, the things I couldn't do—like going to dances. They had their best-friend time. It was a loving and nurturing relationship. The three of us also did things together."

Work was another area that offered relief to Terri. "Getting involved with my job helped me. I'm a director of a day treatment center for the developmentally disabled. I had been very detached for a while. The big downer after work was coming home and looking to see if there were any messages blinking on my answering machine. It upset me because in the past whenever I came home there would always be a message of some sort from Joseph, even if it was only 'Hi, what are you doing? I'll talk to you later.' But there was always a message. We kept in touch wherever we were. When I went on vacation, I would call

Joseph. I could be in the Bahamas or Nassau and I would call Joseph. Ours was the closest friendship imaginable."

Although Terri has her bad moments, she also has discovered she is getting better. "I will hear a song on the radio that Joseph and I used to sing in the car, and I will cry. There are many things in my apartment that Joseph had given me, and they remind me of him. I went to a grief support group and to a therapist for about seven months because I felt very isolated, very alone, very hollow. I don't feel that way anymore. There's a void in my life, a tremendous void, but I'm adjusting. For example, recently I was on my way home from work. I was waiting at the train station and there was a guy on the phone who looked a lot like Joseph. I said to myself, I'm not upset by this anymore, seeing someone who looks like him. I was surprised that I felt that calm about it. In fact, I had a kind of pleasant feeling for the quick memory. I wasn't sad. Actually, I was smiling all the way home because of the experience."

Terri was pleased that she had smiled at what was previously such a painful experience. In the past, even though she and Joseph had a lot of depressing things going on in their lives, they seemed to be able to find a lot of laughter. "We found the kind of laughter that only good friends could find in sorrow. I know if he were here, he would find laughter in his own death. We would laugh, but we would know it was a loving laugh. Even before Joseph was sick, his friends and I would do silly things. I had the keys to Joseph's apartment. Once, when he was unemployed and I knew he was at a job interview, we all took off from work. That afternoon we cleaned his apartment, stocked his refrigerator and cabinets with food, put flowers on the table, and left. We knew it would put a smile on his face. That is what friends do. And that is what Joseph always did—put a smile on our faces."

Even when Joseph was dying, he left his family with a serene and beautiful experience. "An interesting thing happened to Joseph a few days before he died. He was lying in his hospital bed and saw a light coming out of his body. He quickly woke Cynthia up. She had dozed off. He was so excited, Cynthia said. 'I saw my life light leaving me, and I feel so peaceful.' And, of course, Joseph was smiling. I thought that was a beautiful way to end his life.

"Cynthia called me from the hospital to tell me it was time to come. I ran, but when I got there and went to the elevator, I didn't want to get on it. Finally I forced myself to move my feet forward and get on the elevator. Then I didn't want to get off at the floor where Joseph was. I knew it was going to be over, and I didn't know if I could handle that. Cynthia had called because she knew I would want to be there, and now I'm glad that I was.

"I find I can't go to the cemetery. I went there once and it devastated me. It was too empty, too isolated. It was winter, but I was feeling down and blue, so I went. But that was a mistake. I don't need the cemetery to be with Joseph. He's in my heart. I feel his presence around me. Rather than going to the cemetery, it is better to go to our favorite park in Oyster Bay. There I can walk around and feel that Joseph is walking with me, and that makes me feel better. I get comfort by going to pleasant spots that have good and warm memories. They don't have death connected to them."

I N A tragic and uncanny twist of fate, Leonce Chabernaud's parents died two weeks apart—each on their birthday! Leonce was only nineteen. His mother had been fighting cancer, but a heart attack ended that battle. His father died of cirrhosis of the liver. The young man was completely devastated by the double loss.

Leonce's only sister, seven years older, began shooting drugs. After their parents died, the two siblings moved into their house, and it was only a question of time until Leonce was drawn into the web. He realized his only escape was to move out, which he did—leaving his sister and the drugs behind him.

Leonce recalls the circumstances that led to his slipping back into drugs. "I had left our home in Texas and was living in New York at Bailey House, a hospice for people with AIDS. Although I tried not to get close to anyone there, when you have three meals a day together, you get to know who and how they are. I was devastated when so many of them died. When I first started losing the friends I had made there, I was just getting sober from drugs and alcohol."

One particular friend had a profound effect on Leonce and triggered a strong emotional response. "In my first year and a half at Bailey House, Ron lived right next to me. Each person had a room to himself. We became good friends. One day Ron made a conscious decision to die at Bailey House instead of in a hospital. I thought this decision was wonderful, but it was also very hard for me. I visited Ron every day and would sleep next to him in a chair at night. He was the nearest thing to family that I had. One night, it hit me between the eyes that Ron wasn't going to be around much longer. He had stopped eating, stopped his medication, and stopped doing the things that were keeping him alive. That night I stayed in my room. I was crying out very loudly, sobbing. I didn't mean to make a spectacle of myself. All the people at Bailey House were aware of what was going on, I guess, because I cried most of the night. They were there for me, offering support. The next day, Ron died."

After his friend's death, Leonce found it impossible to remain at Bailey House and made efforts through his case worker to be moved to an independent housing unit through the AIDS Resource Center. "My case worker helped me make the change to the Scattered Site Program, which runs Bailey House but also runs this program for people with AIDS who want to live on their own and who think they can handle it. I stayed in one of their apartments for almost a year, and it was during that time that I met my lover, Andy Kruzich. Eventually we moved in together. Andy, like me, is HIV positive. We were introduced by my best friend, Hector Gonzalez. I was working on Fire Island as a house man for a seventy-year-old lady. This woman became a good friend who was there for me at a very difficult time when Hector was admitted to the hospital. I went to see him every day I could. Hector, whom I loved so much, was dying. One day when I went to visit him, the nurses told me he had just died and was no longer in his room. I was in a state of shock. The lady I had worked for was a volunteer at the hospital and lived nearby. I went over to her house and broke down."

Shortly after, Leonce became part of a bereavement program. Initially he felt out of place in the support group. He tells what helped him to feel more at ease. "I was the only one in the group who had not lost a lover or a spouse. I had only lost friends, and I wasn't sure I belonged there. It wasn't until after several meetings that I felt I fitted in. That was because the people in the group understood my feelings. We could also laugh together. During that time I had many friends who were dying, but I wouldn't get in touch with them. I wouldn't go to their hospital rooms. I felt that if I didn't get too close to them, I wouldn't get hurt. In the group, I could talk about all of the things I was afraid of—the shock and pain of losing over one hundred friends. I don't think that people who are straight realize that when gays lose lovers or significant others that it's the same as when they lose their wife or husband. They don't realize that gays can have deep loves and have the same feelings of true devotion. After I got out of the group, I started my life over again."

Leonce philosophizes about the nature of things in a world tainted by AIDS. "The bad side of being a long-term survivor is that you are also a longtime griever. I remember when I was young, my grandmother was in her early seventies and she had lost many friends. But here I am in my early thirties and I have lost six or seven times more friends than my grandmother had. It seems unfair to have lost so many friends at this young age. And it's such a lonely existence. Of course, I have Andy, and I love him very much. But I miss my best friends who have died, and I'm scared to make new friends if they have AIDS. It's like 'I want you so much. I need that love. I want and need your companionship in my life, but I have this tremendous fear of loving you and losing you.' "

One person did penetrate Leonce's veneer of fear. "I have a friend I met three years ago who has just come out of the closet. He was a Christian brother working with the dying in hospitals. That's how he got involved in the AIDS crisis. Now he does an AIDS program in New Jersey. He is so positive and is doing such wonderful things. He feels he is doing the work that Jesus wants him to do. He is really pulling many of us through. He will show up at the hospital and love you, and be there when you need him the most."

According to Leonce, there are no rights and no wrongs

when it comes to grieving. "I don't know if I'm grieving correctly or if there is a right way. I want to be happy and to live the remainder of my life with AIDS to the best of my ability, but it is difficult and very emotional. I don't always know how to deal with my grief in a helpful manner. I don't always look at the bright side, but I'm told that it's normal and human to feel that way sometimes. There are moments when I look at the negatives in my life and, like a lot of people, I beat myself up. When you have AIDS, you have one crisis after the other. The key is to learn how to handle each crisis."

The spiritual part of Leonce has helped him handle the crises as they arise. "I think that my spirituality has saved my life. I'm not a very religious person, but I did the Twelve Step program along with group therapy and special love programs. If I were still on heroin, I wouldn't be around to get AIDS. The drug would kill me first. I feel that as long as I keep myself spiritually full, that will be my survival. I'm going to continue to live as long as I can and keep working on that."

Another inspiration to Leonce has been the loving and caring attitude generated by a nearby church. "I've been going to the Justin Baptist Church at Washington Square Park. I have several friends who also go there, and the wonderful thing is that the church is so positive about the AIDS crisis. The people who have AIDS are being helped so much there, and it has changed my mind about how churches can be down on you. This church is very supportive, and it has a sincere AIDS ministry. They even give out clean needles to drug addicts who are still on IV drugs. It's a very positive step for a church to have a program like that in the fight against AIDS."

Leonce talks about the activities that have helped him in achieving his goals to help himself and others afflicted with AIDS. "I'm also with the AIDS Theater Project in New York and have been very involved in AIDS education. I've known people with AIDS who are into that, and it helps them when they help others. We get out press releases and volunteer at GMHC. I'm like a public figure sometimes, which is good, but it also has an edge to it. I work a lot in the gay community. That's not to say I don't get depressed. I do at times—because I am gay, I have AIDS, I feel old, and am sick and tired of dealing with the bereavement of friends dying all the time. But I'm trying to do the best I can. I have a large support system. I do one-on-one therapy with a Visiting Nurses home. Andy and I are also doing couples counseling. Being in the group with Kathleen Perry, the social worker at St. Vincent's, was a very big help. She's a wonderful person, very sensitive and caring. She was very helpful to all of us in the group. I realize that my problem is not that I just need help once or twice, but that I am in a continuing state of bereavement. I can't release myself from the people who give me support and love, but I wish I could. I wish there was no need."

I N   T H E next story, we hear from a woman whose best friend was her business partner as well. When Bob Ward died in 1993, Deborah Klensenski felt a double loss. Deborah and Bob were both photographers and had been friends for thirteen years. Bob was Deborah's sounding board, the one person she could go to for anything she needed or any time she wanted to talk. As his care partner, Deborah discovered that their friends were the only ones they could count on for support. Bob's family, outside of a nephew, were distant both in miles and in attitude. However, once his illness progressed, Deborah felt it was her duty to make the family aware of it.

"Bob had a brother and sister-in-law in Pennsylvania, but he wasn't very close to them. They didn't even know he was gay, so the whole idea of AIDS wasn't one he felt comfortable talking to them about. But once his condition became serious, I felt it was necessary to alert them to that. Bob's nephew came in from Pittsburgh to visit with him a couple of times. I know that Bob talked to his brother on two occasions. Although they loved each other, neither of them could quite handle the situation—the gay issue and the illness. His nephew, who is twenty-one, was very understanding of what was happening. However, he found it difficult to see the change in Bob. He felt his uncle Bob was always this free spirit, living in New York and being an artist type. He never thought anything like this could happen to him. We openly discussed that Bob was gay, but there was a lot his nephew couldn't comprehend. He was very patient and accepting, and willing to do whatever he needed to do because he really loved his uncle a lot. I spoke with Bob's sister-in-law. She was more worried about the impact it would have on them in Pittsburgh where they lived. If people in the area found out Bob died of AIDS, they would then think that her husband had it, too. She was very worried about that. She was sympathetic toward Bob, but she made no effort to see him, either."

At their business, Bob's clients fell by the wayside one by one as Deborah tried to pick up the slack to keep the studio going. "He didn't have the strength or stamina or even the will to continue with the photography. That was a terrible and emotional time for both of us. Physically, it was awful for Bob because he was wasting away slowly. When Bob died, I was left with a business that was no longer flourishing as it once had been. I think I must have worked on autopilot, trying to take care of him and the business as well. Some of my clients are sympathetic and others aren't. I think that may be more the case that people don't know what to say or how to deal with an AIDS loss because it hasn't touched their lives. So, although I think they want to be sympathetic, they don't know how."

After Bob was diagnosed as positive, Deborah started psychotherapy. Bob's illness was like the proverbial straw that was going to break the camel's back. "I had a lot of other issues that I'd never worked through, and this was just one more. I thought, I'm going to go crazy if I don't sort this out and make some kind of organization in my life. So I started seeing a psychotherapist. I asked Bob if he would come along with me to help with certain things, and he did, which meant a great deal to me. Our friendship grew stronger just by the fact that he shared my problems and helped me work them out. My therapist permitted this. She thought it was important for me."

Once the topic of AIDS came up at the therapist's office, Bob's denial came to the fore and allowed Deborah to express her anger at this. "Bob was in a state of denial about his illness. He never made any business plans so that I would have an easier time of it when he died. He never came to grips with his own mortality. I was angry about that for a long time. He realized how upset I was, and he apologized. But then I concluded, Well, that was Bob. He never did plan for anything. He didn't know how to deal with many things. How would I react in a situation like that? I don't know."

As the disease progressed, Bob became angry at Deborah. "Things were getting pretty bad with his dementia and the PML. He appeared to want me to disengage myself and would say, 'I don't want you to be my nurse.' I would respond, 'But Bob, that's the position I'm in, and you're not helping me because you're not telling me what's going on.' He would try to act as if everything were fine and wouldn't tell me when he had been vomiting all night or had terrible diarrhea. I would call his doctor and find out through him how to help Bob. I think Bob realized he was going to die and that he couldn't keep up that front or say that everything was fine and have me cheerful. I couldn't join him in his denial by saying 'Oh, don't worry. Everything's going to be okay.' I guess he got angry with me about that, too. So there was a lot of emotional stuff that went on. But just before he died we had a conversation and he told me that he loved me and I told him I loved him. This was in the hospital, a few days before he lost the ability to speak and swallow. I was glad that we'd had that chance to talk."

One of the things that surprised Deborah was the attitude of friends and business associates. "So many people are still afraid of AIDS and don't understand the disease. Some try to be supportive and others don't have any concept of what the disease is like. Another thing that annoys me is they don't want to understand. They want to put blinders on and think it's all going to go away. It's never going to touch their lives. That makes me feel like a leper, because I went the extra step and took care of this man. Not because I had to, but because we considered each other family. It's almost like saying I condone AIDS. I can't believe they can be so judgmental."

Although Deborah encountered a lack of understanding in some quarters, she was warmed by the compassion and caring extended to her by Bob's gay friends. "We both taught at the Fashion Institute of Technology, teaching photography to advertising design students. We knew a lot of the same people and shared many acquaintances. But as far as good friends were concerned, he had four close gay friends and I was his only straight female friend. His last lover moved out about five years ago, and

Bob had reached a point where he didn't want anybody new in his life. He said, 'Friendships are the most honorable relationships.' So his friends meant a tremendous amount to him. And he meant a great deal to them, as was exemplified from the care they extended to him during his illness. I would go down in the morning and bring him some breakfast. Another friend would stop by in the afternoon and check on him. Another would go in the evening, and then arrangements would be made for someone to take over later on. After he died, I didn't think his friends would want to keep in touch. I thought, 'Well, what would they want to talk to me about? I'm a straight woman.' But several of them called me up and asked me how I was doing and if I'd like to have dinner. That's very nice. I feel accepted by them, and that means a lot to me."

Shortly after Bob died, Deborah decided to join a bereavement support group. It was there she was able to share the panic she was experiencing. "At the first session, everybody explained what had happened to them, whom they had lost, and everybody just cried. That was good because it united us in our tears and our grief. At the second session, we started expanding more on how we felt and what our lives were like because the people we loved were no longer around. I had inherited Bob's possessions, so I had to clean out his apartment, take care of his legal matters, the hospital bills, and so on. I tried to deal with the apartment as quickly as possible. I felt if I could finish everything while I was in a state of shock, it would be a lot easier for me. Now the work part was over, and emotionally I was faced with the fact that I would never see or talk to him again. One of the things that surfaced in the group was that I had submerged a lot of the panic and the emotional loss I felt after he died. For the three years that Bob was so sick, I had someone else besides my problems and life to concentrate on. Now I have my own life back with all the same old problems. I'd rather have Bob back to worry about."

Deborah still feels the void and wants to reach out. She recently decided to visit a friend in Maryland for a weekend to work in the garden. "Bob and I used to do that in Rhinebeck." She is also reaching out to family members. "I have two brothers in California, and I was thinking of taking a trip out there to try to reestablish a relationship with them. I feel I need to have somebody else in my life. Bob had filled up so much space for so long. I want to reach out and make contact with people."

I N T H E previous story, a friend began to reach out after her loss. The next account we hear is of another woman who began making efforts to reach out after being disappointed by "no show" friends.

Six months after her close friend Ramon died, Sharie Schon decided to seek counseling and was astonished at the insight of her counselor. "I had such a big hole in my heart. I missed Ramon so much. At his six-month anniversary, I made arrangements to go to counseling to help deal with the pain. The counselor said to me, 'You know, you minimize this. You say you were such close friends, but you stress that it's been six months. It sounds to me like you think it should be done with because it's been six months, that you should be better by now. From what you say, it seems to me that you were as close as a spouse or a lover. The two of you had a very deep and special friendship, and you both bonded. Don't minimize that!'"

Sharie was a psychology major in college, where she minored in Spanish and was looking for someone with whom she could converse in that language. "Ramon and I met at a Twelve Step program. He was born in Puerto Rico, and initially our knowledge of Spanish drew us together. But later we became close in many ways, not as lovers, but more like soul mates. Although I'm originally from New York and Ramon was from New Jersey, we were living in Williamsport, Pennsylvania."

Before Ramon became ill, Sharie was helping her former husband, whose lover had died from AIDS complications. "I'm still friendly with my ex-husband, who is also HIV positive. I'm bisexual, so I could deal with some of the issues he had. In fact, I considered his lover to be like a brother-in-law. When I found out that Ramon had AIDS, I became his caregiver because he was my friend and everyone else abandoned him. That experience made all others in my life pale by comparison. The day-to-day caregiving to someone with AIDS is overwhelmingly intense."

Sharie found one of the hardest things to deal with as a caregiver was finding herself alone with AIDS. "You think, Wow, I thought I had such close family, such close friends. Where is everybody? When you're changing the diaper on a thirty-five-year-old man, you would welcome a helping hand. People would give a thousand excuses. 'I don't want to come over there because I can't stand to see him like that.' Ramon had the wasting syndrome and had lost about one hundred pounds. I would respond to them, 'If you would come around more often, you wouldn't see the drastic changes.' But the thing that hurt me most is that it upset Ramon that they didn't come. He would say, 'I can understand why they may not want to visit me, but why don't they call?' I guess if they called him, they would have to apologize and offer an excuse for not coming over. Or they were afraid he might say, 'Why don't you stop over?' "

Even after Ramon died, these friends were not there for Sharie. "After this experience, I don't even like to call them my friends anymore. I called somebody to talk about it and they changed the subject. I said, 'Do you realize I'm trying to talk to you and you've changed the subject?' He said, 'Yes, I'm aware that I'm doing it, but I just don't want to talk about it.' There were not too many people to whom I could turn to help me in my grief. One person who was very kind was Ramon's case worker, Christine Cole. She was always there for me."

Sharie began making efforts to reach out and make new friends. AIDS Resources, one of the community organizations for AIDS, was instrumental in offering a support system to Sharie. "They have a buddy system in place, which really helped me. The buddy system is a national one. In fact, I officially took Ramon on as a buddy. After being asked to stand out in the hall at the hospital because I was 'just a friend,' I went to the director, Nancy West, at AIDS Resources and asked to be assigned to Ramon. Being a buddy made it possible for me to help him more at places like the emergency room."

With the help of one special friend and two neighbors, Sharie was later able to share the caretaking responsibilities. "Ramon lived by himself, and the hospice was threatening to pull out services because there was no primary caretaker. They're not there twenty-four hours a day, seven days a week like some big cities. Ron Sawyer, a friend Ramon met about six months earlier, learned of the situation and moved in with Ramon, which I think was such a humane gesture. The guy has a real pure soul and did it just because he knew Ramon needed help. He hadn't even known Ramon for long, yet the people who had known him from before backed out as soon as they knew how much care was entailed. There were also some Dominican neighbors who lived a few doors away, Fred Brown and Rita Nuñez. So the four of us, Ron, the neighbors, and myself, shared the care for Ramon."

Sharie believes Ramon knew he was dying. "He must have sensed his time was drawing near because he sent for his son two weeks before he died. The boy was twelve. Ramon called his ex-wife and said he would like to have his son here, and she sent him. So when Ramon died at home, with me were his son, his friend Ron, and the hospice worker. I had my hands on Ramon's feet when the nurse said, 'He's gone.' And I was like, 'Wow, where did he go? When did it happen? Did it happen when I moved to go to the front of the couch? Did it happen as I was holding him?' When you have your hands on somebody and they breathe their last breath, that's such an incredible experience."

Sharie is trying to work through her grief. "One of the things I did to help myself since Ramon died was to coordinate an AIDS memorial service for a female friend of mine. I did it in that capacity through AIDS Resources. It was a beautiful service, and the family really liked it. Also, I helped to design an educational program for the inmates in prison."

Because she loves to write, Sharie hoped she would be able to put her thoughts onto paper, but for the first six months she could not do so. However, things have improved. Sharie has been able to go forward in many areas. "Now I find that I am able to write down my thoughts, and that is very comforting to me. I've also gotten some paints and plan to dabble a little to see if that helps release some of the anger. I'm still angry at the friends who said they were friends but who never showed up for Ramon and me. But the new friends I have made have been very supportive just by listening. And they let me be where I'm at. They don't judge and they don't minimize my pain. I'm trying to move on with my life, helping others and doing what I can to help educate people about AIDS."

Sharie also derives comfort from her religious views. "I'm not affiliated with any synagogue, but in my own way I'm an observant Jew. Being Jewish is more than a religion. It's a lifestyle, too. I believe that Ramon is somewhere, but I don't know where. In *The Tenth Good Thing About Barney,* the bottom line of that little book is that in the end, Barney [the little boy's cat] becomes part of the garden, and he continues on because flowers grow and he's part of the earth. And that's what I think happens. I don't believe in a heaven or hell per se. I believe in an energy pool. We all come from that, and we all go back to it."

I N T H E preceding pages, we read how a young woman became involved as a buddy in order to better help her dying friend. In the next segment, we hear from a Toronto-based attorney who also became a buddy and who had to cope with the fact that he and his lover were HIV negative, while so many of their friends were HIV positive and were dying.

Paul Rapsey specializes in poverty law and explains how that relates to AIDS. "A lot of people with AIDS are very poor and rely on Social Assistance. Or, often, it's fighting with Social Assistance, appealing decisions and getting the people onto drug benefits and government pensions. Other times, it's trying to facilitate clients leaving Canada so they can obtain treatment out of the country but not lose their benefits at home. I also help with drawing up a will, power of attorney, and things of that nature."

After his first experience with AIDS, Paul became part of the buddy system and subsequently facilitated groups for people with AIDS as well as bereavement groups for parents and family members. He shares his first exposure to AIDS and the ripple effects.

"The first person who died was the nephew of a friend of ours who had been abandoned by his immediate family. My lover, John, and I took over and were there when he died. Since that time, I have lost twenty-five friends. I became involved with the AIDS Committee in Toronto and had a buddy assigned to me, a one-on-one person with AIDS. I was with him for two years until he died. Through the AIDS Committee, I went into a facilitator training program."

Paul remains in contact with others who are part of the buddy system and talks about the support network provided. "They have a very close network. You are required to go to what I call a debriefing once a month, getting rid of problems or dealing with issues you may not be quite sure how to handle. Say you are seeing a problem about to erupt. We talk about it and discuss the alternatives. After the death, there is a period where you are taken under the wing of the AIDS group, a nurturing period if you will."

Paul describes the effect of multiple losses on him and the difficulties for those who have worked with people with AIDS. "John and I are both HIV negative. I think what is hardest for us is we tend to be in the twenty-five to fifty age range and we are losing people at a constant rate, the same way my parents in their eighties have lost and are losing their friends. So if you have lost twenty-five friends in the past ten years, and these people have been significant in your life, you reach a point where you become reclusive. You may feel that you want to be on your own and that you will just live life fully. You may decide that you will do it alone and not with other people because those people may die. And that's hard. After ten years of being immersed in AIDS work, I know I think, 'Do I really have the energy to get involved with this person, because they may have AIDS or they may be dying?' I don't know if I have the same energy I had ten years ago to deal with that."

It is Paul's belief that dying can be made better, and he offers some suggestions for survivors who may be HIV positive and concerned about their own future. "Since we will all die ultimately of one thing or another, isn't it an easier road to make your dying better if you can? For example, just by having a healthy attitude about life, being satisfied with what life we've got, and reaching out. There are all kinds of support networks out there now. But the number of people who won't reach out is phenomenal. An unbelievable number of people who should know better still hide it and won't tell their closest network of friends that they are dying or that they are ill. It's understandable, but it's unfair to the people who are close to them. I had one person who said, 'What can they do about it even if they know?' Well, there's probably not a great deal we can do in terms of giving you life back, but what we can do is be there, be supportive, and to a certain extent give you a sense of humor or a sense of quality in the life that's left. But, to spring your illness on people when you are in bad health, rather than to allow people to get used to the idea gradually, is cruel."

After the loss of so many friends, Paul was stricken at the inability to reminisce with them and has built up a shield to help him cope with that additional loss. "It's very hard losing your friends. The way I view it is you've lost your history at an early age because of all the things you've done together, usually as an adolescent or as a young adult. You've got no one to go and giggle with about the silly things we used to do. John and I have had different friends in our lives. There's nothing worse than going out with the friend of your partner and listening to them reminisce. And reminiscing is so important. So at this point, John and I allow each other to go out and reminisce alone with our friends because that's a very personal, private sharing with those people. When you've lost the ability to reminisce, it's very difficult because it's a dual loss. You've lost the person as well as being able to reminisce with the person. So to deal with the loss of so many, part of it is building up what I call a shield around myself. A shield in the sense that you simply accept death as part of life, and whether it happens now or in thirty years, you are going to lose these people."

Paul makes an analogy about reminiscing and the age factor. "Friends who are dying in their thirties and forties may have many more things to reminisce about than, say, people like my parents, in their eighties, because those dying so young have learned to make every moment count and use every minute to make life worthwhile."

Normal fears and apprehensions have surfaced after so many losses in his life. At times Paul has even envied the friends who have gone ahead. "Sometimes I wake up and I'm envious that my friends are somewhere else. Sometimes I really think I'd like to be with them. For example, for the last year my job has been terribly difficult, very stressful. I used to think, Life's not going to get better from here on in. It's going to become more difficult, more aches and pains, and harder to wake up in the morning. My job is never secure, and you probably have more debts than you would like. You sometimes wonder, 'It's so unfair that they've left me behind.' That's something that comes to me, not often, but on occasion. It's just a longing for all my friends. It never worries me because I know you wouldn't be human if you didn't miss them and long to see them all."

Although there are some somber moments for Paul, there are also many pleasant contemplative periods. He describes some of these peaceful moments which help him cope. "With our friends, we have wonderful photo albums, and there are priceless memories. I have kept everybody's birth date and everybody's death date. I reflect on those days, and sometimes I just sit in my office for a bit and think about that person, or I go out for a walk at lunch. Other times I've gone away for a weekend if it was someone who was particularly close and reflected on that person. Or I've done something that we had done or shared together. For example, one friend used to go canoeing with me up north. So, on occasion I've gone canoeing in that locale by myself to reminisce. There are different ways of keeping the person's memory alive, and they remain with me in thought."

W H I L E T H E survivor in the last testimony lost over twenty-five friends, the next account tells of a female rabbi who lost one close friend. "Everything was planned and in order, all accounted for, a neat package except for my grief," the rabbi wrote in a poem dedicated to her friend. "We forgot to figure on that. I'm slow these days. I can't face your ghost. . . . I didn't think it would be like this."

The Thanksgiving before her friend Carol died was an awful one for Rabbi Patricia Philo and her husband, also a rabbi. A long, narrow table had been set up, and Carol had invited close friends to dine with her. A video was taping it all, and the scene was a gloomy one. Everyone present knew this was the last Thanksgiving they would be together. Each knew that Carol would not be alive the following Thanksgiving, but the videotape would remain.

Carol was Patti's next-door neighbor for twelve years, and frequently the two women would jog in the early mornings before work. Carol, a divorced mom of two, supported herself as a vocation rehabilitation therapist and had a thriving private practice. When her children went off to college, Carol began to travel extensively, primarily on professional study tours to Europe. After her last trip, she returned home with what was thought to be "traveler's distress." Patti describes the events that followed this early sickness. "For months and months Carol was ill and began a premature and rapid menopause. As her friend, I accompanied her to various specialists and hospitals for tests. She got weaker and thinner and was so tired. Finally her lungs were affected, and after many tests she went for a bronchoscopy. From that procedure, she was so weak and cold, she couldn't walk. I carried her to bed and covered her with every blanket and coat I could find. She shivered in a very deep sleep."

The doctor had advised Patti to stay with Carol, and he called early the next morning to say he had very serious test results. He told Patti to bring Carol to the hospital immediately. "I had to call a friend to help me get her into the car. At the hospital, we first had to go through endless forms with Carol barely conscious. Yet when I was asked what my relationship to her was (I having answered most of the questions), Carol spoke up and said, 'She's my rock.' Once in the room, her doctor was there waiting. He told her that she had PCP and asked if she knew what that was. Carol, in shock, replied very professionally and stated the full name of the rare pneumonia and its implication of HIV. Carol was forty-seven years old when she died. She had given the names of her lovers to the public health department. They were few in number, and all were well. Only her fiancé, who had died in a traffic accident in Latin America years earlier, wasn't tested. He had been a Peace Corps worker in Africa. The best guess of when Carol had been infected was eight to eleven years before."

At first Carol kept her diagnosis secret. She was concerned about the effect on her work if word got out. When she finally told the public she had HIV, she did it with power and commitment. "She went to schools and synagogues and to conferences. Simply seeing Carol made people realize HIV could infect your mom, sister, daughter, neighbor. She also wrote a column in the city's newspaper here in Petaluma, California, about living with AIDS. And, as she feared, her business dwindled to almost nothing."

In seeking help for heterosexual women, she found few services available. The gay community provided the most valuable care and love during her illness. Even close friends were new friends. "Looking around," Patti remembers, "we noticed our running buddies weren't there. Our book group wasn't there. These new folks were great, but it wasn't the way it used to be."

Patti felt anger that Carol had been taken from her. "She left our normal friendship and dove deeply into treatment, research, projects, symptoms. The lightness, the forever aspect of friendship, was gone. Sure, her humor remained, and so did mine, but we were careful now not to joke in more and more areas. I lost her, my best friend, long before she died. Our lives were altered, and we couldn't make it go away. We used to eat out and enjoy sushi. Now she couldn't eat that. So many things changed. Nothing remained but her body and mind—but not the easy, unfettered friendship."

Only now is Patti beginning to reclaim Carol, years after her death. "I had to get the disease of those last years out of my memory. I still miss her and often think of her. I remember jokes she would love, or situations where we would have dissolved into gales of laughter and savored later." Carol even dealt with her impending funeral plans with a dry humor. "My husband was her rabbi, and he said the final prayers with her, though she seemed comatose. She actually mouthed the central prayer. Carol had requested a full Jewish Orthodox funeral and burial service. And, with a twinkle of her characteristic humor and defiance, it was followed days later with a Buddhist memorial service with the big bell for friends and the community."

There are times when Patti still remembers how valiantly Carol fought. "Carol's big fear was about the progression of the disease and whether she would go blind or have dementia. Unfortunately, both happened rapidly, and she was aware of it. After that, she declined rapidly. I felt the awesomeness of love and trust when on her last day I had to help move her. I had pledged to keep her dignity. Carol was comatose, and I told her we were going to turn her and it might hurt for a few moments. She held my arm, then groaned as we turned her. Then she stroked my arm twice, comforting me. She knew it hurt me, too. Finally we had our signal. She had been afraid she would let go of life and not fight her way back during the various illnesses of HIV. Sometimes she was too weak to speak or respond, so we developed a signal. I would hold her foot and she would push against it—to connect with life. It would remind her to live and would signal me that she was trying to live. That last day I held her foot and she pulled it away. Later I did it again, and she pulled away. We discontinued all medication except for pain. Her doctor knew and understood. We all left the room and cried."

Carol did see her daughter get married and both of her children graduate from college, but she had a few dreams that were never realized. She had wanted to go to Russia where her family had come from two generations ago. And she had wanted to go to Israel. Patti explains a sense of having helped to fulfill that dream. "Carol has a 'square' on the AIDS Quilt. I didn't help do it—not one stitch. I was asked again and again to come and help. I couldn't. I was mad at death. I haven't been to her grave since the gravestone unveiling [a Jewish custom at the one-year anniversary of the death]. However, I have been to Russia, and to Israel. Carol's quilt went to Israel, too."

Today Rabbi Philo continues in her work as hospital and hospice chaplain, helping to ease the pain of others. She describes where she is with regard to Carol. "I still eat sushi, now with a different friend. I still miss her. I still laugh at her humor. I still cry. But it's much easier."

c h a p t e r 6

•

CHILDREN

(ADULT/YOUNGSTERS)

THE death of a parent isn't something that happens to only a few people. Unless we predecease both of them, the death of a parent happens to all of us at some time in our lives.

But adult children somehow don't think of losing a parent to AIDS. Neither did Rita Jirak, yet *both* of her parents died from the disease. Rita explains what happened. "My father had a blood transfusion in 1981 during surgery. He died in 1985. He had been sick for approximately a year and then became quite ill ten months later and began to go downhill. Doctors could not find anything physically wrong with him. They suggested that he could not adjust to retirement and was depressed. However, one night my father was unable to write his name or sign checks to pay bills. He was then admitted to the hospital, and after four weeks they found there was a cancer in his lungs. Supposedly that was the cause of his illness. He died within two weeks after the diagnosis of cancer. It didn't make any sense to my family, but in 1985 we weren't thinking of AIDS."

Rita tells of her mother's subsequent remarriage after her father's death and the surfacing of AIDS in her mother's life. "My parents had been sexually active, and my mother contracted the disease from my father. However, she had no knowledge that she was infected. Two and a half years after my father died, my mom married a widower. All during that time she had been in good health and was living in a retirement community in New Jersey. There was some concern that her new husband might have been infected by her, but so far he seems to be okay."

The loss of both their parents brought Rita and her siblings closer together. "We have a large family. There are seven of us, and I am the oldest. We range in age from thirties to late forties. Three of us live in the New York City area. The rest are scattered throughout the country, but all of us bonded after the loss of our parents. We have kept in closer touch, and we've talked about the upheaval that the deaths brought to our lives. Nobody ever really expects a parent to die or is ready for it. Both of them were very healthy people. I think the way my mom handled the AIDS itself was a help to the family. After she recovered from the PCP, she regained some of her normal living patterns and managed to do some of the things that she had wanted to do. This included traveling by herself to visit two of my brothers in Minneapolis and seeing her grandchildren. I don't think she ever thought she would do that again, but she did."

On her mother's birthday, Rita had a very difficult time. To a certain degree she had experienced a sense of closure after her mother's death, but differences between the two women gave Rita pause. "I celebrated her birthday by myself by going out to the grave. I just needed to be alone, and that seemed to help. I'd had a very complicated relationship with my mother, but it became clear to me how much more complicated it was after she died. I'm the oldest, and it had not been quite clear to me how well I was connected to her. Throughout my life I had taken on many responsibilities in terms of being helpful to the family. My own identity was very much tied up with being the oldest child. It was also complicated by the fact that I am not married and have no children. I think that my mom and I had a good relationship in spite of the responsibilities that I had to bear. But I'm very sad about the fact that she died and so we can't go through this now. Thinking about her life has made me able to see some of the strong connections that we had."

At the time when her mother was beginning to lose her mobility and was approaching her final days, Rita encountered a crisis about AIDS in another quarter. "As a school psychologist, I work on a crisis response team in our district. We also maintain a trauma tream and have an adult education program in the district. One of the teachers was ill for a while and died suddenly. It was only then that the staff found out he had AIDS. They were in total shock and unable to function. Our crisis team was called in to help the staff and the adult students with their shock over not knowing, and their anger at his not having shared the nature of his illness so they could have expressed their care and concern. That was a very hard crisis for me, actually, to try to help people deal with an AIDS death just as my mother was dying from the disease."

Another area of difficulty for Rita was the secrecy surrounding her mother's illness. "My mother's new husband didn't want anyone else to know the nature of her illness. Consequently none of her neighbors ever really knew. I differed greatly with his view because I firmly believe that the more people know about this disease, the sooner there will be the possibility of overcoming it. My mom also believed that, and when she was interviewed in the local newspaper anonymously, she spoke about it. She mentioned the struggle she had with talking about her illness. She said, 'You feel very alone, out in left field. If you had something else, you could talk about it. You just can't talk about this like you would another illness.' "

Although Rita wants to become more active in AIDS activities, she still finds herself cloaked in secrecy to some extent. "There is something so isolating about this disease. It is not yet generally accepted. There is a sense of isolation you don't feel when someone has cancer. I still talk about it carefully. I find myself measuring my words with a number of people. These are not very close friends, but are primarily people at work, people I don't normally measure my words with. However, when I am asked questions like 'Was your mother ill?' there is a certain protective barrier that goes up like a red flag. I have the sense that what I say will not be generally accepted in the same way as another kind of death, like cancer."

Rita speaks of the spirituality that helped guide the entire family through the difficult moments. "We were all raised within the Catholic church. That spirituality helped us, first with the actual deaths and then with the burials and the funeral mass. Originally my mom wanted to have a simple funeral mass in the church she had been attending in New Jersey, but that was not where any of us lived. So it was decided to have a one-night wake in New Jersey and one in New York as well, where we had grown up. The funeral mass was held at the parish church we had attended for many years and where there were people who knew her. The priest who had known our family for over twenty years was the celebrant for the mass. The ritual connected with that definitely helped us a great deal. That was also true for my father's funeral. He was living in New Jersey, but the funeral was in New York. The ability to have a farewell in a church that we felt connected with made a great deal of difference to us. I have always felt that the Catholic ceremony around funerals, if it's really given some space, does help people say good-bye in a very meaningful way. The organ music allows you to cry, and that was something I'd had several conversations with my mother about—how crying at funeral masses and the ritual of the Catholic church permit your feelings to run freely."

Rita finds she has also been able to work things through in a therapy group and by talking with close friends. "What really seems to help the most is just talking to people. There are seven of us in the therapy group, and we meet weekly. I also think time is a key factor as well as starting to do some of the things I've always wanted to do. Now there is a sense of my needing to move on and resume some of my responsibilities, both at work and toward my future life. I'm starting to do that now. Recently I had a week off, and during that period I spent some time sorting through my mother's jewelry. Her things were not very valuable, just some costume pieces, but filled with a lot of memories. I tried to see how I could distribute the jewelry to all of the family members who would want something. Distributing her possessions among all of us and not just holding on to them myself gave me a sense of being able to move on in my own life."

A s w e learned in the above account, many seniors with AIDS are fearful of talking about it with friends or neighbors. Most think, "They would be horrified and afraid to be near me." That is why the support group is so crucial. AIDS is not like other debilitating illnesses; it cuts into the ability to receive sympathy and support. One woman said, "If I had an ulcer or a gallbladder problem, I would be able to talk about it with everyone. But I can't talk about AIDS. People are too frightened, and I would feel that rejection."

In some cases, the parent who has died is also a grandparent, and telling the grandchildren is another decision facing adult children. In the next pages, we hear from experts in the field who indicate some of the problems involved with children and death.

M a n y m i s c o n c e p t i o n s arise in a child's mind after the death of a sibling, parent, or grandparent. Dr. Roberta Temes, clinical assistant professor, Department of Psychiatry, SUNY Health Science Center, in Brooklyn, New York, and author of *The Empty Place: A Child's Guide Through Grief,* offers some suggestions in understanding the needs of surviving children and urges that the term *dead* be used:

> Children need to be told that the person is dead and that death is final. Other "stories" do not work.
> If you plan to explain the concept of heaven to a child, you must choose your words carefully. Children calmly take things literally. Stewardesses report that each plane to Disneyland has at least one child peering out the window trying to locate the grandma who died. Children have been known to ask, "If brother went to heaven, why are you burying him in the earth?" One young child thought that

bodies were "planted" in the ground so that new ones would grow.

The grief of a child for a parent or sibling can be especially painful. To a child, death may be seen as the ultimate rejection. In their magical thinking, death occurs because of a deed or a wish. Some children, convinced that they caused the death, feel guilt for the remainder of their lives.

While most adults begin the first stage of mourning immediately, children usually begin mourning several weeks or months or even years later. Children should not be criticized for caring, selfishly, about their own personal needs. They sometimes postpone mourning until they are assured that all their needs for survival will be taken care of. Once they are positive that their physical and psychological security will not be snatched from them, they will relax and feel, and weep, and begin the mourning process.

Dr. Temes explains the tremendous fear children have of AIDS. "AIDS is extremely frightening to children. They imagine it a grotesque disease (which, of course, it is) that can overtake them at any time. Children have been known to fear for their lives after coming in contact with an innocuous drop of blood or a classmate's vomit. The death of a friend or a family member from AIDS is often a child's first experience with the unfairness of life, with the devastation of disease."

In the past, children's fears of a parent's death were explained by stating that people usually die of old age and there are many, many years ahead. That no longer is the case, Dr. Temes comments. "Nowadays, children have witnessed young people, including young parents and young teachers, die because of AIDS. The children have lost their innocence and sometimes their faith, too."

What can help children in battling their fears? Dr. Temes says children are helped by talking about their anxieties and by learning as much as possible about the disease. "Ignorance fuels misconceptions," Dr. Temes believes. "Information creates feelings of security and control. Schools may establish a bereavement counseling group for everyone in the school community (administrators, teachers, paraprofessionals, students, parents) who wishes for the opportunity to talk about the recently deceased and to talk about the personal impact of the death."

W E N O W hear from a grandparent who not only had to explain the death of their parent to her grandchildren, but also had to tell them that they, too, were HIV positive.

Along with the other mothers, grandmothers, and fathers in her bereavement group, Ada Setal steeled herself to the barrage of questions asked by their young children and grandchildren. "Why do we have to take needles? Why does blood have to be drawn? Why do we have to come to this clinic? What is wrong with us?"

Three of Ada's grandchildren were HIV positive. This valiant grandmother describes the directness with which she answered the children's questions. "When they asked for explanations about what was happening to them, I had to be very direct. I loved them and showed how much I cared. I told my grandchildren what was going on and why. 'You have a disease called HIV, which eventually will turn into AIDS. This means you may get sick and you may even die. The reason you have it is because both your mom and dad got infected. How they got infected, I don't know. You became infected through their bodies.' As we went along, I talked to the children step by step and got them to understand that HIV is something you have to live with—something we all have to live with. I explained that we are all going to die one day, whether it's from HIV or something else. I tell them continuously it's not something to be afraid of, that it's something nobody wants, but now that it's here, we have to deal with it."

Two of Ada's grandchildren have died. The remaining little boy, Jesse Michael, whom she has adopted, is now eight. Ada thinks back on her life before AIDS came into it, when she was a home health nurse caring for patients.

"I was traveling back from a vacation in Georgia, where I had driven a disabled woman in a wheelchair to see her mother, who was very sick. It was a long twenty-four-hour drive from

New York. Coming back, I felt I had to see my son Eddie, one of my seven children, and visit with him. It was then that I found out his children were no longer living with him. I was told that his common-law wife had abandoned her one-month-old baby in the hospital. I didn't even know she'd given birth. When I learned the children had been removed from their home, I was in shock. Apparently their mother was HIV positive and too ill to take care of herself, much less another child. So she walked away, leaving her baby in the hospital in the hope the child would be cared for there. The Bureau of Child Welfare had been notified by the doctors from the hospital, and they came and took the kids."

Ada tells us what happened next. "In all, there were five children, three by my son. Those three tested HIV positive. Since my son was not into a life-style that made him a candidate for AIDS, the doctors said he'd probably contracted it through sex with his wife, who did not know she was infected. Later it was discovered that her first husband had died of AIDS. She believed that she contracted the disease from him. However, to my knowledge, her other two children are not HIV positive. They are now being take care of by their grandmother."

Because Ada's son was too ill to take care of his children, they were put into a foster home. His wife had isolated herself from her family, so they were not involved, Ada explains. It was then that Ada's son contacted her to ask if she would take the children. Still reeling from the trauma, Ada didn't know what to do.

"I said I had to think about it. I was working. How would I care for three sick children? What would be best for them? I just couldn't believe this nightmare was happening to my family. I had never faced anything like that in my life. It was really a hard blow.

"At that point I was in a state of shock. I had to come home and pray in order to get an answer. I didn't know if I could deal with it. Finally I stopped crying, dried my eyes, and made the decision to take the children. And I've been at it ever since. At first, it was very hard. The stigma was almost too much to bear. Ultimately I had to come to grips with that. I told myself, Hey, this is something you've got to deal with, and it's not going to go away. Just hold your head up, look the people in the face, and let them know that it could have been them. I determined that I was going to stand up and face the music. This is a problem that the world is going to have to face. Everybody is going to be affected one way or the other—whether they are infected or affected. So I decided, Well, I'm affected, and I cannot turn my back on these children. I can't turn my back on my family."

Ada describes a visit to the hospital where she saw her month-old grandchild for the first time. "The moment I saw the baby, her eyes met mine and I fell in love with this child immediately. The doctor said to me, 'You are the first member of the family this baby has seen.' I felt great about being able to pick her up, hold her, and love her. I kissed her and talked to her. She gave me such a smile. She warmed my heart immediately with that smile. Her name was Angela, and I brought her home. I had her for one year.

"She was such a beautiful little girl. Angela died on her first birthday, and it broke my heart. I almost went with her. I broke down from the stress and the realization that I had dealt with it for one whole year, seeing them suffer, too. I had to deal with three children with AIDS in my home. I had to be there for them twenty-four hours. Each time I heard one of them cry, I would jump out of my bed. The baby would cry all night, and I would hold her. When she lay on my body and felt the warmth, she would go to sleep. It seemed that I was giving her life, so we became very close—so close that I literally lived for her. When she died, there were no words to describe my devastation."

Ada reflects on the aftereffects of her despair. "Just a few days after the baby was buried, I wasn't able to walk anymore. I was hospitalized for almost a week. When I came home, an old spinal injury flared up and I couldn't straighten up my back. The stress took me back to that injury, which had happened fifteen years ago. My son and his wife were still alive when the baby died. They were both very sick and trying to take care of each other. The baby's death was very hard on both of them. It was especially rough on my son because he thought he was responsible for giving the disease to the children. He was in so much pain, both mentally and physically. As for his wife, it was not only hard for her to lose her child, it was also hard to come to grips with what was happening in her life."

To combat the stress she was under after her first grandchild died, Ada decided to make a trip to Myrtle Beach, South Carolina. She asked her mother to oversee the children until her return. Ada tells of the incredible transformation that took place on the trip.

"My mother thought I was crazy. She didn't think I could do it, driving from New York to Myrtle Beach. I was determined to overcome what had happened to me. I had a niece and another granddaughter who came here and helped me drive to North Carolina, where they lived. Then I drove from there to South Carolina. I spent a night in a hotel in Myrtle Beach all by myself. Then, at six o'clock in the morning, I went down to the beach and I rebaptized myself in the water. I lay in the water and prayed and rolled in the water. When I got up, I left all my problems and stress in that water. I came back to New York as a new person. I drove seven hundred and fifty miles with no pain, no stress, no nothing. All the while I was driving, I was singing and praising God. I had gained real strength, and when I got back I had no more problems walking."

Although Ada had summoned new strength in Myrtle Beach, when she returned to New York there were not many people to whom she could talk. "I had one friend I could confide in, but eventually even she dropped out of the picture. It was probably because of her family. I knew my friend didn't mind it, but she was living with her daughter and grandchildren. I guess when they found out about AIDS, she was not allowed to continue the friendship. That meant I had to make all new friends. Mainly I met them at the support groups and at the clinic where I took the children. This was at the Children's Hope Foundation, where they also had parties and different events for the families."

Ada explains what led to the development of the support group at the clinic and some of the problems the families encountered with the doctors there. "At the clinic, there were mothers, grandmothers, and also quite a few fathers who brought their children. Some men came with their wives, and others came because their wives had died. I remember at least four fathers who came. Initially, while we were waiting for the doctors to arrive, the social workers and nurses invited us to come over and talk to them. One thing led to another and we soon got to talking each time. As a result, they decided to start up a support group. Those of us who met at the clinic and were sitting there waiting ended up going to Suite I (Eye), and that is how we began our support group. All of us looked forward to those meetings every Friday. Most of the people there were anticipating bereavement, but I was the first person to have lost a child.

"The doctors tried to be helpful, but after we formed our group, we had to educate them on how to be sensitive to our needs and to those of our children. We explained that we felt very stigmatized and uncomfortable about coming to the clinic. They wore gloves, and in the early stages you got the distinct impression they didn't want to be with either us or the children. Some were loving and kind. Others had a lot of fear and didn't understand what was happening. So a lot went on at the clinic that made us feel bad."

It was not only with the doctors and her friends that Ada encountered fear and apprehension about the disease. Her own children were reluctant to be near her. "At first my other children were afraid and embarrassed, but when I sat down and talked to them, they accepted that this was something we all had to deal with. They have seen me get involved, so they fell in and got involved themselves."

Ada's second grandchild to die was Faith Vanessa, at age eight. She had lived with Ada since she was four years old. During that time, Ada explains, the child endured many heartaches apart from the actual physical illness.

"Her last years were miserable, especially her last few months. She couldn't go to school. She had no one to relate to, and it was the most unhappy period of her short life. I promised myself that if it was within my power, that would never happen to another child. She was just two weeks short of being nine years old. She was the oldest of the three children, but the second child to die.

"One of my goals is to be able to establish a day care center in memory of Faith Vanessa for children with special needs. It would focus on children with HIV and their siblings. If anyone wishes to contact me about this project, they can write to me in care of P.O. Box 175, Brooklyn, New York 11224."

Ada says one of the things that helps her most is reaching out to other families, touching their hands, and trying to bring a little joy into their lives. She has become an AIDS advocate and helps others face what she had to go through. She also works as a health educator on how to prevent AIDS. "I go to clinics and hospitals, to whoever calls for my services. I have a personal relationship with God. I went into the field of ministry and studied theology. My purpose in life is to minister to others and help educate the public about AIDS."

●

The kinds of difficulties experienced by teenagers surface when they are given the opportunity to talk.

• Why is this happening? What's going to happen to me if my mother dies?
• How come I survived and my sisters didn't? Why wasn't it me?
• I get this tight feeling in my chest and throat. I can't concentrate on anything. I must be crazy to feel like this.
• I can't tell anybody, not even my best friend. I don't know if they can keep it to themselves, and they may be thinking that I'm HIV positive, too.

Adolescents find a safe haven in New York City at the Adolescent Health Center of Mount Sinai Hospital, where there is a bereavement support group geared specifically to their needs. The youngsters range in age from thirteen to seventeen and are referred to Mount Sinai by schools, community agencies, hospitals, and the Mt. Sinai staff. The teenagers may have come to the attention of teachers and guidance counselors because they are not functioning well. Social worker Rori Shaffer explains in more detail what brings the adolescents to the Mount Sinai group.

"They may start to do poorly in school. Perhaps they are getting into fights, or are even suspended in some cases. Often they feel depressed. Many of the kids will not tell the school what's going on. I'm sure there are a lot of adolescents out there—more than we know—who are living with a parent who is either HIV positive or whose parent has died of AIDS, and they will not talk about it. The kids may say their parents died of cancer or a heart attack or a brain tumor. But when I hear that a thirty-five-year-old died of a brain tumor, I suspect that HIV may be the cause of death."

Because of gossip in the schools, adolescents are afraid of the stigma. Rori explains that a major problem for teenagers is the fear of talking about what has happened in their lives. "The adolescents are often too frightened to share their parents' HIV status, even with their closest friends. They say, 'The group is the only place I can talk about this. Even my best friend doesn't know.' Often there is nobody who knows what's going on in a kid's life. These adolescents have been terrified of talking about this."

To help the adolescents through the pain of not being able to talk about their fears, Rori makes an evaluation of each teenager before they come into the group. "I try to see if they would feel comfortable talking about this subject in a group and whether this is an issue they could admit openly. Some adolescents aren't at that stage yet. They may indicate that it's a big secret and may feel uncomfortable talking about it even on a one-to-one basis with me. They may need to be seen a few times individually before they are able to 'go public' with it in the group."

The teenagers who come to the support group have either suffered the loss of a parent from AIDS or their parent or parents are currently HIV positive. In some instances younger siblings have also died from AIDS or are HIV positive. "It's very difficult for the adolescents to talk about this issue," Rori explains, "and we try to make access easier for them. We meet once a week in the conference room at the Adolescent Health Center. To make that first step less stressful for them, they don't have to announce why they are coming. We tell them they can just go automatically into the room, and in that way nobody would know they were here for the bereavement group. Many of the adolescents want to deny what is happening. They don't want to deal with it. By coming to the group meetings, they are forced to look at the reality."

Rori brings home that reality. "If the adolescents don't want to talk, they are in the group setting and will hear other adolescents in the group talk about various problems. That can be very upsetting to new participants. Let's say if somebody's mother is HIV positive and another child's mother is also HIV positive and is in the process of dying, the reality of what will happen to their mothers is terrifying for the teenagers who don't want to look at what is happening. They may not return for the next session, but may come in and out of the group, depending on how threatening it is to them."

Although initial visits to the group may be difficult, Rori points out the benefit the group provides to the adolescent farther down the line. "When the time comes that one of the parents is very advanced with the disease, or dies, the adolescent will already have a support network there. They would know other kids in the group and would benefit from seeing that other adolescents could still live, still make it and go on, even though their parent has died. *The focus is that you can cope and you can recover.* Often the teenager who has already lost a parent has been very helpful to the others who may be in the process of losing their parent. That was the rationale of why we combined the group into kids with HIV positive parents and those who had lost a parent to AIDS." Rori found that after the actual death of the parent, many of the teenagers have trouble coming to the group. "It's too raw, too fresh, and a lot of times we have to see them individually. And then, eventually, they are able to move into the group."

Rori cites some of the extraordinary issues these adolescents face. "The group has talked about what it was like taking care of their parents at home, what it was like sitting in a class hearing about AIDS prevention, what it was like to be in a hospital and negotiate with doctors and nurses. They have told of the burdensome responsibilities they have had to assume. Often the adolescents have to make sure their parents take their medication on time or that the parents eat properly. If the parents were very sick and still living at home, the adolescents may have had to take care of younger siblings, do all the household chores, even help their parents get to a hospital. In effect, they had to take on a parental role—a caretaking role. Often they become resentful at this because they can't concentrate on school or on situations with boyfriends and girlfriends. One girl had to drop out of school because she was so busy taking care of her mother and too worried about that situation to focus on anything else. The school was aware of the problem and was generally supportive in trying to help this girl."

Another issue that Rori hears about from the adolescents focuses on the lack of attention from a parent or the fact that the parents thought more of drugs than they did of their children. "Because many of the parents have been involved in drugs for a long time, a lot of these kids were either taken care of by an aunt or a grandparent, and were living with a relative—maybe with the parent living in the house as well. What we hear from many of the adolescents is, 'My mother didn't love me enough to stop drugs,' or, 'My dad was more interested in doing the drugs than being with me.' These kinds of statements reflect the sadness and anger because the parent didn't measure up to the kid's fantasy of the kind of parent they wished they could have had. So in addition to mourning the actual loss of the parent, there is also a mourning of the loss of a parent they never had— the mother or father they would have liked and the relationship they never had with the parent. Lots of these kids come from a long history of being abandoned or neglected because of the life-styles their parents had chosen, mostly drugs. These teenagers didn't have what you might think of in terms of optimal parenting. Because of that, there is a lot of ambivalence toward the parent, particularly mothers who were IV drug users."

Rori points out that the issues voiced by the adolescents often mirror what society thinks. "They complain that if the parents hadn't done drugs or hadn't led a gay life-style, this terrible thing wouldn't have happened and they would still have their parents. Instead, they say, they are in a group talking about parents who were dying or who had died."

Rori clarifies that the group discussions were not all centered on HIV and bereavement but dealt with many other topics. "We would talk about a variety of issues—school, relationships, coping with parents and grandparents, boys, girls, sex, everything. But, ultimately, the HIV or bereavement would come out because it was such a powerful issue. I think there was a lot of relief that they could talk about it freely. They knew they were in a supportive and safe environment where nobody was judging them. And they felt secure in the knowledge that the kids in the room were the only kids who knew about what was happening in their lives. This is one of the reasons why a support group is so terrific, because a lot of these adolescents think they are the only ones. And there is a lot of shame involved with that, a lot of stigma. But in the group, the kids discover they are not alone."

Some of the more specific issues are described in detail by Rori. "One boy, whose father had been gay, was sixteen when his father died. There were a lot of confusing thoughts around his own sexuality and about his father. He wished he and his father had had a better relationship and that his father were here to guide him. We helped this teenager talk about his own feelings about homosexuality and to sort through his feelings about his father. There was a lot of anger and resentment. His father left home when the boy was ten, and the youngster felt a sense of abandonment. After being in the group for two years, he was able sufficiently to work through his grief and is college bound. I thought he had done very well in resolving his grief, and I felt he was on his way."

Another major fear expressed by the teenagers is that they may be HIV positive themselves. Rori comments, "I had boys who wouldn't tell girls about their parents' HIV status because they were worried the girls might think they were HIV positive, too. Similarly, girls were reluctant to speak of it to any of their boyfriends for fear of being shunned. Even though they know through education that you don't get AIDS through sharing a glass of water or from using the same toilet seat, these kids have incredible fears that they may be HIV positive. A number of them have gone to be tested even though they have not participated in high-risk behavior."

An offshoot of the fears adolescents have of being rejected often results in the need to lie about the disease, even in their own families, Rori states. "One girl told how she lied to friends, saying her father had another type of illness. She would not say that her father was HIV positive. There was also another problem—the father had never told the daughter that he was HIV positive. She overheard her father and mother talking about it. So even in the family it was secretive and not something that was discussed. Because of this 'family secret' syndrome, the girl never confronted her parents with this. She said she had always suspected it, though. People often don't give adolescents credit. They hear so much about this subject in school, and certainly it's all over the media. It doesn't take much for kids to pick up on telltale signs." In this particular instance, the adolescent was perpetuating the fear of discovery by lying to her friends. In a sense, she may have felt she was protecting her parents, protecting their secret. But it was a secret she could share in the group."

In some instances the youngsters who come to the group are left as orphans. Rori talks about the pain of one such adolescent. "One teenager who was in the group never knew her father. Then her mother died of AIDS. She had no grandparents and was put into foster care. The girl got pregnant, which is not uncommon. The wish to be pregnant can be seen as a replacement for the loss of the mother. When she became pregnant, she went to live with her boyfriend, the father of the baby, and his family. Unfortunately, a lot of the adolescents end up in foster care because a grandparent may be unable or unwilling to take care of the child. Or there may be no other relatives. Or the relatives who do exist may not provide a suitable environment for them to go into, or are not able to offer care."

Another issue that comes up in the group is the loss of a sibling. Rori shares the effect this had on one sister. "This particular teenager was sixteen when her younger sister died. The mother is currently dying. There were no other children. The teenager shared that while her sister was ill and hospitalized so frequently, there were lots of times when she didn't feel like seeing her sister. She was hanging out with friends and didn't want to go to the hospital. Then, when her sister died, it was very hard for her. There was a lot of guilt that she hadn't been a better sister. She was sorry for all the times she felt her sister was annoying her or being a nag. There was also a lot of sadness in that she wished she had been there for her sister when she needed her." Adolescents tortured with survivor guilt may think,

Why did I survive and my sibling did not? Why didn't it happen to me? It's a difficult task for adolescents to come to terms with the fact that sometimes things happen that defy explanation, that are unfair, and that we don't always know "why."

In the case of the surviving sibling mentioned above, Rori tells of some of the difficulties the sister encountered. "There were lots of feelings she had to work through because her sibling died so young. This girl will probably live with her grandparents, but she had been having a very difficult time. She was acting out, not going to school, smoking a lot of marijuana. Unfortunately, a lot of these kids have used alcohol or marijuana as a form of escape. This teenager admitted she was using drugs. We spoke about that and how painful it was for her to talk about her feelings, how hard it was to prepare for her mother's death, to talk about her sister who had died, how alone she felt, how helpless she felt, how she couldn't do anything to help them, and how angry she was. She shared what it was like to get high and told how that was a way of running away from the reality of the problem. She said even though the euphoria was short-lived and then she wasn't high anymore, it was a way of not thinking about her sister's death, for however long the high lasted. We sympathized with how hard it was to come into the group and that it is so much easier to hang out with your friends and get high or watch television."

The good thing about the group in the above situation, Rori states proudly, is that the other kids were there to make helpful comments. "When hearing that the sixteen-year-old sibling had been using marijuana, a couple of the other kids said, 'Getting high is not the answer.' If I had said that, I would have come off as the older person preaching or being judgmental. But with the kids in the group saying it, it had a powerful impact."

Rori points out the indicators that show the adolescents are benefiting from the group experience. The very fact that these kids are able to talk about all of the things they might otherwise suppress is a sign they are being helped, Rori states. "These kids are able to cry about what's happening in their lives. They become more in touch with their feelings. When they get support from the other kids, you notice the change immediately. 'Yeah, I know what you mean' is a magical phrase, and when they hear someone in the group say that, it immediately lets the kids know they are not the only ones who felt that way. Someone else may say, 'I went through that with my mother, too. I know how you feel.' When the kids hear that, something very positive is happening in the group. These teenagers are sharing, knowing they are not alone or helpless and that they're getting support. The group may be the only place they can cry or talk about their fears. The group is not judging them, but being supportive. Another way I see that they are getting better is when they start functioning in their outside world—they're going to school, maintaining their grades."

Rori emphasizes that when the adolescents decide to leave the group, one of the things that is understood is they know they can call or come back at any time. "It's a long-term group, a continuing, open-ended program, and there is no time limit," Rori stresses. "We are there to support the kids through all phases—from the beginning of hearing about the HIV positive diagnosis all the way through. And even when they are in the group, the kids know they can call on me at any time or ask to see me on an individual basis. They can come here until they are twenty-one years of age."

chapter 7

●

THE HIDDEN GRIEVERS

A N N Blake, a single parent, faced one of the hardest decisions of her life. Her only child, Dolores, had died of AIDS—but few people knew the cause of her daughter's death. Sitting at the memorial service being held for her child, Ann bristled at questions she knew would be asked later. "What was wrong with your daughter?" "What did Dolores die from?" Ann debated with herself now, just as she had for the year prior to Dolores's death. "Shall I say she died of pneumonia? Should I tell them she had TB? Or should I say she had leukemia?"

When Ann first learned her daughter had AIDS, she was reluctant to talk to anyone about it but decided to confide in her two best friends. "I told two really close buddies of mine. One of them stuck with me through the whole ordeal, but the other one—a friend of thirty-five years since childhood—simply turned away from me. She stopped calling me. When I called her, she would be very distant. Prior to my telling her about

Dolores's illness, she visited my home quite often. When that stopped cold, I felt the sharp separation. All our years of friendship evaporated in the face of this disease."

After the hurtful experience with her friend of long standing, Ann became more cautious. "A peculiar process of evaluating emerged. I asked myself questions. 'Who was I going to tell that Dolores was sick? Could I tell them what she was sick from? Was I going to tell them she had another illness, like cancer? And *who* was I going to tell that she had *AIDS?* If I decide to tell anyone, can I trust them? Will they show any understanding or compassion?' I became very selective, and it was the one time in my life when I had to reassess everyone's relationship with me."

Ann became so apprehensive, she was reluctant to speak to anyone about her daughter's illness because she was fearful of losing the relationship. At her job, although there were over fifty co-workers, many of whom she was friendly with, Ann chose to confide in only one person there whom she felt would respect her wish for privacy.

"In the circle of my other friends and family, I was afraid to talk about Dolores's illness because a few of the people I had confided in began to treat me as if *I* had AIDS." In fact, when those individuals began to shy away from her, Ann tells of an extraordinary emotion she experienced as a result of their actions. "I was so upset when people stayed away from me, I actually began to feel that I *had* AIDS!"

Ann mustered her strength for the memorial service, still struggling with her hidden grief. In the church she deliberated about what she would say to the people. She tells of the decision she made on that day. "I thought of all the people who must be living with the same kind of fear I was trying to deal with, and all those survivors who were being stigmatized for loving and mourning someone who had died from this terrible disease. Right then and there, I decided what I was going to do. I had asked if I could say a few words at the service. When it came time for me to speak, I got up and said, 'My daughter, Dolores Blackwell, died from complications of AIDS.' And I have been saying it ever since."

Later, Ann decided to explore a support care group and

began attending meetings. She tells what took place there and how being with others helped her.

"It was a small group. Most of us had lost a loved one to AIDS. I would look at somebody in the group and know that he or she felt the way I did. We were all going through grief at various stages. So we understood each other, and we didn't hurt each other's feelings as some people unwittingly do. I admired the people in my group so much—they were so strong and had gone through much anguish, embarrassment, humiliation, and suffering. Yet there they were, sitting and talking and sharing and caring. When I realized I was part of that group, I too became strong. I was able to acknowledge that I had been through a lot of suffering, that I have courage, and I came to respect myself because I respected the group. As a result, after eight weeks I walked out of those meetings a much stronger person."

Ann believes there is no right way to grieve, only *your* way. "All of us are at different stages of grief. Although we grieve individually, grief is universal. Out of our loss, we connect with all humanity, for we are one with everyone who has ever mourned. We are all one family of survivors. We can raise the consciousness of others by helping those who struggle against this dreadful disease and those who have lost loved ones to AIDS.

"I want to celebrate my daughter's life, not mourn her death. Dolores made me a mother when she was born, and when she died I became a better mother. She taught me the true meaning of unconditional love. As I become a more helpful, loving person, I receive more love and the healing process continues."

Ann now shares with us one of the issues that she encountered in her new role as a trained bereavement volunteer for the supportive care program at St. Vincent's Hospital in New York. "There is a lot of hidden grief in so many AIDS survivors. I have seen it and I have heard it. This hidden grief runs cross-country. Recently I received a call from Georgia. From all walks of life, people are afraid of being hurt more, of having to face the embarrassment or rejection because of the stigma attached to AIDS.

When I speak to hidden grievers, I tell them that there are a lot of ignorant people walking around who have misconceptions about how you can get AIDS. They simply don't know the facts—that you cannot get AIDS from casual contact. The public has to be educated so that AIDS survivors won't have to contend with this additional factor of being afraid to say what their loved one died from."

KEITH WORKED for a major communications company in Ohio for seven years and had earned the enviable title of vice president at age thirty-one. He seemed to have the world by its tail. Until AIDS.

From time to time in his office, Keith had heard snide comments about gays. But these were not everyday occurrences. Now, however, on almost a daily basis, newspapers and magazines blared with headlines about movie stars, television actors, musicians, and others in the arts who, because they had AIDS, were thought to be gay. Now there was a lot of snickering in the office. Still, none of this touched Keith until his lover contracted AIDS.

"I knew that everyone in the office thought I was straight. No one seemed to think it was strange that I hadn't married because I was still young—and I put on a good act. I flirted with the women in the office. Whenever there was a company party, I danced with them. At the office picnic, I partied with them. So I was tagged a 'ladies' man.' They never knew of my private life, and I didn't want them to know. I wanted to safeguard my job."

When his lover had to be hospitalized, Keith faced another set of problems—what to say in the office about his lateness and absenteeism. "I was petrified they would find out the truth. If they discovered that I was gay and that Gary had AIDS, they would be afraid to come near me. It was a story I'd heard many times from friends. So I maintained my silence. I felt paralyzed and couldn't do otherwise. As a result, when Gary became sick, I had to think up a good story to explain my being out of the office so frequently. I told my boss and others at work that my uncle was dying and that there was no one else to care for him or be with him. Then I had to continue the farce and say my uncle died. It was sheer torture just to go to work. The only way I could handle my pain was to talk about it with my friends. They knew how much I was hurting."

I n t h e above story, we learned of a survivor who was fearful of exposing the news of his lover's death to his co-workers. We now hear from a bereaved sister who was forced by her siblings to keep the knowledge of her brother's illness from her mother while her brother was alive; she also had to maintain that silence after his death.

Merri Armstrong appeared on national television with me in Canada, at which time we were both guests speaking on the loss of a parent. After the program, I spent some additional time with Merri. She confided that she really wished she had been able to talk about her brother on the show. It was then that she told me how she and the other members of the family had hidden her brother's illness and subsequent death from her mother.

"When my brother Ross contracted AIDS over ten years ago, very little was known about treatment for the disease. But we believed there might be a better chance for Ross in Toronto, so my husband, my four-year-old son, and I moved there with Ross from Edmonton."

Merri was one of eight siblings. Her mother and father had divorced when she was in her teens. Four of her siblings went with their father, and the other four, including Merri and Ross, remained with their mother. "Later, when Ross got sick, my brothers and sisters were adamantly against telling my mother. She had been ill herself, and they felt that news of Ross's deadly disease might cause her health to fail more. I had to go along with them because they outnumbered me. We led her to believe that Ross's job kept him traveling and so he had been unable to visit her. We would read his letters to her. When Ross died, my siblings again outvoted me and insisted that if we told our mother of his death, it would be nailing her coffin. As a result, she never knew of her son's illness or his death, and we had to hide our grief from our mother. But it bothers me to this day that my mother never knew her son had died."

One of the ways Merri has helped herself survive the loss of her brother is by imparting the message to others that families and friends shouldn't be afraid to be near an AIDS victim or AIDS survivor. Merri stresses in her message that neither she nor her husband nor her child contracted AIDS in caring for her brother.

C H R I S T O P H E R W A S twelve when his father and mother were divorced. "My mom said that my dad decided he wanted to live a single life and was moving to Dallas, but that he would still come to see us in Houston. I found out later that my dad was living with another guy. It was hard to understand how my dad could do this to us, to move in with some guy instead of staying with us. My dad told me that it was very hard to love someone and not live with them. I remember asking if he still loved Mom. He said he loved her like a close friend. Then he said he would always love me and that his love for me would never change. I asked him how he knew that when his love for Mom had changed. He said his love for me was different, that I was his child and that his love for me would always stay the same."

What Christopher's dad couldn't prepare his son for was the advent of AIDS and the effect it would have on all their lives. "I didn't know my dad was sick. Then later, my mother told me he had pneumonia. But a couple of months after that, she said my dad was real sick and might die. She asked me if I wanted to go see him. She said he had gotten worse and that he might not pull through. So I went to see him. He had lost a lot of weight, and he didn't seem like my dad. My mom said that diseases can do that to people, make them lose weight. She said my dad needed to rest a lot, so I didn't get to see him much after that. Then, my dad died. We went to the funeral. I was waiting for my mom. She was talking to my dad's old boss, who had come to the funeral. I heard some people talking nearby. They were saying they thought my dad had AIDS. When Mom and I got in the car, I told her what the people had said. She began to cry and said people could be very cruel."

When Christopher returned to school the following week,

he encountered more comments. "At school, one of the kids said his parents had been talking about my dad and they wondered if my dad died of AIDS. I told him my dad died of pneumonia. But when I went home, I asked my mom why this kid's parents thought Dad died of AIDS, the same as the people at the funeral. Then Mom broke down and told me that I must never tell anyone that Dad died of AIDS because they would treat me different from before. They wouldn't want me to come to school or play with me or be my friend. And she said that she might be fired from her job if they found out. So she made me promise not to tell anyone and said that if anyone asked me, I was to say my dad died of pneumonia."

Christopher's grades began to plunge. Noting this, and his malaise in class, a concerned teacher spoke to the school psychologist, who in turn spoke to Christopher. Seeing the fear in his eyes, the psychologist contacted the boy's mother. In a meeting between the two women, the school psychologist was able to effect a warm rapport, and a trust was established. "When I spoke to Christopher's mother, I could see how hard it was for her to discuss the issue, but my sense was that she really did want to talk about it. She told me she had read an article by Elizabeth Glaser, the wife of the television actor Paul Michael Glaser. Then she paused and waited for a reaction by me, I suppose to see if I knew anything about Elizabeth Glaser. When I nodded yes, she opened up, saying, 'When Elizabeth Glaser found out she was HIV positive and that she had passed the virus on to her two children, she and her husband went to great lengths to keep that information confidential. They were afraid if word got out that she and her children had AIDS, they would be treated as if they had the plague. She said when she told her yoga teacher about it, the woman stopped seeing Mrs. Glaser. And her doctor literally told her that the world wasn't ready to understand the family's situation. She also said that when she did tell some of her close friends, no one would let their kids come play at her house, and most of them wouldn't let her children come to their house. They were afraid there might be a risk to their children. Every time the Glasers told someone, they were frightened that that person might put them in jeopardy by telling someone else. I was trying to protect Christopher from all of this heartache. I knew it was going to be hard on him either way, but I felt it would be worse if people started rejecting him, or pointing a finger at him and keeping away from him, or teasing him unmercifully. I was afraid he might become such a lonely child if the truth leaked out. And even though I know that Elizabeth Glaser has now gone public and is a fighter for AIDS victims, I'm afraid I don't have her courage. I only have one son, and I'm terrified to tell *anyone* that his father died of AIDS.' "

The school psychologist was sympathetic to the woman's fears and suggested it might be helpful if the mother would see a grief therapist, which she agreed to do. The mother also consented to let the psychologist speak with Christopher about his father in order to give the child a place to talk.

M A N Y A I D S survivors have indicated that religious beliefs can be contaminated by personal prejudice and judgment, especially where AIDS is concerned. Seeking a religious leader who is a sensitive and nurturing counseler is extremely important. According to Dr. William J. Worden, professor of psychology at the Rosemead Graduate School of Psychology and former research director for Harvard Medical School's OMEGA project, which included bereavement studies, it is imperative for clergy and other caregivers to understand special features of an AIDS death that may affect the mourning process.

Dr. Worden states, "An AIDS death tends to carry a stigma whether the victim happens to be homosexual, heterosexual, an IV drug user, a child infected through transfusion, or an infant infected in utero by the mother. Because of this stigma, some survivors fear they will be rejected or judged harshly if the cause of the death becomes known. Persons may lie and attribute the death to cancer or to something other than AIDS. This may get them off the 'AIDS hook,' but such deception takes its emotional toll in the fear of discovery, anger that this seems necessary, and possible guilt over what they have done."

In *Caregivers Quarterly,* Dr. Worden cites an instance of a couple who lived in a small midwest town. Their only child died of AIDS in San Francisco. The parents had been uncertain of their son's life-style, and after his death they felt uneasy about disclosing the cause. Instead they concocted the story that their son had died in an automobile accident. However, months later they were so guilt-ridden about the invented story that they decided to speak about it to their congregation. Instead of being rejected or hearing judgmental statements, the couple were embraced by their congregation. In fact, their disclosure enabled two other couples in the church to speak of concerns they had about their own children's life-styles. Dr. Worden offers a suggestion to the clergy: "Clergy can help survivors deal with this perceived stigma and to reality test what might happen if others found out or knew the real cause of death. They can also assist survivors to find appropriate persons and more comfortable ways to share the circumstance of the loss."

A L M O S T   D A I L Y , AIDS survivors make choices as to whether they will speak openly or remain hidden grievers. One such survivor was contemplating going to a meeting for bereaved parents. "How are the other parents at the meeting going to feel when they find out my son died of AIDS?" was the question asked of Abraham Malawski, who runs a hot line for The Compassionate Friends, a national self-help group for bereaved parents, with over 650 chapters.

Mr. Malawski receives calls from all over the country from parents who have lost a child to accident, illness, suicide, murder, and, in more recent years, to AIDS. He remembers the first call he received four years ago when a mother asked the question above.

"This parent was very nervous, and it was obvious from her voice that she was apprehensive about the possible reactions of other parents who would be at the meeting. She asked me how their children had died. I explained that at each chapter the parents had children who died of various causes. But I also explained that the common denominator was what brought all bereaved parents together—they had lost a child. I encouraged her to attend the group meeting and told her that ears were just as important as mouths. By that, I meant that while it is important for parents to talk and to say why they are there, it is also helpful to parents who may not feel like talking to at least be able to listen to what other parents are sharing.

"I sensed the woman wanted to go to the meeting, but that she was fearful of rejection by the other parents. So I asked her, 'What have you been saying to other people about your son's death?' She replied, 'Well, he died of pneumonia, a complication of AIDS, so I just say he died of pneumonia.' I made a suggestion to her: 'Perhaps you may want to follow that route when you first go to a meeting. Then, after you are in the group for a while, and you feel you can trust them and you want to tell them the actual cause, then that is entirely up to you.'"

Mr. Malawski doesn't know if this particular parent chose to go to a meeting or not. In handling the hot line, he gives the name and address of the chapter located nearest to the caller, as well as again extending the telephone number of the hot line as a resource for parents who want to call and talk with him at a future time. He offers encouragement and hope in suggesting that bereaved parents attend meetings but indicates that often parents will gravitate to groups specific to their needs.

"Organizations such as Survivors of Suicide and Parents of Murdered Children were founded because those parents felt more at ease with others who had suffered a similar loss. The same holds true for parents who have lost infants, and groups such as SIDS (sudden infant death syndrome) and SHARE have been formed to help young parents. And I know there have been parents who have sought out AIDS support groups, where they were more comfortable in being able to identify the facts and were able to say their child died of AIDS. But that was an evolutionary outcome that developed over the years.

"My own experience with AIDS parents during the time I attended meetings was that they were reluctant to say their child died of AIDS because they didn't want to have any more pain than they were already having. The parents didn't want the additional factor of being ostracized. People were uninformed about how AIDS was transmitted, and they didn't want anyone who was 'contagious' in their proximity. In fact, there are still a lot of people today who don't know how AIDS is transmitted, and they don't want to have any contact."

For those parents who are fearful of encountering rejection, Mr. Malawski urges them to reach out for help and not to become hidden grievers. "No matter what the cause of death, or the age of their child, bereaved parents need to talk. They should try to find help wherever they can. The most important thing is to locate a place where they will be comfortable, either in a group or on a one-on-one basis, and not be afraid or concerned about their surroundings. Groups are not for everyone, but most parents find talking and sharing with others to be extremely beneficial to their recovering. Many times in a group meeting you will hear an astonished parent say, 'I didn't know anyone else felt that way, too.' There is an outpouring of pain, but there is also an outpouring of love and compassion."

●

THE PROFESSIONALS SPEAK

● *A twenty-two-year-old in the group, whose lover had died, was distraught about mounting medical costs. Reluctantly he wrote to his family for help. At the meeting, he broke down. He was totally humiliated when his father sent him a can of tuna fish! He asked that his family not be notified if he died. They weren't.*

● *In a New York hospital, a nineteen-year-old was expected to live for only a few days. A nurse contacted the social worker, concerned that the young man would die all alone. When the man's family in Puerto Rico was contacted, the father's response was, "Send him home in a body bag!" The mother was brought into the country secretly to be with her son.*

● *"How can you be so self-indulgent?" asked an HIV positive survivor. His question was directed to an HIV negative survivor, who told of a guilt so severe that he wanted to end his life. "How can you talk about ending your life when all of us who are positive are fighting so hard for ours?"*

• *At a group meeting interspersed with gay lovers, wives, parents, and siblings, one woman spoke of her husband's prejudices. "He didn't want anyone to know he had AIDS because he was afraid he would be thought of as less manly." The gay participants didn't bat an eyelash. It was no news to them.*

• *"My daughter was an innocent victim," cried a mother. "No," admonished a grandmother. "My grandchild was the innocent victim! Your child had a choice." "No," exclaimed a sibling. "My brother and anyone else who has died of AIDS were innocent victims! No one sets out to be murdered by a disease!"*

AIDS carries with it a host of complex and unique problems for its survivors. A major issue is the prevalent attitude of blaming the deceased for his or her own illness. Jeri Woodhouse, AIDS policy analyst in the Manhattan Borough President's Office and a social worker who facilitates groups for those who have suffered a loss to AIDS, explains in more detail.

"We encounter attitudes about people who have sex, and attitudes about people who use drugs. Some people say alcohol is a drug. And how many have sex? I often hear talk about persons who are HIV-infected, intimating strongly that 'it's their own fault.' 'They did it.' 'They brought it on themselves.' Or 'If they were not gay . . . ' 'If they had not shared needles . . . ' 'If they had not done blah blah, they wouldn't be sick.' The implication is that they had control over their actions, and therefore they brought the illness on themselves. No one chooses to become ill. No one goes out and says, 'I'm going to perform an act or engage in an activity that will cause me to contract a potentially fatal illness.' Often what people are doing is simply having sexual relationships, which are part of normal human behavior. They are having relationships like almost everyone else in society."

Ms. Woodhouse claims this blaming of the victim carries over to the bereaved. "Survivors will hear comments such as 'If your son had not been gay' or 'If your sister had not been going with that guy using drugs' or 'If your father hadn't been such a runaround,' that beloved relative would not be dead. And the implication here is 'Therefore, you don't deserve the sympathy that someone else—whose loved one was killed in a car accident, or was drowned, or had a heart attack or cancer—deserves."

In the group setting, Ms. Woodhouse talks about that attitude with the survivors. "We talk very specifically about the fact that this is a medical problem. It is not a moral issue. We are all at risk. However, because we have been educated to think that only certain groups of people are at risk, the fear of stigma carries over to the group meetings. It's not uncommon to hear a mother say, 'Well, my daughter wasn't gay. She got it because she had sex one night. She's an innocent person, as opposed to . . . ' "

Elaborating on the effect social stigma has, Ms. Woodhouse explains how incredibly difficult it is for people to talk about what is going on in their lives. "It's so hard for them to find support from people around them, from their friends, their family, their neighbors, and their community. Invariably, the people who come to the support group say, 'There is no one else I can talk to, and that's why I'm here.' In one group recently, it turned out there were three families who had come, all of whom lived within a three-block radius of each other, and yet none of them had known that the other was living with this illness."

One of the reasons support groups work so well, Ms. Woodhouse believes, is that as new members keep coming in, older members have a place where they can share what they know. "I find that the people in the group want to do something to help other people, and that's a wonderful legacy to their loved ones."

DIANA MCKENDREE, psychotherapist/consultant, works very closely with Casey House in Toronto, Canada. At this hospice center, she trains and supervises the volunteer facilitators of self-help support groups, focusing on recovering from the death of someone with AIDS. Ms. McKendree points out that a number of participants have found great comfort in realizing that the death has brought them an awareness and a consciousness of what is really important in life. "The consciousness of the moment is the most important value, and loving is all that really matters—over and above success, materialism, and consumerism. And *that* seems to give them relief and a new energy. They have come to realize that what really matters in life is caring about another human being and that it's far more important than being president of the corporation and owning a fancy house. Apart from a sense of hopelessness felt by AIDS survivors, the loss also opens people to the realization that the focus is about living fully. And that seems to be one of the main gifts that comes through in the groups that I've seen. Although I've seen that in other grief groups, the AIDS issue intensifies the awareness."

Survivors often seek help from the clergy. However, except for those who have the opportunity to work in a hospital setting, perhaps as a chaplain, or in an area where they encounter grief, the clergy may not have been given the chance to have any in-depth study or association with grief. Ms. McKendree comments on the role the clergy plays in AIDS.

"Because of the lack of exposure and the unrealistic expectation that society generally places on them, there is a lot of pressure on the clergy. People expect them to be experts in the area of grief and bereavement. The reality is that individuals are all unique. Some may have the gift of being able to work with the dying or the bereaved, while others find it quite terrifying and at best uncomfortable. Working with the bereaved and the dying is not work for everybody."

However, Ms. McKendree stresses, there are ways in which any person can help the bereaved. "The greatest gift we can give to others is to allow them to be fully who they are in their experience right now, and we must withdraw our own personalities and permit the bereaved to tell their story. We must listen and not try to 'fix it' or convert them, but rather be there to receive, to hear the story, and to offer support. This may include practical matters such as financial, somebody to walk the dog, or a drive to the grocery store because the deceased always did that. Those who are grieving need someone who won't try to take away their grief. They need someone to listen to their story and honor their grief simply by being present."

Ms. McKendree believes there is a specific task for the clergy today. "The challenge to the clergy is to examine the issues and in some cases to transcend the homophobia within themselves in order to be able to receive the wounded person. Lifestyle should have nothing to do with a person's need for spirituality. I think the thing that prevents the clergy from being effective around AIDS issues is their own personal homophobia or the Church's doctrine about that. If nothing else, AIDS is really challenging the Church as well as individuals to look at that—and what that's really saying about the doctrine and the dogma. I have always equated AIDS to leprosy in the Bible. We certainly didn't treat lepers well, and I don't think we treat people with AIDS a whole lot better. I hope we're improving, but there are still too many terrible stories that can be heard. Horrible things are done to people in the name of religious righteousness.

"An example is a woman whose son died of AIDS. She had never really made it known in the community. He had attained a certain public status, and she was fearful of the stigma. Her son had moved away and lived in another part of the country. No one knew he was gay. When he became ill, she went to his home and cared for him. When she returned, it came out in the media that her son had died of AIDS. Nobody spoke to her about her son in church. She was given a very clear message: 'We don't want to hear this' and 'You're not really welcome here with that.' This was the only community she had known in her life. She isolated herself with two individuals who were lifelong friends, but she wasn't doing very well emotionally. I encouraged her to confront it and maintain her own integrity by speaking the truth. If that meant leaving her locale, maybe that's what should be done. Perhaps she could discover a place where she would be able to be who she was in her truth. But not to run away from speaking the truth in the place that was rejecting her because they didn't want to hear it. I think she was trying to do that. However, I've lost touch with her because she moved far away. I believe she was trying to find a place where she could live openly with her grief."

In the end, Ms. McKendree believes, it comes down to speaking the truth and not worrying about what others think. "It's not about judging that this was a bad person because they were different from us. This is a disease that has taken someone we have known and loved and been involved with. I think people tend to get very clouded with all of the baggage that goes around being gay or having AIDS. They are operating from a place of fear rather than a place of risking love or being open to receive. In working with those who have lost a loved one to AIDS, basically I provide a sounding board for them to express all of the feelings that need to be released. What we usually end up with is coming to the place of loving the person for who they are and that their sexuality should have little or nothing to do with it. Parents have based their love on a relationship with their son, and the fact that he has a gay life-style, which may have been secret to them, is something they have to come to terms with. Unfortunately, some don't. Men seem to have more difficulty than women. Mothers seem to be able to transcend the differences, but most fathers have a lot of problems confronting issues and fears about sexuality. It's often not about their son."

Ms. McKendree offers a cautionary note to survivors who may have lost not only the person in the physical sense, but also the potential of a relationship. "They rejected them long before they died. There is a big loss of what could have been, the loss of a dream, and the feeling that maybe one day they might have worked it out differently. Whenever we cut somebody off emotionally, there is a part of us that believes it will be different someday. Then, when they die, we have to grieve the death of that desire also. The death of the dream that maybe one day it will be resolved."

DR. DIANE Grodney, associate director of field work at New York School of Social Work and a private practitioner, is also the co-leader of the Walk-In Bereavement Support Group at the Gay Men's Health Crisis. Dr. Grodney emphasizes that the beauty of the walk-in group is you don't have to become a client of GMHC and you can utilize the service in a way that serves your individual needs. "If someone wants to come to a group meeting, all they do is walk in. There is no fee for the service." Although the group consists mostly of gay men who have lost a lover, others who come include mothers, sisters, brothers, friends, children, and other family members.

"Unfortunately," says Dr. Grodney, "I cannot recall one father ever attending. Fathers seem to have a harder time reaching out for emotional support."

Each week the facilitators begin the meeting by asking the mourners to give their names and to indicate whom they are grieving. "We also ask them to say something about what they would like to get out of the meeting. At the same time, a sign-in sheet is circulated on which the participants in the group write their names and telephone numbers, thus encouraging members to communicate with one another after the group meetings if that is their wish."

The "go-around," Dr. Grodney explains, offers an opportunity for introductions, helps those in the group begin to identify their own needs, and allows members who are further along in the process to tell how they have been helped by the group. This is an extremely important element in the healing. "Because it is a drop-in group, people who have been attending for a while can help the newly bereaved by assuring them, 'No, you're not going crazy. Many of us have had similar thoughts and feelings.' This process helps both parties. By helping others, the members help themselves. It also allows new members to develop hope and confidence in the group, while at the same time allowing the core members to communicate, albeit indirectly, the norms and rules of the group. Finally, in going around, the group members begin to identify strongly with one another and begin to recognize they are all sharing the common denominator of pain—an AIDS loss." Dr. Grodney states that despite the pain, the members are anxious for the contact with others and the chance to talk about their loss. "Because of the need to talk with others who have 'been in the same boat,' they display a high degree of openness at the meetings."

The walk-in group at GMHC functions as a support group. While it is not a psychotherapy group, it *is* therapeutic. "It is focused on the resolution of bereavement," Dr. Grodney states. "Some people attend for just one session. Others come many times. Others use it in conjunction with therapy. Although the group is informal, there is a clear focus on bereavement. The members talk in very personal ways about the nightmarish events and memories that haunt them. Sometimes people who come for the first time just sit and listen. This may be their first group experience, the first time they have talked to strangers about their loss. Or they may be afraid of being overwhelmed by the intensity of the emotions. We don't push people into participating if we think it may be too much for them. We try to engage them, but not be intrusive. Since we don't know anything about a person prior to their first meeting, we rely a lot on nonverbal communication as to what a person is ready for. Many members have said that just listening and discovering that they are not alone has been extremely helpful. Each group is like a renewal because there is always at least one new person, and the longtime members help that person get engaged in the group. They convey to the newcomers that this is a place where they will get understanding and where people can trust one another. There are always people who come back."

Dr. Grodney comments on the facilitator's role when specific difficult issues arise, such as in cases where a person in the group is suffering from severe depression. "If we discern that a person needs additional help, we take him or her aside after the meeting, talk about the issues, and try to refer the person to a therapist for additional help. In terms of allaying fears about depression, new members often ask how everyone else 'has gotten through it' and 'if it gets better.' When the older members see a new member in pain, they are very generous in demonstrating empathy and understanding. They share similar experiences and offer suggestions as to what has helped them cope. Usually, just finding out that you are not the only one who has suffered from the flashbacks, the crying jags, fears of being alone, and so on, provides enormous relief."

It is not only the newly bereaved who come to the walk-in group. Dr. Grodney tells of a man who came in whose lover died eight years ago. "He realized he had not gotten involved in another intimate relationship because he had not resolved his grief and decided it was time that he did. We also have people who come in whose lovers have died only two days before. But the usual pattern is for people to come in a few months after the death when they feel that they are beginning to become a burden to family and friends.

"Many people have put their lives on hold while they are

acting as caretaker for the person with AIDS. When they get to the group, they have a great need to talk about the trauma." Dr. Grodney has noticed that group members continually speak about how amazed they are that, as depressing as the group is, they leave feeling greatly relieved. "What my co-leader, Cecelia Marcus, and I try to convey at the meetings is that what the members are experiencing is 'normal,' and that they are having 'normal reactions' to a very traumatic situation."

Some of the reactions experienced early on include denial, such as believing, at times, that the person is still alive, says Dr. Grodney. "It may be expressed in fantasies such as thinking of the loved one as 'being on vacation' or visiting someone and soon will return home. But more often the denial of the loss is perceived when the person goes home to an empty house. There is also tremendous pain and sadness that can hit you out of the blue. When you are walking down the street and see someone who resembles the person who has died, you are shocked. Or you may wonder how the world can be going on now that your lover is dead. Recovering is not a straight upward line. There are times when members feel they have suddenly lost progress they thought they had gained. This usually occurs when the griever becomes aware of yet another way in which the loved one's death has affected them."

Many other issues surface during the meeting, such as anger about why the person they loved suffered so much pain before dying. "Others are angry that the government is not doing what it should be, or that doctors feel helpless. There are feelings of guilt for surviving. Were they there when the person died, or were they not there for whatever reason? If they're HIV positive, with their partner gone, who is going to take care of them now? There is also a lot of anger at families who abandoned them while they were so ill. Some express they had to take care of their lovers as if taking care of a baby. In the AIDS epidemic, people are experiencing one loss after another with little, if any, time or opportunity to resolve previous losses. Often, members of the group have lost many friends, or another lover has already died and they are going through 'round two' of grief. The entire gay community has suffered innumerable losses."

Dr. Grodney states that for some people who have lost

many treasured loved ones to AIDS, the impact is like what is experienced during times of war, and they may suffer from post-traumatic stress. However, she adds, "most of the group members are deeply affected by a specific loss, and we see them go through the normal stages stages of grieving, including shock, numbness, disorganization/despair, reorganization, and resolution and recovery.

"You can see people are recovering when they go on to another relationship," Dr. Grodney indicates, "or when they become more engaged in life. When that progress occurs, they may or may not choose to remain. The group is open-ended in that one may begin in the group and remain for as long as one wishes and may return at a later time if they feel the group can be helpful again. It is a drop-in in the sense that anyone is welcome and there are no admission requirements. Members may come regularly, sporadically, for a few sessions, or only for one session. Not attending isn't treated as resistance. Rather, the members are warmly welcomed back. The open-door policy, lack of fee, and the 'no strings commitment' make it possible for many people to join who would otherwise be unlikely to utilize bereavement services."

T H E R E V E R E N D John K. Saynor, an Anglican priest at Saint Simon's Church in Toronto, Canada, indicates that social stigma remains a major issue clouding the progress of many AIDS survivors. "It is crucial to the recovering of AIDS survivors that they gain the knowledge that their grief is valid and worthy."

This knowledge is obtained through hearing other survivors of AIDS who have lived through the stigma and finger pointing, Reverend Saynor maintains. It is also provided by those in the caregiving professions who are educating people about AIDS and helping to calm their fears, helping to free them from prejudice. Some of this prejudice erupts at support group meetings. Reverend Saynor describes what happened at one particular meeting.

"In a group of six gay men and one woman, the woman made it clear that she was out to 'reform' the six men and took on the role of being their mother. These were grown men, mourning lovers. They were not coming to a support group to be chastised about their life-style. It is best when gay men share openly in a group where they will feel totally comfortable. And most parents prefer to attend a separate group where they are not privy to the warm expressions and jargon often shared by gay men. Generally, it seems to work better when the groups are not mixed."

The author of many books on bereavement, including *Genesis, Dead Is a Four-Letter Word,* and *Saying Goodbye,* Reverend Saynor is also licensed as a funeral director. As a result of his twenty-five years in funeral service, he became aware of the gaps in follow-up after a death and now conducts grief seminars and workshops in that area. "The first group I did with the AIDS Committee of Toronto was an open and ongoing group that lasted for two years, but hardly anybody at the end were people who had been there at the beginning. They all sort of moved out. The most recent group was designated for ten weeks but went for sixteen. Now, the participants meet in their homes about once every six weeks, taking turns at having the meeting. It's almost like a social event, and they enjoy suppers together. I found that the fellows really bonded."

Another issue that comes up in the group meetings centers around families. Reverend Saynor explains, "I've had meetings where the participants would just sit there and rage over their own family members and the family members of the person who died. People were literally going back to the lover's home after the funeral reception, going through things in their home, saying, 'I want this and this.' Many times the families are just wonderful until the death comes, and then they turn sour."

Reverend Saynor comments on the problem survivors have of establishing new relationships. "This is not an uncommon problem to any widow or widower, but many of the fellows are HIV positive, and it's an added situation to deal with in trying to establish a permanent relationship. A lot of men who are not HIV positive are not at all interested in taking that on. The HIV positive men often gravitate to each other and find ways to cope with their own illness and the death of their lover, ways that enable them to resume normal activities. If I were to bring in the most recent group right now, you would see a group of people who are functioning really well. A lot of them were a mess when the group started. No matter how long I'm in this work, I'm still amazed at what groups do for people and at the change. I've seen how much the groups help."

In other areas, Reverend Saynor has been instrumental in trying to educate professionals in the field and to reduce homophobia. "Gay people do not always look like they are from another planet, and their jargon is sometimes misunderstood. It took me the longest time to convince a funeral home that it was okay to put into the newspaper obituary 'the lover of so and so.' One of the funeral directors said, 'Well, we don't call our husbands or wives "lovers." Everybody assumes we are lovers.' I replied, 'In the gay community, that is the term that is used.' He continued, 'What's wrong with using "friend"?' I replied, 'They might be a friend, but they are also a lover.' So, it is the jargon that people sometimes feel uncomfortable with. I suspect they might be even more uncomfortable if the obituary column for the death of a lover read 'husband' or 'wife.' Also, a lot of people who don't feel uncomfortable at seeing two women embrace or kiss will feel very uncomfortable at seeing two men openly hug or kiss. People have to be educated. There is too much that people misunderstand or simply don't want to know about gay people."

As a clergyperson himself, Reverend Saynor makes an assessment on other men of the cloth. "By and large, the clergy is doing a much better job than I thought they would. I really have to commend a lot of them who rise to the occasion. On the other hand, I've seen clergy say, 'Well, if there is anything I can do, let me know,' and make no attempt to keep in touch with the individual. By the time the person has died, the family calls somebody else to do the funeral service. They don't even call their own parish priest because they have been so put off."

Reverend Saynor believes it is crucial for counselors to be available to do some one-on-one talking with the survivors. "It's so important to talk individually. If you just spend a couple of sessions with a person, you can be of tremendous help letting them know that they are not nuts, that they are perfectly normal. And if a survivor who has lost someone to AIDS—particularly in small towns—realizes that someone else shares their secret and accepts them, that is an enormous help and relief to them."

In larger communities, Reverend Saynor explains there are different issues to address, such as continuing losses. "In the gay community, people often don't have time to change from their clothes at one funeral before they are going to the next. I conducted two funerals back to back recently where after the first funeral, over half the people went out to smoke a cigarette on the front lawn and were back to attend the second funeral. There are many factors that influence grief. In this instance, it's the overwhelming number of losses and the fact that everywhere you go, you live with memories rather than the people. Too, with the volume of deaths, there isn't any time to deal with it. It's not at all uncommon in Toronto in a gay bar to see a man sitting at the bar in tears. And you assume you know what it's about. I urge all those who have lost a loved one to AIDS to reach out, find someone you can talk to, and let the tears flow. If there is a support group near you, don't be frightened. There are loving, caring people just like you."

During holidays and other special days, Reverend Saynor finds that participants are very attentive to each other in the groups. "For example, one of the guys may say, 'My lover's birthday is coming up,' and the other participants will often give him a call on the day. And I encourage them to do something on special days. If a group is going on over a holiday, I will usually do something. I think it is important to keep the group running over Christmas. I will usually suggest that we not have a meeting that week but have a Christmas dinner instead, or a party together. It is important for people to learn that it is okay to party. On the last night of a group, I have a pot-luck supper. I always do this. It's one way to get off the heaviness of the group and to say, 'We are moving on from here.' After one such dinner, a bereaved parent commented, 'It's been so nice to be able to sit down and laugh with people who felt it was okay for you to laugh.' "

T H E S P E C I A L issues of seniors who are gay is addressed by a group formed specifically to meet their needs. Greg Anderson, social worker and grief counseler for SAGE (Senior Action in a Gay Environment), is literally putting something back into the pot by working with men who have lost lovers. Greg also suffered such a loss, but to a homicide. Because there was no support group available to him that addressed that type of death, Greg was warmly welcomed by participants in an AIDS survivors group. It saved him from drowning in the abyss of pain. Now Greg is helping with problems that arise in the lives of older gays. Having experienced a similar loss, he is in tune with their despair and offers a compassionate ear and guiding hand.

As supervisor of individual services at SAGE, Greg has a mixed case load but works almost exclusively with older gay men. "The men are over sixty, and a third of them are living with AIDS. I provide general counseling among the aging concerning loss and run several open-ended support groups for older HIV positive men. We also have a bereavement group for survivors. Because we have only a small staff, we utilize a lot of volunteer professionals. Our bereavement group is run by a priest who works with us. He is highly skilled, charismatic, and very effective. The group meets weekly and consists of ten to twelve participants."

Greg talks about some of the problems that worry older gays. "One of the major concerns is dealing with their own illness at this age when their lover—the person to whom they could have looked to for care and comfort—has died of AIDS. Although this concern is not unique to older gays, it weighs heavily on their minds that younger men will have more chances of meeting new partners. And they are extremely cautious about attempting new relationships, fearful that they may not work out. While our psychological self has to be nurtured, our physical body yearns to be touched and held. It's human nature to seek warmth and comfort."

Greg has observed that most of the men have never come out to their families. "They are very secretive about their health status. When it comes to sharing their pain with family members, they usually say, 'I don't want any of them to know until it's over.' And that's sad because some of their family could be very supportive and take care of them when they need it the most.

But they are too scared to risk a break in their family ties. This is a generation that didn't come out about their sexual orientation, and equally they are not at all comfortable with the thought of coming out about their HIV status."

Another issue that surfaces is that the men who come to SAGE feel more comfortable with gay men who are their own age level. "They come here to be with their peers, who will understand their problems better. When they go to other groups, there are primarily younger gay men who say, 'You have no right to complain because you've had a full life.' It is implied that they are 'over the hill,' so to speak, and not entitled to continue living with the same wishes and desires of younger men, who feel so cheated. But whether you're twenty, forty, or sixty plus, if you know you are going to die of AIDS, you feel cheated. So we help deal with some of the issues that older men feel are not properly or adequately addressed in groups with younger men."

Talk of suicide is also not limited to older men and comes up in almost any bereavement group at one time or another. "I stand aside and let them handle it, and they do it pretty well. They generally keep it abstract. But they also say, 'I can understand how you are feeling because all of us think that at some point.' And you can see everyone breathe a huge sigh of relief that the issue is something they can talk about, just as they can talk about any issue that is of concern to them. That's what is important—being able to come to a group and not be afraid they will be taunted or laughed at. The mutual respect shines through."

S T I L L   A N O T H E R segment of AIDS survivors are those who have suffered multiple losses within a family unit.

Sheila Crandles, MSW, M. Ed., and coauthor of "Development of a Weekly Support Group for Caregivers of Children with HIV Disease," works with survivors who have suffered or will suffer multiple losses to AIDS. She tells of the pain of one of those survivors. "A grandmother came to our program after her daughter had died of AIDS. Two of the woman's grandchildren are HIV positive. This woman desperately needed to talk to others who were having the kind of pain she was experiencing. 'Who is going to take care of my daughter's children? I'm trying, but I don't know if I can handle this by myself. Is there anyplace I can get some help? I've had to cope with my daughter's death, and now I'm facing the loss of two of my grandchildren. There isn't even time to mourn!' "

Ms. Crandles, who works with the STAR Program (Special Treatment and Research Program) at the State University of New York Health Science Center at Brooklyn in New York, also explains that there are innumerable complicating issues surrounding the AIDS deaths when young siblings are involved.

"Because of these issues, we are really only in the beginning stages of understanding what is needed in developing adequate programs for survivors—especially those with multiple losses. One major issue is the wish for secrecy. Often, when a child has died of AIDS after contracting it from the mother, the remaining family members may not wish a surviving sibling to know the cause of death. This puts a whole other complexion on how to best help the surviving sibling and still respect the family's wish for confidentiality."

According to Ms. Crandles, the child is often the first in a family to be identified with the HIV virus, and in cases of perinatal transmission, not only the children but their mothers are infected with HIV. It is also possible their fathers and siblings may be infected as well. The support group was set up to help the primary caregivers of children with HIV disease in coping with depression, anxiety, and multiple losses. She comments, "Our goal was to help provide a social support system for them, something akin to a surrogate family."

The group includes biological parents who may be either HIV positive or negative, foster parents, and grandparents. Ages range from their twenties to their sixties. There is a mix of types of caregivers as well. Some are single parents who have lost their partners to AIDS. Some are anticipating the death of one or more children, or perhaps a spouse. The children may have lost one or more parents and are under the care of a grandparent or foster parent. Some of the foster parents have left the group after their foster children died or were taken from their custody. There are primarily females in the group. When the first male participant, Alberto, joined, two of the women were opposed, as they felt they wouldn't be able to be as open as they had been in the past. Ms. Crandles explains how other members of the group convinced the objectors that a man in their midst wouldn't hamper their style.

"The rest of the members held their ground and stated they were interested in having a male perspective. Alberto felt comfortable in the group, since he was accustomed to being the only man in many situations. His wife had died of AIDS six months earlier, so he had to be both mother and father to his three children, two of whom have HIV. Alberto was especially grateful to the members of the group for listening. He said he could get advice from many sources, but it was very hard to find people who would just listen. So what the members had in common far outweighed the gender difference, and Alberto was accepted into the group."

The group is facilitated by two social workers. In addition, there is a physician assistant who treats HIV-infected children and who offers updated medical information to the participants. A third social worker is available to conduct a play group for the children while their caregivers attend the group meetings. Often the caregivers may have spent the previous night in the hospital with a child who was ill, and a light breakfast is provided to them. Although the group functions as a support group, it also acts as a therapy group in some ways. "The participants talk about the previous session at the beginning of each group meeting. In so doing, the members increase their interest in and concern about one another, which helps to build the group's history." The group leaders also established some ground rules: to respect each other's opinions and confidentiality, to listen to each other with sympathy and understanding, and to be on time, attending as regularly as possible.

During the early meetings the group leaders ran into prejudice and discrimination regarding how their children became infected with HIV. Ms. Crandles explains the need for clarification to the group. "One grandmother spoke of her two daughters in different terms. The youngest, who became infected through a tainted blood transfusion, was described as being the 'good daughter,' whereas the older daughter, who was a drug user, was designated as being the 'bad daughter,' who had brought her illness upon herself. We stressed that AIDS is a disease in which everyone is equal and there is no guilt or innocence. The grandmother was encouraged to examine her anger and frustrations in connection with her daughter's addiction. In that way, the group concentrated on her self-scrutiny rather than debating who was and who was not to blame for AIDS."

As losses in the group began to occur, the focus of the group expanded to include not only anticipatory mourning, but also bereavement. Some of the issues included the concern about the effect the death of their infected children would have on their uninfected children. Another issue addressed was anger toward men and relationships. "One mother who discovered she was HIV positive when she was six months pregnant spoke openly about her rage at her deceased husband for having had extramarital affairs and for infecting her and her baby. Through her ability to express her anger, more reticent women were able to release their feelings once they recognized they could do so without fear. Others of the HIV positive women gave support to one another in continuing relationships with men, wondering how and when to talk about the use of condoms and when and how to disclose their status to their partners."

One of the most important outgrowths of the group was an increase in contact among the participants outside the group atmosphere. Many times they became exchange baby-sitters and were available to each other whenever an emergency arose. Another important aspect was the fact that HIV positive mothers began to become concerned about their own health issues. "It had been noted in the group that often participants were so involved with their children's health care that they were not mindful of their own. Regardless of basic religious differences, or moral and life-style choices, the group members inevitably bonded and supported one another." Ms. Crandles stresses that death is an integral part of life for the group members, but they believe they can still hope and still enjoy some measure of happiness even though AIDS has impacted on their lives.

M ICHAEL MILLER, ACSW, is a psychotherapist and director of the Bereavement Center of the Family Service

Association of Nassau County, New York. He speaks directly to a problem being encountered by survivors throughout the country: finding the right support group. He stresses that while in theory it would be nice to have separate groups geared to specific needs, in practice this isn't always possible. Consequently, providers and mourners often have to transcend their differences in order to get help and to give help. He indicates that many support groups have evolved against the backdrop of the AIDS crisis. "There has been the beginning of a grass-roots movement that is sometimes professionally led, sometimes not, involving different populations. I have encountered many people who simply have not known where to turn because the resources are so few and far between. The major organizations are ones that people have known about, but often mourners are reaching for supports and are not really quite sure of where they belong. Some groups are more evolved to help partners, some to help parents, some to help spouses, some to help the extended family in terms of bereavement. It can be confusing when people reach for help and encounter one group that has evolved in one direction and then another in a different direction, all falling under the umbrella of AIDS care.

"What all this suggests is that some standards need to be set in terms of care. Who is qualified to run a certain group? What happens when issues begin to get complicated? Do groups include people who, for instance, are gay partners along with heterosexual spouses? These kinds of group issues need to be examined. Professionals are wary of mutual support groups that may not look at the group composition in terms of mutual identification and other factors that may be important for group cohesion. However, the available resources may be so sparse that by the time mourners reach each other, these distinctions appear secondary. What matters initially is being able to acknowledge what they've been through and to share the support that's there."

From a professional point of view, Mr. Miller comments on the possible difficulties within bereavement groups. "In terms of group composition, it may be difficult to include people who are vastly different in their relationship to the deceased, in their psychological issues, as well as in their sociocultural backgrounds, because it may make for a difficulty in being able to share within the group. And the issues of secrecy are there to begin with. But in reality I think people who do come together are in so much pain that differences become secondary. In one group, one participant was HIV positive and had lost his lover to AIDS. He was still in a drug treatment facility at the time, alongside his attendance in the bereavement group, and he was receiving methadone. The issues that were complicated for this group were that some mourners had spouses who had died of a drug overdose, and these mourners had histories of substance abuse themselves. In the course of their own Twelve Step work, they evolved a style of defense that was like a teetotaler's stance. Some people who are alcoholics and no longer drink don't want to be around people who do drink because they're afraid of falling off the wagon. Similarly, because some of the participants were drug-free now, anything such as methadone use represented a potential threat and was considered anathema to them. The underlying issue here was to help the group identify that bereavement is a situation that, for some people, involves a great deal of anger and unpreparedness. As a result, anger sometimes gets displaced from the original sources and onto other mourners within group settings. A lot of displacement anger goes on despite the fact that there is a tremendous need for support. Some people enter a group with preconceptions about whether or not they can trust anyone or whether or not group participation will just involve a further loss to them. They are extra careful about whom they choose to identify with. In many cases it even boils down to members scanning the group in order to identify some aspect of those people that they *cannot* identify with in order to confirm a preconceived assumption that there is no one to whom they can relate. It's a way of self-isolating in grief because the pain is so enormous. And I think there is a great fearfulness around being able to trust again. Their fear is that if you allow someone to be close to you, it means you can lose them as well. So the bottom line is that the beginnings of group membership itself can be fraught with difficulties that sometimes get played out on other members."

As a professional group leader handling mixed grief meetings, Mr. Miller believes it is first important for group members to develop a feeling of trust in their group leader and for the group leader to encourage participants to begin to find places where they can have the safety to express themselves. In addition, he prepares the group for each new person coming into the fold.

"I prepare the group, indicating that we have a new member who will be joining the group who is HIV positive and/or that their loved one recently died of AIDS. I make that basic statement, and then I ask if anyone has any discomfort with that. And we explore the reasons for that discomfort. So far, we haven't encountered any blocks that we couldn't deal with. The main thing to combat is ignorance and lack of education about AIDS. Among the other mourners in the group may be the fear of getting AIDS, of catching it. Once those fears are dispelled, we are able to move on. In the group setting, participants are confronted with the task of talking about their grief publicly. By doing so, they alter the course of their grief and start on the road to reconciliation and reentry into the world at large."

MANY GROUP leaders have similar concerns about AIDS survivors who become part of general bereavement groups. Patricia Corrigall, program coordinator for bereavement services and community education for the Humphrey Funeral Home in Toronto, Canada, talks about difficulties melding into the group.

"We generally have five or six groups operating at the same time. Because of the many AIDS organizations within the city offering groups to meet the needs of AIDS survivors, we try to refer people to those groups. If for any reason they don't want to go, we welcome them into our groups. But often the AIDS survivors found it very difficult to acknowledge what they were there for. It takes quite a while—if ever—to be able to share with the group what the cause of death was. *Actually, this is often why they come to our groups in the first place, as opposed to a group that openly acknowledges that the group is there for AIDS survivors.* They are people who are having difficulty dealing with the fact that their loved one died from AIDS. This is especially true if they are not a gay partner. It applies particularly to parents who might feel uncomfortable with, and possibly be very angry toward, other members of the group who are gay. The parent of a son who died of AIDS might be harboring anger and resentment toward other members of the group who are gay, and often there is a reaction by the gay men against the intolerance of the parents.

"Sometimes a parent may be willing to say their child died of AIDS and sometimes they are not. It's almost a catch-22 situation. They *don't* want to go to a place where they *can* say why they are there, and when they come to one of our groups, they *won't* say why they are there. Basically, it is not coming to terms with the cause of the death, or not coming to terms with their deceased child's life-style. These are people who are very much in need of talking and are pretty much in a limbo situation. Some go through the entire nine weeks that the group meets and *never* disclose what they are there for or what the cause of death was. We encourage participants to be comfortable with what they are dealing with and discourage them from keeping to themselves. We explain the benefits of disclosing and sharing and receiving the support of the group. It's more of a long-term education process than a matter of being able to respond to their needs at this point in a straightforward way. It is often a hidden area in many people's lives. There is the goal of educating them to become more tolerant and aware of AIDS within our society and to not feel they are the only ones facing the issues they're involved with."

At the moment, lots of groups tend to fall between the cracks, says Ms. Corrigall. "We have had HIV positive drug users come to the group. They didn't feel they belonged in a gay group. They are another group of people who often don't have a lot of places to turn to. The question is, is it more beneficial to develop individual groups to address each particular need or is it better to look at the bottom line, which is they are all AIDS survivors?"

I N S O M E of the preceding passages, we have heard from professionals who have encountered problems or have expressed concern about mixed groups. We must remember that the groups involved were for the most part *general* bereavement groups. Kathleen Perry, CSW and director of the supportive care program at St. Vincent's Hospital in New York City, focuses on the needs of groups geared specifically to AIDS survivors. She shares with us what it's like to attend a *bereavement supportive care group* for those who have lost a loved one to AIDS and explains what the facilitator does, what is asked of participants, and what some of the issues are—ones that surface during the meetings.

"Because space is limited, our group model consists of a maximum of ten participants and two facilitators. It's a *closed group* and *not* a walk-in type, *so when participants come they will see the same people for the eight weeks of meetings.* There is no charge, and the group is open to *anyone* who has lost someone to AIDS. The first night is very hard for everyone, coming from their own pain. The way I try to help them past this is by saying, immediately, that each person is free to say who they are and for whom they are grieving. I suggest, 'If you can, tell us who died and anything you would like to say about that person. Perhaps you'd like to share about their illness—or their death. Perhaps you'd like to talk about what it's been like since they died and any issues you have currently.' That's kind of a sweeping mandate, and people don't answer all of those things. But someone usually goes first, saying, 'Well, I'll just jump right in there and tell you about . . . ' and so they begin. Generally, on the first night, participants will spend three or four minutes each to tell what happened and who died. Sometimes you will have a person who likes to talk a bit who will expand for a while longer. The bonding comes quite easily. One of the most important aspects of the group is that usually the participants have not been in another setting where they were free to talk openly in a safe and confidential place or where they have heard stories that were similar to their own."

Ms. Perry believes it is important in the beginning for the group leader to give the participants a little grief education. "Many people think that their reaction is so profound that it can't be normal. So I try to incorporate a little grief education, but not formally. I do provide some handouts and a bibliography for those who may want to read. It is also especially nurturing to the group for the facilitator to let them know their efforts are recognized. It is very comforting for participants to hear from the group leader that grief is hard work and that they are doing a good job simply by experiencing the pain and not avoiding it. For example, doing a lot of drinking or not talking about it would be avoiding the grief. By not avoiding it, they are doing the very difficult work of grieving."

We have read throughout this book about hidden grievers. Ms. Perry reinforces much of what has been said but also offers some concrete suggestions to survivors. "It's hard enough with deaths other than AIDS. For example, I still work with people who have had a family member die of cancer. But at least here, people get support on their job. They can talk openly about the illness to their family or friends. But when the family or life partner finds it too frightening or too painful to talk about an AIDS illness, this prevents the normal supports in life from taking place. It makes the situation so much worse and the recovering so much harder. It's a lot of heartache to bear to learn a loved one has died of AIDS. So what I often say is, 'If you could only tell one person, who would it be?' In that way, I let the grieving person open the door in their mind as to whom they could tell. Then that begins to let them see that maybe if they told one trusted person, they would feel better. Sometimes they will tend to tell a sister or brother, or perhaps an aunt. If you help the survivor see that they really need the support and will need it even more in the future, that is making an inroad."

In other instances, members of the group have complained of feeling pressured by friends or family members about getting on with their lives. "One person may say, 'So and so calls all the time and wants me to go out, do things that will get me out of the house, or back on my feet and things like that.' Then you may hear a few other people in the group say, 'Oh, yes, I know just what you mean. My family says to me, 'You can't sit home all the time. You're brooding, and that's not good.' So the group leader can make a connection for the participants here, saying, 'What you both seem to be talking about is that you're very sad, yet what people are seeing on the outside is anger. And that's keeping them away from you, keeping them from supporting you."

Ms. Perry explains to the group that it is their job to

educate friends and family as to how to support them. "I tell participants how to help with that problem. 'You need to educate people not to call and say, 'If I can do anything, let me know.' You really have to be very direct with people about what will help and inform them about what you really need. Think about how you would feel if the situation were reversed. Would you want your friend or dear close family member to tell you how you could help? Perhaps you could indicate some specific things that might help, like 'I'm bringing over some dinner' or 'I'm bringing some stamps and envelopes in case you need them' or 'I picked up the laundry and I'll help you put it away.' Then this usually elicits additional comments and a greater opening-up among the participants."

Ms. Perry points out that there is another tragic aspect for some parents after the loss of a child. "Often, they have lost an adult child and soon after may lose a spouse, usually a husband. Women have called me who have lost their sons, and I've gotten to know them and help them struggle through that loss. A year or two later a husband may die, and they are bereaved all over again and very much alone in the world. There are literally thousands of women who have lost their families by having lost an adult child and then their husbands.

Participants in the group also talk about spiritual experiences that they are not comfortable sharing with others, indicating that the person who died has come to them either in a dream or when they were "daydreaming." Many of the group members say they've had an "eerie" experience. "It's very reassuring to them," Ms. Perry states, "when they hear others in the group say they, too, have had that kind of an experience."

Because so many of the gay men in the groups have voiced their fears about their own HIV status, St. Vincent's recently started a bereavement group for people who have suffered a loss and who are also HIV positive. Ms. Perry expands on the benefits of the new group.

"Now, when people call to inquire, I say we are offering *two* kinds of bereavement groups—the regular group and the group for people who are HIV positive. In that way, people can self-elect into that group without anyone asking, 'Are you HIV positive?' "

Ms. Perry talks about the plans and hopes for HIV positive survivors. "Many people, while they are still working, begin to really plan how they can be helped. One man, an interior designer, has literally lined up women friends because, as far as he is concerned, they are not going to be disappearing from his life at the ratio he has been losing his male friends. He has spoken to some of his female friends and has asked, 'Will you be available to me? Could you move in and take care of me if I got sick?' These are lifelong friends. Rather than turning to his present circle of friends, his thought is, Although they are well now, will they be around when I need them? He feels that unless they get hit by a truck, his female friends will be there for him. Another man who has KS [Kaposi's sarcoma] told how he was able to turn to his family. 'I would have gone my full life not discussing my being gay or anything related to my life-style if this hadn't happened.' Fortunately his family responded favorably to his needs."

Many parents have come forward to help their children once the illness was made known to them. But there have also been dreadful stories when parents have devastated their children with shocking responses to pleas for help. Ms. Perry tells of two particular incidents.

"One fellow from Texas, who came from a well-to-do family, asked his father for financial help to meet the mounting medical costs after he discovered he was HIV positive. His father sent him a can of tuna fish! Just the idea that this was his father's response was so humiliating. He said, 'I grew up with this man, and a part of me says this is what I expected, but I really did hope that since this is a situation where I am going to die from this disease, that maybe the impact of that information would have helped draw us together.' This young man died here, at home, which is what he wanted. His friends had a service for him. He had never contacted his parents again, and indeed, he specifically said he didn't want them notified.

"In another incident, a young man was in the hospital, completely alone and dying. This happens often, and the nurses express great concern, asking if there isn't anyone they can contact. Sometimes the patients will say, 'There's nobody I can tell,' or "My family wouldn't take me back.' We have volunteers who come in to be with them, and we try to extend ourselves in any way we can so at least they have some sort of a loving presence at the end of their life. With the young man mentioned above, who was from Puerto Rico, he felt there was no one he could call upon but had specifically been asking for his mother in his last stages. Through friends of the young man, the telephone number of the family in Puerto Rico was obtained. The resident called them to say their son was critically ill and that he had been asking for them. The father's reply was, 'Send him home in a body bag!' There is a happy ending to this story, however. We took further action, and the patient's friends called their own parents in Puerto Rico. They were able to raise the money that would allow the mother to come, which was her wish. The friends put the mother up, took care of her needs, and enabled her to ease her child's dying days."

Ms. Perry expands upon the issue of rejection by families. "In the gay culture, because there is so much rejection in their own families, they have established their own sort of family group. In the meetings, participants tell of shattering experiences. They learn that there may not be any solution and it is something they have to learn to live with. By being in the group where they can share their life, and talk about their feelings, they begin to really care about one another and say, 'What are you going to do about this or that?' They begin to have an intimacy, more than camaraderie—and that is pretty miraculous. All of life is really about connections with one another and relationships. I think many men in our groups would say that their priorities in life aren't always to have money and homes, but that what really matters is to have honest relationships in your life and people who care about you—and whom you care about. One of the things I've grown to appreciate out of groups is that it's another intimate circle to be with. Also, it is very life affirming and very inspiring to hear stories of real love in action—how people care for one another. And then you see it actually enacted in the group as people reach out to one another. You see such compassion, human kindness, and caring, and people receive warm nurturing from each other."

Ms. Perry speaks of hope and what that word really means to HIV survivors. "Some of the men in the group have been diagnosed positive for eight or nine years. So we are dealing with two issues—how to cope with being HIV positive and how to continue to have hope. How do you keep up your hope for the future? And what does hope mean to each person? The thing that most of them have evolved to is that hope is extremely personal. For a long time, people hope for a cure. They hope to stay well. If that is no longer possible, they hope they can manage this whole thing, that they will be financially able to do that. Your hopes change according to where you are on the whole spectrum of things. Then, as things get closer, they hope to have one more summer, hope for not too much pain, or hope they won't go blind. Hope is one of those things where people say, 'I'm feeling hopeless,' but then when you get to what's behind that feeling and ask what they mean, it's do they get discouraged, or frightened, or tired. And suddenly there is the realization that they really do have hope and it sort of pulls them through. It's like you have faced something and now you are hoping for something else. And, in the end, it's usually 'I hope for a peaceful death' or 'I hope to have loving people around me.' And I suppose that is what we all hope for eventually."

EPILOGUE

A I D S . Is it Armageddon?

In writing this book to help those who have lost a loved one to AIDS, the question keeps surfacing.

No—it isn't Armageddon.

In the Middle Ages, not everyone who got the bubonic plague died from it. It was a deadly disease, but it did not end the world. Similarly, not everyone who gets the flu, a virus, dies from it. Yet at the end of World War I, a worldwide epidemic of influenza killed more than ten million people in a single winter.

To those who ask about Armageddon now, permit me to present briefly some encouraging research. At the Harvard School of Medicine, studies that have been under way for over twelve years among HIV positive gay men have revealed that over 5 percent have survived without developing AIDS for more than fourteen years. Their immune system has not collapsed. The research suggests there might be a natural immunity to AIDS.

In other words, the immune system among some gay men may be stronger than the virus. And this immunity may be enhanced with medical help such as vaccines that strengthen the immune system.

Initially, the studies were conducted among ten thousand gay men. Studies now in progress among heterosexual men and women may show a similar natural defense against HIV. If these statistics are borne out in continuing studies, it would stand to reason that although AIDS is indeed a plague, it is *not* Armageddon.

And, historically, man has eventually triumphed over plagues.

Let us take hope.

PART TWO

HELPING HANDS:

Description and Directory

of Organizations

AIDS HOT LINES

National AIDS Hotline	(800)342-AIDS
Hearing Impaired AIDS hot line	(800)243-7889
Spanish AIDS hot line	(800)344-7432
National AIDS Information Clearing House	(800)458-5231
Drug Abuse hot line	(800)662-HELP
AIDS Clinical Trials Information Center	(800)TRIALS-A
Project Inform (AIDS) Experimental Drug Information	(800)822-7422

AIDS HOT LINES
IN THE UNITED STATES

—

Alabama	228-0469
Alaska	478-AIDS
Arizona	334-1540
Arkansas	445-7720
California (N)	367-AIDS
California (S)	922-AIDS
Colorado	252-AIDS
Denver	(303)333-4336
Connecticut	342-AIDS
Delaware	422-0429
District of Columbia	332-AIDS
Florida	352-AIDS
Georgia	551-2728
Atlanta	(404)876-9944
Hawaii	922-1313
Idaho	(208)345-2277
Illinois	243-AIDS

Indiana	848-AIDS
Iowa	445-AIDS
Kansas	232-0040
Kentucky	654-AIDS
Louisiana	992-4379
Maine	851-AIDS
Maryland	638-6262
Baltimore	(301)333-AIDS
Massachusetts	235-2331
Boston	(617)522-4090
Michigan	872-AIDS
Minnesota	752-4281
Mississippi	826-2961
Missouri	533-AIDS
Montana	233-6668
Nebraska	782-AIDS
Nevada	(702)687-4804
New Hampshire	342-AIDS
New Jersey	624-2377
New Mexico	545-AIDS
New York	541-AIDS
Albany	962-5065
New York City	(212)340-4432
North Carolina	342-AIDS
North Dakota	472-2180
Ohio	332-AIDS
Oklahoma	522-9054
Oregon	777-AIDS
Portland	(503)223-AIDS
Pennsylvania	662-6080
Puerto Rico	765-1010
Rhode Island	726-3010
South Carolina	322-AIDS
South Dakota	592-1861
Tennessee	525-AIDS
Texas	255-1090
Utah	537-1046
Salt Lake City	(801)538-6094

Vermont	882-AIDS
Virginia	533-4148
Washington	272-AIDS
West Virginia	642-8244
Wisconsin	334-AIDS
Wyoming	327-3577

Hot line information source:
American Association for
World Health (AAWH)
2001 S Street, Suite 530
Washington, D.C. 20009

MAP (Mothers of AIDS Patients) has an excellent newsletter.
For information on a chapter in your vicinity:
        (213)542-3019
        P.O. Box 1763
        Lometa, Calif. 90717-5763

PFlag (Parents and Friends of Lesbians and Gays, Inc.)
        P.O. Box 27605
        Washington, D.C. 20038-7605
        (202)638-4200
For information about PFlag by region, see below:

Pacific Northwest	(503)233-5415
Pacific Southwest and Metropolitan Los Angeles	(213)472-8952
Mountain	(303)333-0286
Great Plains	(402)435-4688
Central	(502)454-5635
Southern	(318)984-2216

Metropolitan New York	(212)752-4220
Northeast	(413)352-4883
Mid-Atlantic	(703)768-0411
South Atlantic	(704)922-9273

ADDITIONAL NATIONAL NUMBERS

For further information contact any of the following national resource organizations:

AIDS Action Council
2033 M Street NW, Suite 802
Washington, D.C. 20036
(202)293-2886

American Foundation for
AIDS Research
1515 Broadway, Suite 3601
New York, N.Y. 10036
(212)719-0033

American Red Cross National
Headquarters AIDS
Education Office
1709 New York Avenue NW,
Suite 208
Washington, D.C. 20006
(202)639-3223

Centers for Disease Control
National AIDS Information
and Education Program
1600 Clifton Road NE
Atlanta, Ga. 30333
(404)639-0965

Coalition of Hispanic Health
and Human Services
Organizations
1030 15th Street NW
Washington, D.C. 20005
(202)371-2100

George Washington University
Intergovernmental Health
Policy Project
2011 I Street NW, Suite 200
Washington, D.C. 20006
(202)872-1445

Lambda Legal Defense and
Education Fund
666 Broadway, 12th Floor
New York, N.Y. 10012
(212)995-8585

National AIDS Network
2033 M Street NW, Suite 800
Washington, D.C. 20036
(202)293-2437

National Association of People
With AIDS
2025 I Street NW, Suite 1118
Washington, D.C. 20006
(202)429-2856

National Gay and Lesbian
Task Force
1517 U Street NW
Washington, D.C. 20009
(202)332-6483

National Hemophilia
Foundation
SoHo Building, 110 Greene
Street, Room 406
New York, N.Y. 10012
(212)219-8180

National Leadership Coalition
on AIDS
1150 17th Street NW,
Suite 202
Washington, D.C. 20036
(202)429-0930

National Minority AIDS
Council
300 I Street NE, Suite 400
Washington, D.C. 20002
(202)544-1076

U.S. Conference of Mayors:
AIDS Program
1620 I Street NW, 4th Floor
Washington, D.C. 20006
(202)293-7330

OTHER RESOURCES

●

(United States)

AIDS Center at Hope House
19–21 Belmont Avenue
Dover, N.J. 07801
(201) 361-5555

Bailey House
180 Christopher Street, 6th
Floor
New York, N.Y. 10014
(212) 337-3054

Bereavement and Loss Center
of New York
170 East 83rd Street
New York, N.Y. 10028
(212) 879-5655

Body Positive Magazine
2095 Broadway, Suite 306
New York, N.Y. 10023
(212) 721-1346

The Center for Attitudinal
Healing for Children and
Siblings
19 Main Street
Tiburon, Calif. 94920
(415) 435-5022

Center/Bridge Lesbian and
  Gay Community Services
  Center
Grief Support Groups
208 West 13th Street
New York, N.Y. 10011
(212) 620-7310

Children's Hope Foundation
HIV/AIDS Children/Loss of
  Parent
295 Lafayette Street Suite 801
New York, N.Y. 10012-2722
(212) 941-7432

Children's Quilt Project
1478 University, Suite 186
Berkeley, Calif. 94702
(510) 548-3843

The Compassionate Friends
  (self-help for bereaved
  parents and siblings)
National Office:
P.O. Box 3696
Oak Brook, Ill. 60522-3696
(312) 990-0010

Damien Center
1350 N. Pennsylvania
Indianapolis, Ind. 46202
(317) 632-0123

Elder/Family Services
The Spectrum Program
464 Ninth Street
Brooklyn, N.Y. 11215
(718) 788-2461

Gay Men's Health Crisis
Walk-In Bereavement Group
129 West 20th Street
New York, N.Y. 10011
(212) 337-3694 or (212) 807-
  6664

Hollis Hills Jewish Center
Bereavement Support Group
210-10 Union Turnpike
Hollis Hills, N.Y. 11423
(718) 776-3500

Henry Street Settlement
(services for children who
  have lost parents to AIDS)
40 Montgomery Street
New York, N.Y. 10002
(212) 233-5032

Horizon Teen Center
710 Bergen Avenue
Jersey City, N.J. 07306
(201) 451-6300

Hospice, Inc.
34 Label Street, Walnut Plaza
Montclair, N.J. 07042
(201) 783-7879

Jewish Board of Family and
  Children's Services
Children's Loss and
  Bereavement
Brooklyn: 26 Court Street,
  Room 800
Brooklyn, N.Y. 11201
(718) 855-6900

New York: 120 West 57th
Street, 11th Floor
New York, N.Y. 10019
(212) 582-9100 x 2720

Leake & Watts
Foster Care Agency for
Orphaned Children of
AIDS
487 S. Broadway, Room 201
Yonkers, N.Y. 10705
(914) 376-0106

LIAAC—Long Island
Association for AIDS Care
Box 2859, Huntington
Station
New York, N.Y. 11746
Hot line (516) 385-AIDS

Mount Sinai Hospital
Adolescent Health Center
1 Gustave Levy Place,
Box 1005
New York, N.Y. 10029
(212) 241-5241

Oceanside Jewish Center for
Parents of PWA/HIVs
2860 Brower Avenue,
Oceanside, N.Y. 11572
(516) 536-6112
Or call Arlene Binkowitz,
(516) 678-6936

The Orphan Project
121 Sixth Ave., 6th Floor
New York, N.Y. 10013
(212) 925-5290

Notes from the Underground
PWA Health Group
Newsletter
150 West 26th Street
New York, N.Y. 10010
(212) 255-0520

PI Perspective and Fact
Sheets
Project Inform
347 Delores Street, Suite 301
San Francisco, Calif. 94110
(800) 822-7422

Pittsburgh AIDS Center for
Treatment
University of Pittsburgh
Medical Center
200 Lothrop Street
Pittsburgh, Pa. 15213
(412) 647-PACT

Pittsburgh AIDS Task Force
905 West Street, 4th Floor
Pittsburgh, Pa. 15221
(412) 242-2500

PWA Coalition Hotline
31 West 26th Street, 5th
Floor
New York, N.Y. 10010
(212) 532-0568 or (800) 828-
3280

PWA Coalition *Newsline*
(magazine)
31 West 26th Street, 5th
Floor
New York, N.Y. 10010
(212) 532-0290

PWA Mothers Bereavement
Group
222 West 11th Street
New York, N.Y. 10011
(212) 532-0568

SAGE
Senior Action in a Gay
Environment
208 West 13th Street
New York, N.Y. 10011
(212) 741-2247

SIDAhora
Quarterly bilingual
publication/PWA Coalition
31 West 26th Street
New York, N.Y. 10010

St. Vincent's Hospital
Supportive Care Program
Groups for AIDS Bereaved
and for Bereaved HIV +
153 West 11th Street
New York, N.Y. 10011
(212) 790-7508

Transition Bereavement
Program of Nassau and
Suffolk County
410 East Main Street
Centerport, N.Y. 11721
(516) 488-7697

The Warm Place
(Affiliated with Cook–Fort
Worth Children's Medical
Center)
Grief support for children
1510 Cooper Street
Fort Worth, Tex. 76104
(817) 870-2272

OTHER RESOURCES

●

(Canada)

Bereaved Families of Ontario
Les Familles Endeuillées de
 l'Ontario
214 Merton Street
Toronto, Ontario M4W 3H1
(416) 440-0290

Casey House Hospice
Bereavement Services, AIDS
 Families/Friends
9 Huntley Street
Toronto, Ontario M4Y 2K8
(416) 962-5147

Compassionate Friends of
 Canada
Les Amis Compatissants
Chapters throughout Canada
 for bereaved parents and
 siblings
National Office:
685 William Avenue
Winnipeg, Manitoba R3E
 0Z2
(204) 786-2460

LIFT (Living Is for Today)
Open-ended support groups
Bereavement Services and
   Community Education
   Division
Humphrey Funeral Home
1403 Bayview Avenue
Toronto, Ontario, Canada
   M4G 3A8
(416) 485-6415

Treatment Update
517 College Street, Suite 324
Toronto, Ontario M6G 1A8
(416) 944-1916

Vancouver PWA Society
   Newsletter
1447 Hornby Street
Vancouver, British Columbia
   Canada V6Z 1W8

AUTHOR'S NOTE

To Survivors:

If you have been unable to obtain help from any of the resources in this book or from anyone in your vicinity, please write to me and I will try my best to help network:

Katherine Fair Donnelly
c/o St. Martin's Press
175 Fifth Avenue
New York, N.Y. 10010

To Professionals/Volunteers:

If you have a group you believe should be listed in this "Helping Hands" section, please write to me at the above address, and I will do my best to include it in the next updating of the book.

BOOKS OF INTEREST

Becker, Ernest. *The Denial of Death*. New York: The Free Press, 1973.

Caine, Lynn. *Widow*. New York: Bantam Books, 1974.

Corr, Charles, and Donna Corr. *Hospice Care*. New York: Springer Publishing Co., 1983.

Cousins, Norman. *Anatomy of an Illness*. New York: Bantam Books, 1980.

——. *Head First: The Biology of Hope*. New York: Dutton, 1989.

Davidson, Glen, *Living with Dying*. Minneapolis: Augsbury Publishing, 1975.

Donnelly, Katherine Fair. *Recovering from the Loss of a Child*. New York: Berkley Publishing Group, 1994.

——. *Recovering from the Loss of a Parent* (by the adult child). New York: Berkley Publishing Group, 1993.

——. *Recovering from the Loss of a Sibling*. New York: Dodd Mead, 1987.

Grollman, Earl. *Living When a Loved One Has Died*. Boston: Beacon Press, 1976.

———. *What Helped Me When My Loved One Died*. Boston: Beacon Press, 1981.

Gunther, John. *Death Be Not Proud*. New York: Modern Library, 1953.

Jampolsky, Gerald. *Teach Only Love*. New York: Bantam Books, 1983.

Krementz, Jill. *How It Feels When a Parent Dies*. New York: Alfred A. Knopf, 1981.

Kübler-Ross, Elisabeth. *To Live Until We Say Goodbye*. Englewood, N.J.: Prentice-Hall, 1978.

———. *Death: The Final Stage of Growth*. New York: Touchstone Books, 1986.

Kushner, Harold S. *When Bad Things Happen to Good People*. New York: Schocken Books, 1981.

Lerner, Gerda. *A Death of One's Own*. Madison, Wisc.: University of Wisconsin Press, 1985.

LeShan, Eda. *Learning to Say Goodbye: When a Parent Dies*. New York: Macmillan, 1976.

Lewis, C. S. *A Grief Observed*. New York: Bantam Books, 1976.

Meagher, D. K., and R. D. Shapiro. *Death: The Experience*. Minneapolis: Burgess Publishing Co., 1984.

Miles, Margaret S. *The Grief of Parents When a Child Dies*. Oakbrook, Ill.: The Compassionate Friends, 1980.

Monette, Paul. *Borrowed Time: An AIDS Memoir*. New York: Harcourt Brace Jovanovich, 1988.

Moody, Raymond. *Life After Life*. New York: Bantam Books, 1986.

Parkes, Colin Murray, and R. S. Weiss. *Recovery from Bereavement*. New York: Basic Books, 1983.

Peck, M. Scott. *The Road Less Traveled*. New York: Simon & Schuster (Touchstone), 1980.

Pincus, L. *Death and the Family: The Importance of Mourning*. New York: Pantheon Books, 1974.

Rando, Therese A. *How to Go on Living When Someone You Love Dies*. New York: Bantam Books, 1991.

Saynor, John Kennedy. *Genesis*. Ontario, Canada: W. L. Smith & Associates, 1991.

————. *Goodbye Buddy.* Ontario, Canada: W. S. Smith & Associates, 1990.

Schiff, Harriet Sarnoff. *Living Through Mourning.* New York: Viking/Penguin Books, 1987.

Shiltz, Randy. *And the Band Played On.* New York: St. Martin's Press, 1987,

Siegel, Bernie. *Love, Peace, and Healing.* New York: Harper and Row, 1989.

Tatelbaum, Judy. *The Courage to Grieve.* New York: Harper and Row, 1980.

Temes, Roberta. *Living with an Empty Chair: A Guide Through Grief.* Far Hills, N.J.: New Horizon Press, 1992.

————. *The Empty Place: A Child's Guide Through Grief.* Far Hills, N.J.: New Horizon Press, 1992.

————. *A Leader's Manual* (for laypersons and professionals). New York: Lyons Publications, 1993.

Worden, William. J. *Grief Counseling and Grief Therapy,* rev. New York: Springer, 1993.

INDEX

About the Author

KATHERINE FAIR DONNELLY is the author of *Recovering from the Loss of a Child*, *Recovering from the Loss of a Parent*, and *Recovering from the Loss of a Sibling*. A journalist and an authority in the field of bereavement, she has lectured widely at colleges, community organizations, and bereavement groups, and has appeared on "Sally Jessy Raphael," "Donahue," and "Canada A.M." Katherine Donnelly was born in Texas and currently lives with her husband in New York and Toronto.